THE
OXYRHYNCHUS PAPYRI
VOLUME LXXIV

THE
OXYRHYNCHUS PAPYRI
VOLUME LXXIV

EDITED WITH TRANSLATIONS AND NOTES BY

D. LEITH   D. C. PARKER   S. R. PICKERING
and
N. GONIS   M. MALOUTA

WITH CONTRIBUTIONS BY

A. BENAISSA   D. COLOMO   M. COTTIER   M. GERHARDT
R. HATZILAMBROU   N. LITINAS   D. MANETTI
H. MAENO   P. M. PINTO   P. RIPAT   M. SATAMA

Graeco-Roman Memoirs, No. 95

PUBLISHED BY
THE EGYPT EXPLORATION SOCIETY
WITH THE SUPPORT OF
THE ARTS AND HUMANITIES RESEARCH COUNCIL
AND
THE BRITISH ACADEMY
2009

TYPESET BY
THE STINGRAY OFFICE, MANCHESTER
PRINTED IN GREAT BRITAIN BY
THE CHARLESWORTH GROUP, WAKEFIELD
AND PUBLISHED BY
THE EGYPT EXPLORATION SOCIETY
(REGISTERED CHARITY NO. 212384)
3 DOUGHTY MEWS, LONDON WC1N 2PG

Graeco-Roman Memoirs

ISSN 0306-9222

ISBN-13 978 0 85698 183 8

© EGYPT EXPLORATION SOCIETY 2009

N. GONIS	A. K. BOWMAN
D. OBBINK	R. A. COLES
P. J. PARSONS	J. R. REA
General editors	J. D. THOMAS
	Advisory editors

PREFACE

Section I offers the edition of a single text (**4968**), several leaves of a codex of NT Acts, which is the most significant new addition to the Greek evidence for the Acts over the past hundred years. **4968** shows that the bi-polar concept of a two-text form of Acts can hardly continue to be maintained. At the very least, the history of the text of Acts will need extensive revision.

Section II collects texts of principally medical content, and doubles the number of such papyri published previously in the series; many more are planned to appear in future volumes. The number is significant; did Oxyrhynchus have its own local tradition of medical education? **4969** represents the first published witness to the Hippocratic *De Articulis*, and indicates significant divergences from the transmitted text. **4970** offers rare evidence for the educational use of the Hippocratic *Oath* in antiquity. **4971** describes dietetic treatment closely related to a therapeutic system developed within the medical sect of the Methodists. **4972** records an elaborate and unparalleled analysis of the forms of medical expertise proper to surgery.

Section III publishes documents of the Roman period, grouped by theme. Notable items include the early though fragmentary census returns **4980–82**, the two archive rolls of registrations of children and notifications of death (**4993–8**), the dozen new summonses (**5001–12**). **5013–16** illustrate the public performances which Oxyrhynchites enjoyed, as the oracle questions **5017–19** illustrate their personal crises.

The edition of **4968** was initially entrusted to Dr S. R. Pickering, who produced an advanced draft; this was brought to completion by Professor David Parker, who is responsible for the final version of the introduction and commentary. The establishment of the text owes much to the painstaking and thorough collation of the original by Dr Coles. Section II is chiefly the work of Dr David Leith, and derives from his doctoral thesis (UCL); Dr Leith records his gratitude to the Arts and Humanities Research Council for the award of a doctoral studentship, and to the Wellcome Trust for funding his research fellowship, during which the final revision was carried out. Some of the texts edited in section III were first studied at seminars on documentary papyrology held by Professor Bowman and Dr Gonis in Oxford; others stem from doctoral theses (R. Hatzilambrou and N. Litinas, UCL; M. Malouta, Oxford). The scripts submitted by the individual editors have been further revised and reworked by Gonis, who takes responsibility for any defects.

Professor Isabella Andorlini contributed to the elucidation of certain texts in section II. Professor Thomas read and commented on most texts in section III; Professor Parsons advised on section I and parts of III; Dr Coles read early drafts of **5013–19**; Dr Rea commented on a version of **5013–16**; Dr Amin Benaissa contributed corrections to the penultimate draft of section III. Two PhD students at UCL, Susan Beresford and Antonia Sarri, have helped with the keying of section I, proofreading, and imaging. Dr Leith indexed section II, and Dr Benaissa section III.

As always, we are grateful to Dr Jeffrey Dean for his meticulous copy-editing and typesetting, and to The Charlesworth Group for efficient production; and we remain indebted to the Arts and Humanities Research Council and The British Academy for their manifold support.

This is the last volume in the series in which Dr Coles and Dr Rea appear in the formal capacity of 'Advisory Editor'; we hope that this will not be the last volume to profit from their advice and expertise. Our gratitude for their contribution is easier to express than to measure.

September 2009   N. GONIS

CONTENTS

Preface	v
Table of Papyri	ix
List of Plates	xi
Numbers and Plates	xi
Note on the Method of Publication and Abbreviations	xii

TEXTS

I.	NEW TESTAMENT (**4968**)	1
II.	MEDICAL AND RELATED TEXTS (**4969–4979**)	46
III.	DOCUMENTARY TEXTS (**4980–5019**)	89

INDEXES

I.	Medical and Related Texts	163
II.	Rulers	165
III.	Months	166
IV.	Dates	166
V.	Personal Names	166
VI.	Geographical	169
VII.	Religion	170
VIII.	Official and Military Terms and Titles	170
IX.	Professions and Occupations	170
X.	Measures	170
XI.	General Index of Words	171
XII.	Corrections to Published Texts	174

TABLE OF PAPYRI

I. NEW TESTAMENT

4968	Acta Apostolorum 10–12, 15–17	DCP/SRP	Fifth century	1

II. MEDICAL AND RELATED TEXTS

4969	Hippocrates, *De Articulis* 57–58, 60	DM/DL	Second/third century	46
4970	Prose mentioning the Hippocratic Oath	DL	Second century	51
4971	Medical Treatise	DL	First/second century	55
4972	Division of Surgery	DL	Second/third century	60
4973	Veterinary or Physiognomical Text	DM	Second century	66
4974	Osteological Fragment	DL	Second/third century	70
4975	Pharmacological Manual	DL	Second century	73
4976	Medical Recipe	DL	Second/third century	78
4977	Medical Recipes	DL	Second/third century	80
4978	Medical Recipes	DL	Second/third century	84
4979	List of Items	DL	Second/third century	86

III. DOCUMENTARY TEXTS

4980–4999	Documents addressed to Authorities			
4980	Census Declaration	NG	7 March 34	89
4981	Census Declaration	NG	26(?) April 34	90
4982	Census Declaration	NG	28 May 62	92
4983	Census Declaration	RH	*c.*76	93
4984	Registration of a Loan	AB	98–100	97
4985	Registration of a Sale	AB	Late first century	98
4986–4988	Census Declarations	NG		99
4986		NG	146?	100
4987		NG	146	100
4988		NG	146	101
4989	Census Declaration	MM	25 Feb. – 26 March 175	101
4990	Census Declaration	NL	188/9	105
4991	Census Declaration	RH	215/16	108
4992	Notification of Death	NG	223/4	110
4993–4995	Registrations of Children	MM		111
4993		MM	253/4?	113
4994		MM	26 May / 24 June 254	113
4995		MM	6 January 254	117
4996–4998	Notifications of Death	MM		119
4996		MM	254/5	120
4997		MM	26 May – 24 June 254	122

4998		MM	253/4	124
4999	Registration of a Child	NG	12 August 292	127
5000–5012	Documents relating to Village Police			
5000	Sworn Undertaking	NL	166–9	130
5001–5012	Summonses ('Orders to Arrest')	NG		133
5001		NG	First/second century	136
5002		NG	First/second century	136
5003		HM	Second century	137
5004		PMP	Third century	138
5005		NG	Third/fourth century	139
5006		NG	Third/fourth century	140
5007		NG	Third/fourth century	140
5008		NG	Third/fourth century	141
5009		NG	Third/fourth century	142
5010		MC	Third/fourth century	143
5011		DC	Third/fourth century	145
5012		RH	Fourth century	146
5013–5016	Documents relating to Performers	MS		147
5013	List of Performers	MS	Second century	148
5014	Contract of Performers	MS	Third century	150
5015	Contract of Performers	MS	Third century	152
5016	Contract of Performers	MS	Third/fourth century	155
5017–5019	Oracle Questions	PR		157
5017		MG	First/second century	158
5018		PR	Second century	159
5019		PR	Second century	160

AB = A. Benaissa DC = D. Colomo MC = M. Cottier MG = M. Gerhardt
NG = N. Gonis RH = R. Hatzilambrou DL = D. Leith NL = N. Litinas
DM = D. Manetti HM = H. Maeno MM = M. Malouta DCP = D. C. Parker
SRP = S. R. Pickering PMP = P. M. Pinto PR = P. Ripat MS = M. Satama

LIST OF PLATES

I. **4970**, **4971**
II. **4968** (fols. 1b, 8a)
III. **4968** (fols. 8b, 1a)
IV. **4968** (fols. 6b, 7a)
V. **4968** (fols. 7b, 6a)
VI. **4975**, **4977**
VII. **4982**, **4983**
VIII. **4972**, **5006**, **5007**

NUMBERS AND PLATES

4968	II–V	**4977**	VI
4970	I	**4982**	VII
4971	I	**4983**	VII
4972	VIII	**5006**	VIII
4975	VI	**5007**	VIII

NOTE ON THE METHOD OF PUBLICATION AND ABBREVIATIONS

The basis of the method is the Leiden system of punctuation; see *CE* 7 (1932) 262–9. It may be summarized as follows:

αβγ̣	The letters are doubtful, either because of damage or because they are otherwise difficult to read
. . .	Approximately three letters remain unread by the editor
[αβγ]	The letters are lost, but restored from a parallel or by conjecture
[. . .]	Approximately three letters are lost
( )	Round brackets indicate the resolution of an abbreviation or a symbol, e.g. (ἀρτάβη) represents the symbol ⸏, cτρ(ατηγόc) represents the abbreviation cτρ∫
⟦αβγ⟧	The letters are deleted in the papyrus
\`αβγ´	The letters are added above the line
⟨αβγ⟩	The letters are added by the editor
{αβγ}	The letters are regarded as mistaken and rejected by the editor

Bold arabic numerals refer to papyri printed in the volumes of *The Oxyrhynchus Papyri*.

The abbreviations used are in the main identical with those in J. F. Oates *et al.*, *Checklist of Editions of Greek Papyri and Ostraca* (*BASP* Suppl. no. 9, [5]2001); for a more up-to-date version of the *Checklist*, see http://scriptorium.lib.duke.edu/papyrus/texts/clist.html.

I. NEW TESTAMENT

4968. Acta Apostolorum 10–12, 15–17

89B/1–4 16.5 × 21.5 cm (full page) Fifth century
𝔓¹²⁷ Plates II–V

Assembled from numerous fragments, these remains of eight leaves from two gatherings of a papyrus codex, with two columns to the page, preserve a highly distinctive text of Acts 10.32–5, 40–45; 11.2–5, 30; 12.1–3, 5, 7–9; 15.29–31, 34–6, (37), 38–41; 16.1–4, 13–40; 17.1–10. A page number ($\rho\iota\beta$ = 112) on folio 7a (containing 16.27–35) suggests that the codex began with Acts.

The box in which the fragments were stored contained miscellaneous material only partly from Oxyrhynchus, so that the provenance of **4968** is subject to doubt.

Script and date

The main hand of the papyrus is a relaxed form of Biblical Majuscule that may be assigned to the fifth century. Examples for comparison include 𝔓⁸¹ (ed. S. Daris, *Un nuovo frammento della Prima Lettera di Pietro*, Barcelona 1967, pll. i–ii; LDAB 3068), a papyrus of the Ascension of Isaiah (P. Amh. I 1, pll. iii–ix = *GBEBP* 18a; LDAB 5989), and another of the Psalter (P. Amh. I 5; LDAB 3280). 𝔓⁸¹ was assigned to the fourth century by the editor, but the fifth century was proposed by Turner, *Typology* 17, 150. The Amherst examples were assigned to the early fifth century by G. Cavallo, *Ricerche sulla maiuscola biblica* 72, tavv. 53–4. The former is placed in the fifth, the latter in the fifth or sixth century by Turner, *Typology* 185, 170.

The ink is brownish in colour. The first scribe corrected omission of some letters. There are further alterations in a small hand, in black ink much darker than that of the main text. The script of the page number, added (above 16.31) in a lighter ink, is in much the same style as the main text but could be by a different hand. The scribe occasionally and for no obvious reason wrote the last letter of a line small and high. See for example the three epsilons on folio 6b, column i 6 and column ii 24 and 26.

Physical details of the codex

The breadth and height of the page can be measured from folio 7 as 16.5 × 21.5 cm. This calls to mind the aberrants of Group 6 in Turner, *Typology* 18. The upper margin was a little over 2.5 cm and the lower margin 2–2.5 cm. The outer margin was 3 cm wide; the inner margin was half that, 1.5 cm. The intercolumnar distance is 1 cm. The columns are approximately 16.5 cm high and 5.5 cm wide. In folios 1–3 (Chapters 10–12) the number of lines per column is 22–24; in folios 5–8 (Chapters 16–17) it rises to 25–26; the number in folio 4 (Chapter 15) is uncertain.

The manuscript is unusual among papyrus codices of the New Testament in having two columns. Other examples are 𝔓$^{4/64/67}$, 𝔓^5 and 𝔓^{118} (III cent.), 𝔓^{25} (IV), 𝔓^{50} (IV/V), 𝔓^{84} and 𝔓^{96} (VI), 𝔓^{34} (VII), and 𝔓^{41} (VIII).

The sheets were, as normal, arranged so that the fibres of facing pages run in the same direction. The surfaces of one pair of facing pages (7b, 8a) were consolidated prior to the time of writing (during manufacture?) with several narrow horizontal strips of papyrus, merging with the rest of the material rather than being glued on top. They run across the whole width of the page and are spaced at 3–4 cm intervals. There are several *kolleseis* (showing that the sheets of the codex were cut from a roll), with coinciding lines of breakage.

Traces of some binding holes are visible. Top and bottom binding cords survive, the girth of the ties being sufficient for a number of quires. There is also a third surviving tie, which was added towards the bottom. There is evidence that the codex suffered from wear along sheet folds and at binding points, and was repaired and rebound. In the first place, the folds of two partially extant sheets were repaired with strengthening strips about 2 cm wide (1 cm on either page) pasted across the outside of the folds, running the full height of the sheets (visible on folios 1a and 8b). The strips were affixed with their vertical fibres against the vertical fibres of the sheets. At several points in folio 8b, column ii, the strip covers a small amount of writing. Secondly, the binding points of the conjoint leaf comprising folios 2 and 3 were reinforced with a piece of papyrus about 2.5 cm square wrapped around the fold, on the outside of the sheet (i.e. visible on folios 2a and 3b), both sheet and piece showing horizontal fibres. The third binding cord may also be associated with this renovation process.

Folios 2 and 3 are from a bifolium (a portion of the centre of the sheet survives). Some of the fragments of this sheet are still attached to folio 8 by the binding cords. The position in which they were found suggests that they may have been bound after it. This may imply that the bifolium was at some point wrongly bound in after folio 8, perhaps when the codex was repaired. The fragments of folio 1 are likely to be from a bifolium of the same quire as folios 2 and 3 and to have been similarly misbound. The innermost sheet of the quire is lost. Such a mistake might explain why two non-consecutive portions of the manuscript have been preserved. On the other hand, it may be coincidence that folios 2, 3 and 8 are still attached to the cords.

The two folios 4 and 5 were a bifolium (suggested by fibre matching) and formed the inmost sheet of a quire. The next three (folios 6, 7 and 8) cannot be matched with one another. If it is supposed that the sheets from which they come folded about the bifolium comprising folios 4 and 5, with the lost conjugates holding text prior to 15.29, the quire would have consisted of four sheets or more.

An arrangement by quaternions (which was by this time the favoured but not the only arrangement: cf. Turner, *Typology* 62) is thrown into doubt by the calculation (assuming 12 verses per leaf) that 10 leaves are required for the text between 12.9 and 15.29. These lost intervening leaves cannot be fully apportioned on the supposition that the bifolium comprising folios 2 and 3 is the second sheet in from the middle of a quaternion (which would mean 2 more leaves of the quaternion after folio 3, and so could account for 2 of the 10) and if folios 4 and 5 are taken to be the central bifolium of a quaternion (which would mean 3 leaves of this quaternion before 4, and so could account for 3 of the 10). Five leaves, not enough for a quaternion of their own, would be left unaccounted for. Perhaps a mixture of threes and fours is the answer; such mixtures are attested (cf. Turner, *Typology* 61–2).

The diagram overleaf shows the contents of the leaves, the direction of their fibres and other details of their make-up. About 31 leaves may be calculated to be lost before 10.32, and about 33 leaves after 17.10, if the codex contained only Acts. With the 8 leaves represented by the fragments, the 2 leaves of the bifolium lost after 11.5, and the 10 leaves calculated for the text lost between 12.9 and 15.29, this gives a codex of about 168 pages (84 leaves = 42 sheets).

The text is very evenly distributed, as the table on p. 5 shows (with the average given in the nearest whole number). The only aberrations are in the two shortest fragments, where the figures are the least likely to be reliable.

Scribal habits and diacritical marks

Nomina sacra occur or may be safely restored for θεóc, κύριοc, Ἰηcοῦc, χριcτóc, πατήρ, πνεῦμα, and ἄνθρωποc. There are a few rough breathings (16.14, 21, 17.7) and circumflexes (16.34; 17.2; both added incorrectly). Diaeresis is usually written over initial iota and upsilon (but it is not used in our restorations). The word καί is sometimes abbreviated (more often at a line-end, but also within a line). The page number is in the top right-hand corner of a right-hand page, the only such corner intact. Punctuation consists of oblique strokes (normally after a word, sometimes above its last letter) and points (usually middle, sometimes high, once low). Many of these are in blacker ink, and were added by another hand. Paragraphi occur at 15.30 and 17.10.

The text

This papyrus is the most significant new addition to the Greek evidence since the publication in 1927 of P. Mich. inv. 1571, containing 18.27–19.6, 19.12–16 (Gregory–Aland 𝔓³⁸).[1] Another highly significant discovery of recent times has

---

[1] H. A. Sanders, 'A Papyrus Fragment of Acts in the Michigan Collection', *HTR* 20 (1927) 1–19.

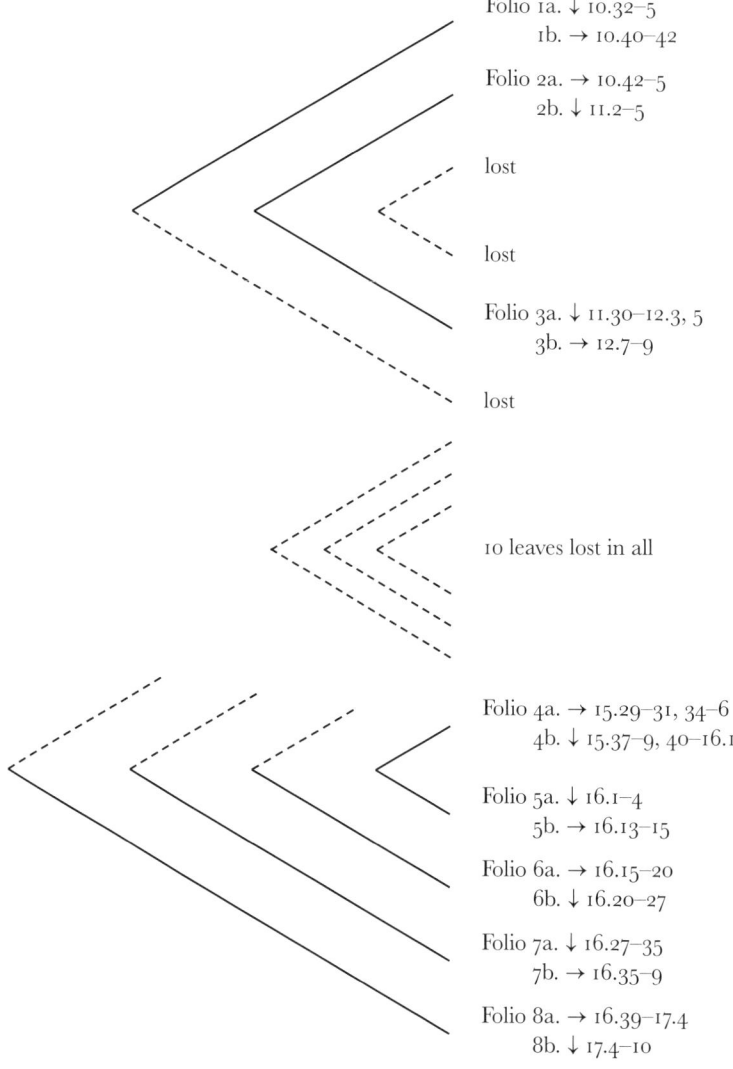

been a manuscript of a Middle Egyptian Coptic version (Pierpont Morgan Library Copt. G^{67}, containing 1.1–15.2) which supports many of the readings found in the longer text.[1] Another important versional witness for this form of text is the marginal readings of the Harklean Syriac.

The papyrus contributes substantially to our understanding of the development of the text of Acts. It has been traditional to divide the older witnesses into

[1] H.-M. Schenke (ed.), *Apostelgeschichte 1,1–15,3 im mittelägyptischen Dialekt des Koptischen (Codex Glazier)* (TU 137: Berlin 1991).

folio	column	lines	letters	average
1 a	1	22	235	11
	2	—		
1 b	1	—		
	2	20[a]	212	11
2 a	1	24[b]	267	11
	2	—		
2 b	1	—		
	2	23	265	12
3 a	1	23	258	11
	2	4	55	14
3 b	1	5	47	9
	2	23	252	11
4 a	1	8[c]	92	12
	2	12	144	12
4 b	1	11	118	11
	2	10	114	11
5 a	1	24[d]	273	11
	2	—		
5 b	1	—		
	2	22	238	11
6 a	1	25	276	11
	2	22	246	11
6 b	1	26	304	12
	2	26	290	11
7 a	1	25	279	11
	2	25	271	11
7 b	1	26	280	11
	2	26	286	11
8 a	1	25	270	11
	2	25	279	11
8 b	1	25	298	12
	2	26	308	12

[a] Not including line 3.
[b] Not including line 24.
[c] Not including lines 11–12, 16.
[d] Not including line 25.

two groups. The one has traditionally been known as the 'Alexandrian' or 'Old Uncial' text, the other as the 'Western'. It has been customary to regard these two forms as championed by two manuscripts; the one by a fourth-century Codex Vaticanus (Gregory–Aland 03), the other by Codex Bezae (Gregory–Aland 05), a

Graeco-Latin copy produced in about 400. This second text has been calculated most recently to be between six and seven per cent longer.[1] It contains alternative wordings, additional details, and longer versions of events. According to Read-Heimerdinger (17–19), there is more variation in narrative than in speeches. On the whole our papyrus happens to be preserved in passages containing a high proportion of narrative, though it does contain sections of Peter's speech in Chapter 10 (often in a very distinctive version). Whether it is similar to Codex Bezae in this apparent respect for apostolic words over Lukan narrative may be hard to establish.

Although a few scholars have suggested that the 'Western' text is original, the majority consider it to be a secondary development. The more recent Byzantine text, represented by the majority of minuscule witnesses, contains some elements of the longer version, but generally offers a version of the shorter. The general view that the longer text is secondary characterizes it as a free recasting of the story. Hitherto scholarship has tended to assume that there was only one such free version. This was because of the markedly different character of Codex Bezae when it was compared to Codex Vaticanus. Other copies, notably the sixth-century Graeco-Latin bilingual Codex Laudianus and the Harklean Syriac, along with vestiges in other versions, bear witness to other forms of text, but in nothing like so pronounced a manner. So it is that scholarship has assumed Acts to be a two-text problem. The papyrus offers a strong challenge to this view, leading rather to the recognition that if a text could exist in one free version, it could exist in many. The fact is that 𝔓 offers a new free version. Although it differs greatly from Codex Vaticanus, it also presents a strikingly different version from that found in Codex Bezae. Like Codex Bezae, it is somewhat longer than Codex Vaticanus, and like Codex Bezae its wording often varies from Codex Vaticanus. But its variations from it are by no means identical with those of Codex Bezae. Take the example of the Philippian gaoler's response to the earthquake (16.27–30). If we set 𝔓 between the two parchment manuscripts, the differences are clear to see:

---

[1] J. Read-Heimerdinger, *The Bezan Text of Acts: A Contribution of Discourse Analysis to Textual Criticism* (JSNTS 236: Sheffield 2002) 6f., argues for 6.6 per cent. W. A. Strange, *The Problem of the Text of Acts* (SNTStudies 71: Cambridge 1992) 213 n. 18, reckons 6.24 per cent. Both explicitly correct older, more inflationary estimates, such as the 8.5 per cent of Kenyon, apparently rounded up to 10 per cent by Metzger.

Codex Vaticanus (03)	𝔓	Codex Bezae (05)
²⁷ εξυπνος δε γενομενος	²⁷ εξυπνος δε γενομενος	²⁷ και εξυπνος γενομενος
ο δεσμοφυλαξ και ιδων	ο δεσμοφυλαξ και ιδων	ο δεσμοφυλαξ και ιδων
ανεωγμενας τας θυρας	ανεωγμενας τας θυρας	ανεωγμενας τας θυρας
της φυλακης	πασας	της φυλακης
σπασαμενος	[σ]πασαμενος	και σπασαμενος
την μαχαιραν ημελλεν	μαχ[αι]ραν ηθελησε[ν]	την μαχαιραν εμελλεν
εαυτον αναιρειν	εαυτον κατακ[ ]σαι	εαυτον αναιρειν
νομιζων εκπεφευγεναι	νομιζων εκπεφευγεναι	νομιζων εκπεφευγεναι
τους δεσμιους	τους δεσμιους	τους δεσμιους
²⁸ εφωνησεν δε	²⁸ εφωνησεν δε αυτον	²⁸ εφωνησεν δε
Παυλος μεγαλη φωνη	Παυλος	φωνη μεγαλη ο Παυλος
λεγων	λεγων	λεγων
μηδεν πραξης σεαυτω	μη ταρασσου	μηδεν πραξης σεαυτω τι
κακον		κακον
απαντες γαρ εσμεν	απαντες γαρ εσμεν	απαντες γαρ εσμεν
ενθαδε	ενθαδε	ενθαδε
²⁹ αιτησας δε φωτα	²⁹ φωτα δε αιτησας	²⁹ φωτα δε ετησας
εισεπηδησεν και εντρομος	εισεπηδησεν και εντρομος	εισεπηδησεν και εντρομος
γενομενος προσεπεσεν	υπαρχων επιπεσων	υπαρχων προσεπεσεν
		προς τους ποδας
τω Παυλω και Σειλα	τω Παυλω και Σιλεα	τω Παυλω και Σιλα
³⁰ και προαγαγων αυτους	³⁰ προαγων αυτους	³⁰ και προηγαγεν αυτους
εξω	εξω	εξω
	τους λοιπους	τους λοιπους
	ασφαλισας προελθων	ασφαλισαμενος
εφη	εφη	και ειπεν αυτοις
κυριοι τι με δει	κυριοι τι με δει	κυριοι τι με δει
ποιειν ινα σωθω	ποιειν [ι]να σωθω	ποιειν ινα σωθω

In each verse a different significant characteristic is visible. In verse 27 we find 𝔓 differing from both manuscripts four times (placing the papyrus' readings first): (πασας) της φυλακης; μαχαιραν] την μαχαιραν; ηθελησεν] ημελλεν/εμελλεν; κατακ[ ]σαι] αναιρειν). Verse 28 contains two distinctive variations: αυτον παυλος against παυλος μεγαλη φωνη (03) or φωνη μεγαλη ο παυλος (05) and μη ταρασσου against μηδεν πραξης σεαυτω (τι) κακον. In verse 29 it provides a variation on the text of 03 without the tautology of 05 (επιπεσων against προσεπεσεν and προσεπεσεν προς τους ποδας). Verse 30 is perhaps the most striking example in this passage: it follows 03 against 05 (εφη against και ειπεν αυτοις), has an addition with 05 against 03 but disagreeing in detail (τους λοιπους ασφαλισας and τους λοιπους ασφαλισαμενος), and differs from both in the beginning of the clause (προαγων against και προαγαγων αυτους and και προηγαγεν).

In this short section, Codex Vaticanus contains 60 words, Codex Bezae 71, and 𝔓 58. In the complete section comprised by folios 6b, 7 and 8 (16.20 ημων – 17.10 εις), the papyrus has 531 words, which compares with 523 in Codex Vaticanus and 591 in Codex Bezae. This suggests that the text of 𝔓 possesses two characteristics that almost balance each other out so far as the length of text is concerned: against expansions similar to those found in Codex Bezae (as in verse 30), may be set a habit of tersely summarizing whole phrases, notably μη ταρασσου in verse 28.

On the evidence presented here and in the commentary, it is hard to see how the bipolar concept of a two-text form of Acts can continue to be maintained. At the very least, the history of the text of Acts will need extensive revision. In the light of the degree of analysis required, the textual notes can offer only a provisional and limited assessment. Moreover, the edition of Acts currently being prepared in Münster as part of the *Editio critica maior* will involve a thorough survey of the whole tradition, along with a fresh collection of the evidence. Once that has been done, we will be in a much better position to understand the entire textual history, and the place of each witness within it. The commentary therefore concentrates on the relationship between 𝔓's text and that of a few other older Greek manuscripts. It is based upon an automatic collation of the papyrus with transcriptions of 03 and 05. Variations in 𝔓 against one or both of the other two are noted. Further evidence is provided from witnesses included in the Institut für neutestamentliche Textforschung's NT Prototypes (http://nttranscripts.uni-muenster.de/)[1] and in printed editions including Ropes and Nestle–Aland²⁷.[2] Versional evidence is only mentioned where it is of particular significance.

It is worth setting out some of the main questions that will need asking in further research.

1. Most striking is the question of the relationship between 𝔓 and Codex Bezae. Do they represent two versions independently derived from a form of text more similar to the Initial Text? Are they both derived from a more free form of text but, inevitably for a free text, showing many differences from each other? There are several ways of answering this. One is by studying those places where either one of them agrees with Codex Vaticanus against the other. Another is to

---

[1] The editors are grateful to the Institut für neutestamentliche Textforschung for the use of their transcriptions of 03 and 05 in NT Prototypes.

[2] J. H. Ropes, 'The Text of Acts', in F. J. Foakes Jackson and K. Lake (eds.), *The Beginnings of Christianity*, Part 1: *The Acts of the Apostles*, iii (London 1926). B. and K. Aland, J. Karavidopoulos, C. M. Martini, B. M. Metzger (eds.), *Novum Testamentum Graece*, 27th edition, 8th (revised) impression (Stuttgart 2001). Evidence concerning Codex Sinaiticus uses the transcription prepared for the virtual edition (www.codexsinaiticus.org).

compare 𝔓 with the Latin column (d) of Codex Bezae, especially in those places where it differs from the Greek column. It has been argued that this Latin column was adapted from an existing translation derived from a somewhat different Greek base containing a shorter form of text than the Greek column of Codex Bezae (Parker, *Codex Bezae* 248–9). A study of these places could be especially valuable.

	05 (Greek)	d (Latin)	𝔓
11.2	δε	omits	omits

This comes within an expansion of the text shared by the two manuscripts, and is therefore especially interesting.

11.5	εκcταcει	in mentis stupore	[εν εκcταc]ει
12.7	omits	in	εν
16.2	Λυcτροιc	Lystrae	[Λυ]cτ[ρ]η
16.34	cυν τω οικω αυτου	cum tota domu sua	πανοικεῖ
17.5	εθορυβουcαν	turbabant	εθο[ρ]υβο[υν]

(05 remains the only manuscript to read this form of the imperfect.)

As may be seen, this is a rather disappointing yield. Generally, it is agreements between 𝔓 and the Greek of 05 against its Latin parallel that are more striking.

| 12.7 | αι αλυcειc εκ των χειρων αυτου | eius catenae de manibus | αι α[λυcειc ε]κ των [χειρων αυ]του |

d shares the word order of all other Greek witnesses, so the agreement of 05 and 𝔓 is striking.

| 15.38 | ειναι cυν | adsumerent | [cυν]ειναι |

In spite of the differing position of cυν, 05 and 𝔓 probably agree together against d, which is best taken to represent cυνπαραλαμβανειν.

| 15.41 | τας εντολας | autem mandatum | ταc [εντολ]αc |

This agreement is found within a passage omitted from other witnesses.

| 16.1 | διελθων δε | pertransiens | [διελθ]ων δε |

This is also in a longer reading.

| 16.16 | κυριοιc | dominis suis | κυριοιc |

This was hitherto a singular reading in 05 (though Swanson also records the reading from 2412, a twelfth-century manuscript).[1]

---

[1] The words δια τουτου in 05 should be taken as a separate embellishment rather than as an

16.34	επι τον θ̄ν̄	in domino	επι τον θ̄ν̄

Again, support from 𝔓 for a reading previously known only in 05.

17.1	Απολλωνιδα	Apolloniam	Ạπολλωνιδạ

Another instance of the same.

17.5	οι δε απειθουντες	adsuptis uero	οι δε απειθου̣ν̣τες
	Ιουδαιοι	iudaeis	Ιουδα̣ι̣ο[ι
	cυνcτρεψαντες	conuertentes	cυν]cτρεψαντες

Yet again 𝔓 reads a previous singular reading of 05.

At other places we find that 𝔓 differs with both columns of 05, namely

12.7	επελαμψεν	refulgens	[ελα]μψεν [απ αυτου]
	τω οικηματι	illo loco	[τω οικημ]ατι
16.3	εκεινοις	suis	εν τω τ̣[οπω]
16.14	της πολεως Θυατειρων	Thyatirum ciuitatis	Θυγατηρ[ων]
	ηκουcεν	audiebat	omits
16.18	ευθεως εξηλθεν	eadem hora exiit	omits
16.21	τα εθνη α	gentem quam	[εθ]η α
16.30	προηγαγεν . . .	cum produxisset . . .	προαγων
	αcφαλιcαμενος	custodiuit	αcφαλιcας
	και ειπεν αυτοις	et dixit illis	προε̣λθων εφη
16.36	τους λογους	hos sermones	omits

At 12.7, neither column of 05 supports the wording found in 𝔓 (see below, note ad loc.). But could the somewhat unexpected *illo* in the Latin reflect a confusion with a form of the text *ab illo*?

So much for places where the text of 𝔓 is certain enough for us to be able to compare it with passages where the two columns of Codex Bezae differ. To treat the matter as a bald matter of numbers, we see that six times it agrees with the Latin against the Greek, eight with the Greek against the Latin, and on eleven occasions it differs from both. If one compares 𝔓 to the two separate Greek bases from which the Bezan texts are derived, it seems that the form of text represented by 𝔓 is not particularly close to either. On the other hand, the first reading at 12.7 suggests that the matter may not be so simple: εν agrees with the Latin *in* and also with the text of Codex Vaticanus (03). This leads to the second question.

2. It is a question that is closely related to the first. How are the two texts of 05 and 𝔓 related to the text of 03? Is one closer to it than the other? Perhaps it

---

alternative for αυτης. Swanson = R. J. Swanson, *New Testament Greek Manuscripts, Variant Readings Arranged in Horizontal Lines against Codex Vaticanus: The Acts of the Apostles* (Sheffield and Pasadena 1998).

would be better to ask how the textual base of 𝔓 (once more recent idiosyncrasies have been removed) may be related to 03. At this point the number of readings that 𝔓 shares with 05 against 03 must lead to the general conclusion that both are descended from a similar form of text.

3. What are the distinctive characteristics of 𝔓? One is very evident, namely, the habit of abbreviating or even omitting material:

10.33	ακου[ϲα]ι τα [προϲ]τετα[γμ]ενα ϲο[ι
10.34	αποκριθειϲ
10.42–3	τουτω παντεϲ (omitted)
10.44	[ταυτα]
11.4	α]πο[κριθειϲ δε] ο Πε[τροϲ ειπεν] αυ[τοιϲ
11.5	[Ιοππη] for πολει Ιοππη προϲευχομενοϲ
12.7	[α]υτου for του Πετρου
12.8	κ(αι) [περιβαλ]ου τ[ο ιματιο]ν ϲου
15.36	ειπεν δε
16.16	[π]ορευομενων [δ]ε ημων
	[η]τιϲ [ε]χουϲα π̅ν̅α̅
16.24	παρ[α]λαβ[ων
16.26	[κ]α[ι] εξαπ[ι]νηϲ [εγ]ενετο ϲιϲμ[ο]ϲ μεγ[α]ϲ
	κα[ι εϲ]αλ[ευ]θη . . . [κ]αι ηνε[ωχ]θηϲ[αν]
16.27	παϲαϲ
16.28	μη ταραϲϲου
16.32	αυτοιϲ
16.36	αυτοιϲ
	απολυθητε for νυν ουν εξελθοντεϲ πορευϲθαι εν ειρηνη
16.37	ελθοντεϲ ουν αυτοι for ου γαρ ελθοντεϲ αυτοι
16.38	απηγγειλαν δε . . . απεκαλουν
16.39	επιϲτ[ρ]αφω[ϲιν]
16.40	απολυθεντεϲ δε
17.1–2	κατα δε το ειωθοϲ Παυλοϲ ειϲηλθεν ειϲ την ϲυναγωγην των Ιουδαιων for οπου ην ϲυναγωγη των Ιουδαιων. και κατα το ειϲωθοϲ ο Παυλοϲ ειϲηλθεν προϲ αυτουϲ (05)
17.10	απελυον δια νυκτοϲ

Omission of the following is noted:

12.3	εϲτιν after αρεϲτον
12.7	αυτον after ηγειρεν
15.38	απ αυτων
	αυτοιϲ after ϲυνελθοντα
16.1	γυναικοϲ

16.3	article before Παυλος
16.14	πολεως
16.15	τω κυριω
16.16	υπαντησαι ημας αυτου
16.19	επι τους αρχοντας
16.23	αυτους
16.24	το
16.27	την
16.32	cυν παcιν τοιc εν τη οικια αυτου
16.35	εκεινουc
16.38	τοιc cτρατηγοιc
17.1	διοδευcαντεc δε την Αμφιπολιν
17.3	εκ νεκρων
17.4	εξ

We thus have an interesting phenomenon: an expanding free text that has a strong tendency to omit. That this is a common feature in manuscripts is undeniable. That it is especially marked in 𝔓 is evident. This makes a striking contrast with Codex Bezae, which rarely omits.

A second feature is changes in the word order:

10.42	και δια[μαρτυ]ραcθαι τ[ω λαω]
10.44	[το] π̅[να̅ το αγιον επεπ]ε[cεν]
12.5	[προc] το[ν θν̅ περι αυτου] ὑπ[ο της εκκληcιαc]
12.7	ιδ]ου αι α[λυcειc ε]κ των [χειρων αυ]του [εξεπεcα]ν
16.3	[cυν]εξελθ[ειν αυτω]
16.14	ονο]ματ[ι Λυ[δια πο]ρφυρο[πωλιc] Θυγατηρ[ων
16.15	μενετε ειc τον οικον μου
16.22	[τα ιματ]ι[α] [περιρηξαντεc]
16.33	[κα]ι εκεινη τη [ω]ρα παραλαβοντεc αυτουc
17.1–2	κατα δε το ειωθοc Παυλοc ειcηλθεν ειc την cυναγωγην των Ἰουδαιων (see also above)

There are other changes in word order shared with 05 (e.g. 12.1 ταc χειραc Ηρωδηc).

In the following passages 𝔓 shares, at least in general, distinctive readings of 05, either of rewriting or of expansion of the text (see p. 9 above).

10.33	[παρα]καλ[ων ελθειν] προ[c ημαc]
11.2	the whole verse
12.2	[και α]νειλε[ν] (m.2 'ν')
12.7	νυξαc

16.1	[διελθ]ων δε τ[α]
16.4	[δι]ερχομ[ενοι] . . . ε[ντολας]
16.22	[κα]ι πο[λυ]ς ο[χλο]ς επε[cτη]κ[ατ αυτ]ων [επικραζο]ντες
16.35	the whole verse
16.36	[ει]cελθων δε ο δεcμοφυλαξ απ[η]γγειλεν αυτοις
16.39	the whole verse
17.4	[πολλοι των] cεβομενων
	[κ]αι γυναικες των πρωτων
17.5	the whole verse

A number of these readings were previously singulars in Codex Bezae. The task of analysing the differences between them in these distinctive readings will be an important task in the re-examination of the tradition.

The reading at 15.41 is a longer form of the text only partially found in Codex Bezae, but fully attested in other witnesses.

4. What is the character of the distinctive readings that are new to us from 𝔓? Why are they new to us? Are they similar in character to the readings it shares with 05? Again, this is too large a task to be attempted here, except to make the general observation that it is not infrequent for these readings to contain strong echoes of material found elsewhere in Acts (for example 15.30 [τα γραμ]ματα). Details are given in the commentary below. There follows a list of some of the more notable of these readings (excluding some of those abbreviations and omissions listed above; since some of the readings have compound features, it is difficult to be precise).

10.33	ακου[cα]ι τα [προc]τετα[γμ]ενα cο[ι]
10.34	απ[ο]κριθ[εις δ]ε Πετρος
10.40	[εποι]ηcεν
10.41	[κοcμ]ω
10.42	ε[cτιν ο ωριcμε]ν[ος τη βουλη και] π[ρογνωcει του θ̄ῡ] (or another expansion)
11.3	με[τα αυτων]
12.3	〚προc〛c[υλλ]αβεcθαι
12.8–9	both the verses
15.30	[τα γραμ]ματα
15.39	beginning of the verse
15.41	Cυρο[φοινικη]ν(?)
16.3	τω τ[οπω
16.14	[ινα] . . . [λεγ]ομε[νοις]
16.16	the whole verse
16.20	και ενεφαν[ιc]αν . . . λεγο[ντ]ες ταρα[cc]ουcι[ν]

16.24	the whole verse
16.25	δεϲμωτα[ι
16.26	[κ]α̣[ι] εξαπ[ι]νηϲ [εγ]ενετο̣ ϲιϲμ[ο]ϲ μεγ[α]ϲ
16.27	ηθελϲε̣[ν]
16.28	αυτον̣ Παυλοϲ
	μη ταραϲϲου
16.30	τουϲ λοιπουϲ α̣ϲφαλιϲαϲ
16.33	the whole verse
16.36	απολυθητε
16.37	most of the verse
16.40	the whole verse
17.1–4	the whole passage
17.6	[ ]ϲτατο̣υντεϲ
17.8	ενεπληϲαν τε θυμου
17.10	ϲυ[ν] τω Ϲιλεα

5. A new historical question to be asked concerns the context in which the form of text found in 𝔓 arose. The fact that it is dated to such a similar period as Codex Bezae, which has most recently been located to around 400 (Parker, *Codex Bezae* 30), is perhaps surprising, given the general assumption that texts tended to be treated more freely in the early stages of their existence. Perhaps we should be looking for a different explanation.

This introduction concludes with an example of the fresh challenges posed by 𝔓. 16.38 shows how 𝔓 provides new ways of reading the textual history of Acts. The differences are most easily expressed by setting the texts of 03, 05 and 𝔓 in a lineated apparatus.

03	απηγγειλαν δε τοιϲ ϲτρατηγοιϲ οι ραβδουχοι τα ρηματα ταυτα
05	απηγγειλαν δε αυτοιϲοι ϲτρατηγοιϲ οι ραβδουχοι τα ρηματα ταυτα τα ρηθεντα
𝔓	απηγγειλαν δε οι ραβδουχοι τα ρηθεντα

03	εφοβηθηϲαν
05	προϲ τουϲ ϲτρατηγουϲ οι δε ακουϲαντεϲ οτι ρωμαιοι ειϲιν εφοβηθηϲαν
𝔓	υπο του Παυλου το̣ι̣ϲ ϲ̣τ̣ρ̣α̣τ̣ηγοιϲ οι δε ακουϲ̣αντεϲ εφοβηθηϲαν

03	δε ακουϲαντεϲ οτι ρωμαιοι ειϲιν
05	
𝔓	οτι ρωμαιο{υ}ϲ αυτουϲ απεκαλουν

Here it may be said that 05 contains elements found separately in 𝔓 and the commonest form of text. But one of these (τα ρηματα ταυτα τα ρηθεντα) might be an abbreviation by 𝔓. At the same time, 𝔓 contains two expansions not present in 05.

It is inevitable that free texts will differ from each other almost as much as from more fixed forms of text. That we now have an example of such a different version of Acts indicates that our theories concerning the early history of the New Testament books remain provisional.

We are indebted to Dr R. A. Coles for his painstaking collation of the transcription against the original.

Folio 1a

↓ Col. i [Col. ii lost]

	με[νος λαλησει]	10.32
	σοι· [εξαυτης]	10.33
	ουν [επεμψα]	
	προ[ς σε παρα]	
5	καλ[ως ελθειν]	
	προ[ς ημας και]	
	συ κα[λως εποι]	
	ησα[ς εν ταχει]	
	και ν[υν ιδου]	
10	παν[τες ημεις]	
	ενω[πιον σου]	
	ακου[σα]ι τα [προς]	
	τετα[γμ]ενα σο[ι]	
	απο τ[ου] θυ· απ[ο]	10.34
15	κριθ[εις δ]ε Πε	
	τρος ε[ιπεν ε]	
	π αλη[θειας]	
	καταλα[μβανο]	
	μαι· οτι [ουκ ε]	
20	στιν προ[σωπο]	
	λημπτη[ς ο θς]	
	αλλα εν [παντι]	10.35

Folio 1b

→ [Col. i lost] Col. ii

[c.12   ]
[c.12   ]
[c.6   ] ημερα   10.40
[και εποι]ησεν
5 [εμφανη] γενε
[cθαι ου π]αντι   10.41
[τω κοcμ]ω· αλλα
[τοιc προ]κεχει
[ροτονη]μενοιc
10 [υπο του] θ̄ῡ· η
[μιν οιτ]ινεc
[cυνεφα]γομεν·
και cυ[νε]πιο
μεν α[υτ]ω· και
15 cυν[ανε]cτρα
[φημεν α]υτω·
[μετα τ]ο ανα
[cτηναι] αυτον·
[εκ νε]κρων μ̄
20 [ημερα]c και ενε   10.42
[τειλατ]ο [η]μιν·
[κηρυξαι] και δια
[μαρτυ]ραcθαι

Folio 2a

→   Col. i   [Col. ii lost]

    τ̣[ω λαω οτι ουτος]   10.42
    ε̣[στιν ο ωρισμε]
    ν̣[ος τη βουλη και]
    π̣[ρογνωσει του θ̅υ̅]
5   κ̣[ριτης ζωντων]
    κ[αι νεκρων οι]   10.43
    π̣[ροφηται μαρ]
    τ[υρουσιν αφε]
    ς̣[ιν αμαρτιων]
10 λ[αβειν δια του]
    ο̣[νοματος αυ]
    τ[ου παντα τον]
    π̣[ιστευοντα]
    ε̣ι̣[ς αυτον ετι]   10.44
15 λ̣α̣[λουντος του]
    Π[ετρου ταυτα το]
    π̅ν̅α̅ το αγιον επεπ]
    ε̣[σεν επι παντας]
    αυ[τους και εξε]   10.45
20 στ̣[ησαν οι εκ]
    π[εριτομης πι]
    ς̣[τοι οσοι συν]
    ηλ[θον τω Πε]
    τρ[ω οτι και επι]

Folio 2b

↓   [Col. i lost]

Col. ii

[ποιουμενο]ς   11.2
[δια των χωρ]ων
[διδασκων α]υτους
[ος και κατηντ]η
5 [σεν εις Ιερ]οσο
[λυμα και απη]γ
[γειλεν αυτ]οις
[την χαριν τ]ου
[θ̄ῡ οι εκ περιτ]ο
10 [μης οντες αδ]ελ
[φοι διεκρινο]ν
[το προς αυτο]ν
[λεγοντες οτ]ι   11.3
[εισελθων πρ]ος
15 [ανδρας ακρο]βυ
[στιαν εχον]τας
[συνεφαγες] με
[τα αυτων α]πο   11.4
[κριθεις δε] ο Πε
20 [τρος ειπεν] αυ
[τοις εγω ημ]ην   11.5
[εν Ιοππη κ(αι) ει]δον
[εν εκστας]ει

Folio 3a

↓ Col. i   Col. ii

   Βαρ[ναβα και Cαυ]   11.30
   λου [κατ εκεινον]   12.1
   δε τ[ον καιρον]
   επε[βαλεν τας]
5 χει[ρας Ηρωδης]
   ο βα[cιλευc κα]
   κω[cαι τιναc]
   των [απο τηc]
   εκκ[λησιαc εν τη]
10 Ϊου[δαια και αν]   12.2
m.2 'ν' ειλε[ν Ιακωβον]
   τον [αδελφον]
   Ϊωα[ννου εν]
   μα[χαιρα και]   12.3
15 ϊδω[ν οτι αρε]
   cτο[ν τοιc Ιου]
   δαιο[ιc η επιχει]
   ρηc[ιc αυτου]   [εν τη φυ]   12.5
   επι τ[ου]ς πιστους   λ[ακη προσευχη]
20 ηθε[λης]εν και   20 δε [ην εν εκτενεια]
   τον [Πε]τρον   γε[ινομενη προc]
   〚προc〛'c[υλλ]αβεcθαί·   το[ν θ̄ν̄ περι αυτου]
   ηcαν [δ]ε ημεραι   ϋπ[ο της εκκληcιαc]

Folio 3b

→ Col. i

Col. ii

[νυξας δε] την
[πλευραν α]υτου
[ηγειρεν] λεγων
[αναστα ε]ν τα
5 [χει και ιδ]ου αι α
[λυσεις ε]κ των
[χειρων αυ]του
[εξεπεσα]ν· ει   12.8
[πεν δε ο] αγγε
10 [λος τω Π]ετρω·
[ζωσαι κ]αι υπο
[δησαι τα] υπο
[δηματα c]ου· κ(αι)
[περιβαλ]ου τ[ο]
15 [ιματιο]ν cου·
[και λαβο]μενος
[τον Πετρον] προ
[ηγαγεν ε]ξω ει
πων [ακ]ολου
20 θει μ[οι ο] δε Πε   12.9
τρος η[κο]λου
θει μη [ει]δως
ει αλη[θε]ς εστι

[επεστη τ]ω   12.7
20 [Πετρω κ]αι το
[φως ελα]μψεν
[επ αυτου] εν
[τω οικημ]ατι·

Folio 4a
→ Col. i   Col. ii

6   .[15.29
    δ[ιατηρουν]
    τες [εαυτους εν]
    πρα[ξετε εν ο]   15.30
10 λιγαις [δε ημε]
    ραις ο[
    δε[[   ]..[15.34
    εις Αν[τιοχειαν]   [αυτ]ου μο[νος]
    και ϲυν[αγαγον]   [δε] Ἰουδας επο
15 τες το [πληθος επ] 15 [ρευ]θη ο δε Παυ   15.35
    εδωκ[αν τα γραμ]   [λο]ς και Βαρνα
    ματα ο[15.31 [βα]ς διετριβον
    ......[[εν] Αντιοχεια
                           [διδ]αϲκο[ντ]ες
                        20 [κα]ι ευαγγελιζο
                           [με]νοι μετα κ(αι)
                           [ετ]ερων πολλων
                           [το]ν λογον του
                           [κυ] ειπεν δε   15.36

Folio 4b
↓   Col. i   Col. ii

                                     7 [υπο των αδελ]φων   15.40
                                        [διηρχετο δε] Cυρο   15.41
                                        [φοινικη]ν επι
                                     10 [cτηριζ]ων τας
                                        [εκκλη]ciac· πα
                                        [ραδιδο]υc τας
     [ ]..[15.37   [εντολ]ας φυλας
     [Μαρ]κον· Πα[υλος]   15.38   [cειν τ]ων απο
     δε ουκ ηβο[υλε]   15 [cτολω]ν και των
  15 το λεγων· [τον]   [πρεcβ]υτερων·
     αποcτατηc[αν]   [διελθ]ων δε τ[α]   16.1
     τα απο Παμ[φυ]
     λιας και μη [cυν]
     ελθ[ο]ντα ει[c το]
  20 εργ[ο]ν εφ ο [ε]
     πεμφθηcα[ν]
     τουτον μη [cυν]
     ειναι αυτοι[c]
     εκ τουτου [ ]   15.39

Folio 5a

↓ Col. i   [Col. ii lost]

νοματ[ι Τιμοθεος]   16.1
υἱος Ιο[υδαιας]
πιστης [π̄ρ̄ς̄ δε]
Ελλην[ος ος]   16.2
5 εμαρτ[υρειτο]
περι τ[ων εν Λυ]
στ[ρ]η κ[αι Ικο]
ν[ι]ω μ[αθητων]
τουτο[ν ηθελη]   16.3
10 σεν Π[αυλος συν]
εξελθ[ειν αυτω]
και λαβ[ων πε]
[ρ]ιετε[μεν αυτον]
[δ]ια το[υς Ιουδαι]
15 ους τ[ους οντας]
εν τω τ[οπω δι]   16.4
ερχομ[ενοι δε]
τας πο[λεις εκη]
ρυσ[σον μετα]
20 παρ[ρησιας τον]
κ̄ν̄ [Ῑν̄ Χ̄ν̄ αμα πα]
ρ[αδιδοντες κ(αι)]
τας ε[ντολας]
των [αποστολων]
και π[ρεσβυτε]

Folio 5b
→[Col. i lost]

Col. ii

[ευχη ε]ιναι· ‵κ(αι)′ κα	16.13
[θισαν]τες συν	
[ελαλο]υ̣ν ταις	
[συνελ]ηλυθυι	
5 [αις γυ]ν̣αιξιν·	
[και ην τι]ς γυνη	16.14
[σεβομ]ε̣νη τ̣ον	
[θ̄ν̄ ονο]μ̣ατ[ι] Λυ	
[δια πο]ρ̣φυρο	
10 [πωλις] Θυγατηρ	
[ων . . .]. ς· ἡς ο	
[κ̄σ̄ διη]ν̣οιξεν	
[την κα]ρδιαν̣	
[ινα πιστ]ε̣υση	
15 [τοις λεγ]ο̣με̣	
[νοις υ]πο το̣υ̣	
[Παυλου] ητις	16.15
[εβαπτισ]θη· κ(αι)	
[c.8].π̣α	
20 [c.8]. . .	
[c.7]·π̣α̣	
[ρεκαλεσεν λε]	
[γουσα ει] κ̣ε̣κ̣ρ̣ι̣	
[κατε με π]ι̣στην	
25 [ειναι ε]ι̣σ̣ε̣λ̣	

Folio 6a

→Col. i

θοντες μενε
τε εις τον οικον
μου· και παρε
βιασατο ημας
5 [π]ορευομενων   16.16
[δ]ε ημων εν τη
προσευχη ʼ(m.2) παιδισκηʼ ⟦η⟧τις
[ε]χουσα πνα ʼ(m.2) πυʼ
[.]⟦[...]⟧ʼ(m.2)[θ]ωνοςʼ (m.1) ητις πολ
10 [λ]ην εργασ[ι]αν
παρειχεν τοις
κυριοις δια του
του μαντευο
μενη. κατακο   16.17
15 λουθο[υ]σα α[υ]
τ[η] πολ[λα] ημων
ε[κραζεν λε]γου
σ[α ουτοι] οι δου
λο[ι] το[υ υ]ψιστ[ο]υ
20 εισιν [οι]τινες
καταγ[γε]λλου
σιν ημ[ιν] οδον
σωτηριας· κ(αι)   16.18
τουτο εποιει
25 ημεραις ϊκα
ναις· vacat

Col. ii

επ[ις]τρεψ[ας δε]
ο Πα[υ]λος τ[ω πνι]
και [δ]ιαπο[νη]
[θεις] ειπε[ν πα]
5 ρ[αγγ]ελλω [σοι]
ε[ν τ]ω ονο[μα]
τι [Ιυ Χυ ε]ξε[λθε]
εξ [αυτη]ς· [ως δε ει]   16.19
δο[ν οι κυρι]ο[ι αυ]
10 τη[ς οτι ε]ξ[ηλ]
θεν [c.8]
αδ. [c.8]
της [εργασιας]
ρ[
15 [
ης [ειχαν δι] αυ
της [ε]πιλαβο
με[ν]οι τον Παυ
λον [κ]αι Σιλεαν
20 ηγα[γο]ν εις την
αγορ[αν] · και ενε   16.20
φαν[ισ]αν το[ι]ς
στρα[τη]γοις
λεγο[ντ]ες οτι
25 οι αν[οι] ουτοι
ταρα[σσ]ουσι[ν]

Folio 6b

↓ Col. i

[η]μων την πο
[λιν] Ιουδα[ι]οι υ
[πα]ρχοντ[ες] κ[α]ι   16.21
[κα]ταγγελ[λου]ϲιν
5 [εθ]η α ου[κ η]μιν
[εξε]ϲτιν [παρ]αδε
[ξα]ϲθα[ι ουτε] ποι
[ειν] Ρω[μαι]οις ϋ
[παρ]χο[υϲιν κα]ι πο   16.22
10 [λυ]ϲ ο[χλο]ϲ επε
[ϲτη] κ[ατ αυτ]ων
[επικραζο]ντες
[τοτε οι ϲ]τρα
[τηγοι τα ιματ]ι[α]
15 [περιρηξαντες]
ε[κελ]ευ[ον ρ]αβδ[ι]
ζειν κα[ι π]ολ   16.23
λας επι[θε]ντ[ες]
πληγας [εβ]αλο[ν]
20 εις φυλ[α]κην
παρηγ[γε]ιλαν
τες τω δ[εϲμ]οφυ
λακι α[ϲφ]αλω[ς]
τηρειν [ο] δε δε   16.24
25 ϲμοφυ[λα]ξ πα
ρ[α]λαβ[ων α]υτους

Col. ii

εβαλεν εις την
φυλακην την ε
ϲωτερω· και τους
ποδας αυτων
5 ηϲφαλιϲατο [ει]ς
ξυλον· κατ[α δ]ε   16.25
μεϲην νυκτα
ο Παυλος και Ϲι
λεας π[ρ]οϲευ[χο
10 μενο[ι] ὑμνο[υν
τον θ̄ν̄· επη[κρο
ωντο δε αυ[τω]ν
οι δεϲμωτα[ι κ]α[ι   16.26
εξαπ[ι]νης [εγ]ε
15 νετο ϲιϲμ[ο]ς
μεγ[α]ς· κα[ι εϲ]α
λ[ευ]θη [τα θεμ]ε
λια π[αντα κ]αι
ηνε[ωχ]θηϲ[αν]
20 αι θυ[ραι] παϲαι·
και π[α]ντων τα
δεϲμα ανεθη·
εξυπνος δε γε   16.27
νομενος ο δε
25 ϲμοφυλαξ· και
ιδων ανεωγμε

Folio 7a $\overline{ριβ}$

↓   Col. i   Col. ii

	Col. i			Col. ii	
	νας τας θυρας			[ι]να cωθω οι	16.31
	πασας [c]πας<u>α</u>			δε ε[ι]πον [αυ]τω	
	μενος μαχ[αι]			π<u>ι</u>cτευc[ο]<u>ν</u> ε	
	ραν ηθελης<u>εν</u>			π<u>ι</u> τ<u>ο</u>ν κ̄ν̄ Ῑν̄ κ(αι)	
5	εαυτον κατακ . [.]		5	[c]ωθηc[η c]υ κ(αι)	
	cαι νομιζων			<u>ο</u> οικος c<u>ο</u>υ· κ(αι)	16.32
	εκπεφευγεναι			ελα<u>λ</u>ηcαν α<u>υ</u>τοις	
	τους δεcμιους·			τ<u>ον</u> [λ]ογον του	
	εφωνηcεν δε	16.28		κ̄ν̄ [κα]<u>ι</u> εκεινη	16.33
10	αυτ<u>ον</u> Παυλος		10	τη [ω]ρα παραλα	
	λεγων μη ταρας			βοντες α<u>υ</u>τους	
	cου· ἁπαντες			ελ<u>ο</u>υcαν απο	
	γαρ εc<u>μ</u>εν εν			των πληγων·	
	θαδε· φωτα δε	16.29		<u>και</u> εβαπτιcθη	
15	αιτηcας ειcε		15	αυτος και παν	
	πηδηcεν· και			τες οι παρ αυτου·	
	εντρομος υπαρ			και [α]ναγαγον	16.34
	χων επιπεcων			τες [α]υτους εις	
	τω Παυλω και			τον οικον πα	
20	Сιλεα προα\(m.2)γα΄γων	16.30	20	ρεθηκαν τραπε	
	αυτους εξω. τους			ζαν· και ηγαλλι	
	λοιπους αcφα			ατο πανοικει	
	λιcας· πρ<u>ο</u>ελθων			πεπιcτευκως	
	εφη κυριοι· τι			επι τον θ̄ν̄· γε	16.35
25	με δει ποιειν		25	νομενης δε	

Folio 7b

→ Col. i

ημερας συνηλ
θο[ν] οι στρατη
γοι επ[ι τ]ο αυτο
εις την αγορα[ν]
5 και [αν]αμνη
σθεντες το[υ]
γενομενου
σεισμου εφο
βηθησα[ν κ]α[ι]
10 αποστελ[λο]υσι
τους ραβδου
χους λεγοντες
τω δεσμοφυ
λακι απολυσον
15 τους ανους
ους εχθες πα
ρελαβες [ει]σελ   16.36
θων δε ο δεσμο
φυλαξ απ[η]γγει
20 λεν αυτοις οτι
απεσταλκασιν
οι στρατηγοι α
πολυθηναι ϋ
μας· απολυθη
25 τε· ο δε Παυλος   16.37
προς αυτους

Col. ii

ειπεν ακαται
τιαστους δειραν
[τ]ες ημας δημο
[σ]ια εβαλον εις
5 την φυλακην
ϋ[π]αρχοντας
Ρωμαιους· και
νυν λαθρα εκ
βαλλουσιν ημας·
10 ελθοντες ουν
αυτοι επαγαγε
τωσαν ημας· α   16.38
πηγγειλαν δε
οι ραβδουχοι τα
15 ρηθεντα υπο
του Παυλου τοις
στρατηγοις οι
δε ακουσαντες
εφοβηθησαν
20 οτι Ρωμαιο(m.2)υ'ς
αυτους απεκα
λουν· παραγε   16.39
νομενοι τε με
τα ικανων φι
25 λων επι την
φυλακην πα

Folio 8a

Col. i

ρεκαλε[c]αν αυ
τους εξελθειν·
ειποντες ηγνο
ησαμεν τα κ[α]
5 θ υμας οτι ε[cτε]
ανδρες δικα[ιοι]
εκ ταυτης δε
πολεως εξ[ελ]
θετε μ[η]π[οτε]
10 επιcτ[ρ]αφω[cιν]
παλιν οι επικρα
ζοντες καθ ϋ
μων· απολυ   16.40
θεντες δε ηλ
15 θον εις την Λυ
διαν· και ιδον
τες τους αδ[ε]λ
φους διη[γ]ηcαν
το οcα εποιη
20 cεν κc αυτοις·
και πα[ρ]ὲ(m.2)ὰκαλε
cαντες αυτους
εξεηcαν· και   17.1
κατη⟦η⟧λθον
25 εις Απολλω

Col. ii

νιδα· εκειθεν
δε εις [Θ]εccα[λο]
νικην· κατα δε   17.2
το ειωθὸc Παυ
5 λος εισηλθεν
εις την cυνα
γωγην των Ϊ
ουδαιων· επι
caββατα τρια δια
10 [λεγο]μενος αυ
τοις εκ των γρα
φων και διανοι   17.3
γων και παρα
τιθ[ε]μενος ο
15 τ[ι το]ν χν̄ εδ[ει]
π[αθειν και α]
ν[αcτηναι και]
ο[τι ουτος εcτιν]
χ[c̄ Ιc̄ ον εγω κα]
20 τ[αγγελλω υμιν]
κ[αι τινες αυτων]   17.4
ε[πεισθηcαν κ(αι)]
π[ροcεκληρω]
θ[ηcαν τη διδα]
25 χ[η πολλοι των]

Folio 8b

↓ Col. i

ϲεβομενων Ε̣[λ]
[λ]ηνων πληθ[ο]ϲ
πολυ· [κ]αι γυναι
κεϲ των πρω
5 των ο[υ]κ ο̣λι̣`(m.2)γ̣ʹαι   17.5
οι δε απειθουν̣
τεϲ Ϊουδαιο[ι ϲυν]
ϲτρεψαντεϲ τ̣[ι]
ναϲ ανδρ[α]ϲ τ[ων]
10 αγοραιω[ν πολ]
λουϲ εθο[ρ]υβο[υν]
την πολιν· και
επιϲταν̣τεϲ τ̣η
οικ̣[ια] Ϊαϲο̣νοϲ
15 εζ̣[ητ]ο̣υν [αυτ]ο̣υϲ
[εξαγαγειν ειϲ]
[τον δημον μ]η   17.6
[ευροντεϲ δε αυ]
[τουϲ εϲυρον Ϊαϲ]ο
20 να και τιναϲ αδ[ελ]
[φουϲ επι τουϲ πο]
[λιταρχαϲ βοω]ν̣
[τεϲ και λεγο]ν̣
[τεϲ οτι οι την οι]
25 [κουμενην αν]α̣

Col. ii

ϲτατουντεϲ ου
τοι ειϲιν· και εν
θαδε παρειϲιν·
[ου]ϲ υποδε[δ]εκ   17.7
5 [α]τοϲ ο Ϊαϲων·
[κ]αι ουτοι παντε̣ϲ
[α]πεναντι των
[δ]ο̣γματων Κα[ι]
[ϲα]ρο̣ϲ π̣ρ̣αϲϲοʹ(m.2)υϲινʹ
10 [ω]ϲ βα̣[ϲι]λεα λε
γοντεϲ τινα πο
τε Ι̅ν̅ ενεπλη   17.8
ϲαν τε θυμου
τουϲ πολιταρχαϲ
15 και τον οχλον
ακουονταϲ τα̣υ
τα· οι μεν ουν   17.9
π[ολι]ταρχαι ϊκα̣
νο̣ν λαβοντεϲ
20 παρα του Ϊαϲονο[ϲ]
και των λοιπω̣[ν]
απελυϲαν· οι δ[ε]   17.10
α̅δελφοι απελυ
ον δια νυκ̣τοϲ
25 τον Παυλον ϲυ[ν]
τω Ϲιλεα ειϲ Βε

For an explanation of the parameters of this commentary, see the end of the introduction. Note that the phrase 'other witnesses' does not indicate all other witnesses, but those which have been included in this survey.

Where there is no explicit comment, punctuation is considered to be by the first hand.

Fol. 1a, col. i
(**10.32**)

1–2 με[νοϲ λαληϲει] ϲοι. The extant letters of the first two lines represent a reading present in most witnesses, including 05, but not followed by 03: the addition of οϲ παραγενομενοϲ λαληϲει ϲοι. For a full list of the evidence see K. Aland et al. (eds.), *Text und Textwert der griechischen Handschriften des*

Neuen Testaments, III.1 *Die Apostelgeschichte* I (ANTF 20–21: Berlin and New York 1993) 503–5 (where however the readings 1 and 1B are reversed with respect to the readings λαλήcει and λαλῆcαι).

2 Point probably *m.* 2.

(**10.33**)

4–6 𝔓 is reconstructed as [παρα]καλ[ων ελθειν] προ[c ημαc], the reading of 05*, with corresponding readings in versions including the Harklean margin and mae. 03 omits.

6–7 προ[c ημαc και] cυ. The reconstruction assumes that the absence of τε (03) or δε (05) requires καί.

8 The reconstruction εν ταχει follows the text of 05 (note that παραγενομενοc is read at the end of the previous verse; see above, 1–2 n.).

9 Reconstruction of και ν[υν ιδου] (cf. 13.11; 20.22, 25) prefers the slightly longer reading of 05 (05^A, 05* reads δου, 05^C ουν) to νυν ουν (03). The reading ιδου should be taken with the omission of παρεcμεν after θεου later in the verse as a possible Semitism (cf. Ropes ad loc.; Moulton–Turner, *A Grammar of New Testament Greek* iii 296, 305).

11 ενω[πιον cου]. The restoration of του θεου (almost all witnesses) can hardly be said to be more probable than the alternative cου (05* d vg sy^p mae).

12–13 ακου[cα]ι τα [προc]τετα[γμ]ενα cο[ι] is a distinctive reading. 𝔓 evidently omits both παντα (found in 02 after cοι and in 𝔓^45 𝔓^74 01 03 and most other witnesses before τα) and τα itself, as well as βουλομενοι παρα cου found in 05*. It thus has a shortened form of the text compared to that found in 03.

14 απο is found also in 𝔓^45 𝔓^74 01^Ca 02 04 05, υπο in 01* 03 and most other witnesses (παρα 08). θ̄ῡ. θεου is read by 𝔓^74 05 and the Byzantine majority. The alternative reading is κυριον.

(**10.34**)

14–16 απ[ο]κριθ[εις δ]ε Πετροc is otherwise unattested in the Greek tradition. Other witnesses read ανοιξας δε Πετροc το cτομα (ανοιξας δε το cτομα Πετροc 𝔓^45 05). The reading of 𝔓 provides a possible Greek source for the reading as it is found in a Syriac fragment. See C. Perrot, 'Un fragment christo-palestinien découvert à Khirbet Mird, Actes des Apôtres x: 28-29; 32-41', *Revue biblique* 70 (1963) 506–55.

14, 19 Points *m.* 2.

18–19 καταλα[μβανο]μαι: καταλαμβανομενος 05*.

20–21 προcωπολημπτηc is the spelling of the majority of older witnesses; προcωποληπτηc is read by 03^C2 and some other manuscripts.

(**10.35**)

22 αλλα rather than αλλ also 02.

Fol. 1b, col. ii

(**10.40**)

3 ημερα. 𝔓 may have read either μετα την τριτην ημεραν (05) or (εν) τη τριτη ημερα (other witnesses), since the papyrus is lost where a superline over the alpha would be. But since there are no examples of superline for final nu, (εν) τη τριτη ημερα is more probable.

4 εποι]ηcεν is otherwise unattested (εδωκεν other witnesses). ποιεω is found for διδωμι in 05 at Mk 3.6; 13.22; Lk 12.51. Hitherto unattested also is the omission of αυτον (αυτω 05), a lost τουτον at the beginning of the verse presumably standing as object both for this verb and for ηγειρεν.

(**10.41**)

7 κοcμ]ω. λαω all other witnesses, but [λα] is too short for the space. [κοcμ] is supplied as a likely fit (cf. 2.47, where 05 reads κοcμω instead of λα).

7, 10, 16, 18 Points *m.* 2.

12, 14 Points probably *m.* 2.

13 There may be a trace of epsilon on a piece of papyrus that is bent over.

14–16 και ϲυν[ανε]ϲτρα[φημεν] with D^B (a corrector of the first half of the fifth century): και ϲυνεϲτραφημεν (05*): 𝔓^45 𝔓^74 01 02 03 04 08 omit. The Old Latin, Harklean Syriac, Sahidic and mae also contain the added phrase.

19–20 μ̅ [ημερα]ϲ. μ̅ is read by 05, δι ημερων τεϲϲερακοντα by 08. The Old Latin, Harklean Syriac, Sahidic and mae also attest the phrase. Use of a numeral instead of the full word is a common feature of Greek New Testament manuscripts.

(**10.42**)

20–21 ενε[τειλατ]ο is restored with 05. All other witnesses read παρηγγειλεν.

21 Point m. 2.

22–fol. 2a, col. i. There is no other Greek support for the word order και δια[μαρτυ]ραϲθαι τ[ω λαω. Other witnesses read τω λαω και διαμαρτυραϲθαι.

Fol. 2a, col. i

4 Since other witnesses read θεου κριτηϲ, 𝔓 evidently contained an addition, of which only the first letter survives. One possibility is that lines 3–4 contained a remodelling based on 2.23, τουτον τη ωριϲμενη βουλη και προγνωϲει του θεου. Although quite a long conjecture, it is followed in the reconstruction.

(**10.43**)

6 𝔓 appears to have omitted τουτω παντεϲ. There is only space for οι or perhaps οι δε.

(**10.44**)

16 ταυτα (restored). All other witnesses read τα ρηματα ταυτα. Abbreviation to ταυτα fits the available space.

16–19 ταυτα το] π̅ν̅α̅ το αγιον επεπ]ε[ϲεν επι παντας] αυ[τουϲ. The reconstruction is otherwise unattested, being a variation in word order from επεπεϲεν το πνευμα το αγιον (preferring επεπεϲεν to the επεϲεν of 02 05), followed by an abbreviation of επι παντας τους ακουοντας τον λογον.

(**10.45**)

22 The restoration of οϲοι (οι 03) fits the available space.

22–3 ϲυν]ηλ[θον. Restoration with -ον (ϲυνηλθον 𝔓^74 02 05 08 al, -αν 01 03 al) accords with the evidence from elsewhere in the papyrus (cf. 17.1).

Fol. 2b, col. ii

(**11.2**)

1–12 The column begins within an expanded version of verse 2. It seems to have had a very similar version to 05. This consists of a revision of the first half of the verse as it appears in 𝔓^74 01 03, which includes a lengthy insertion. Support for the longer reading includes 05, the Middle Egyptian version, the Harklean Syriac (obelized) and some Latin witnesses. The text of 05 fits in as the reconstruction, with three differences:

(i) 4–6 for κατηντηϲεν αυτοιϲ (05), 𝔓 reads [κατηντ]η[ϲεν ειϲ Ιερ]οϲο[λυμα], a reading shared with the Middle Egyptian.

(ii) 9 𝔓 is unlikely to have agreed with 05 in inserting δε after οι, since there seems too little space for it. Note that if this was so, then it agreed with d against 05.

(iii) 10 In the final part of the verse, there is space in 𝔓 for an extra word between περιτ]ο[μηϲ] and [αδ]ελ[φοι]; οντεϲ (see 11.1 (not 05, but d reads *erant*)) seems likely.

For a full statement of all text forms here, see *Text und Textwert* 508–11.

(**11.3**)

17 [ϲυνεφαγεϲ]. One could restore either ϲυνεφαγεν (𝔓^45 03) or ϲυνεφαγεϲ (01 05 other wit-

nesses). There is unlikely to have been enough room for καί, even as a compendium. This suggests the reading εισελθων . . . συνεφαγες.

17–18 με[τα αυτων]: συν αυτοις 05*: αυτοις other witnesses.

(11.4)

18–21 αυτων α]πο[κριθεις δε] ο Πε[τρος ειπεν] αυ[τοις. 𝔓 has a distinctive version of this introduction to Peter's speech. 03 05 and other witnesses read αρξαμενος δε πετρος εξετιθετο αυτοις (+ τα 05) καθεξης λεγων. The version in 𝔓 is a simplification to a formula that is common in the Gospels and Acts.

(11.5)

22 There is no room for πολει (found after Ιοππη in 05 and before it in other witnesses), even with και-compendium in the reconstruction. Elsewhere in Acts πολις is not used with Ιοππη (9.36, 38, 42, 43; 10.5, 8, 23, 32, 11.13).

προσευχομενος after Ιοππη is omitted with 01*.

23 05* omits εν before εκστασει.

Fol. 3a, col. i

(12.1)

4–6 τας] χει[ρας Ηρωδης] ο βα[σιλευς. The word order with τας χειρας before Ηρωδης is shared with 05. Most witnesses read Ηρωδης ο βασιλευς τας χειρας (ο βασιλευς Ηρωδης τας χειρας 01).

9–10 𝔓 agrees with 05 in defining the persecution more clearly with εν τη Ιουδαια.

(12.2)

10–11 [και αν]ειλε[ν] (m.2 'ν') restored with 05: ανειλεν δε other witnesses.

13 There is space at the end of the line for an otherwise unattested word of up to three letters. εν has been supplied (see Lk 22.49).

14 One may restore either μα[χαιρη (03* 05^C etc.) or μα[χαιρα (03^C 05*).

(12.3)

14–15 και] ιδω[ν restored with 05 and most other witnesses: ιδων δε 01 03 08.

16 𝔓 agrees with 01* in error, omitting εστιν after αρεστον.

17–19 η επιχειρησεις αυτου επι τους πιστους is read by 05, as well as three Old Latin witnesses, the Harklean Syriac and Middle Egyptian (reads 'Christians' instead of 'faithful').

20 ηθε[λης]εν: προσεθετο other witnesses. Schenke conjectured προσθεις ηθελησεν behind the reading of the Middle Egyptian. Compare also 𝔓 at 16.27, where it uses ηθελησεν against other witnesses, also in a context of doing to death. For a full statement of all text forms here, see *Text und Textwert* 511–13.

21–2 τον [Πε]τρον ⟦προς⟧'σ[υλλ]αβεσθαί. Other witnesses read συλλαβειν και Πετρον. For the use of the middle, compare 26.21.

23 𝔓 agrees with 𝔓⁴⁵ 03 and other witnesses against 05 and the majority of manuscripts in not including αι before ημεραι.

Fol. 3a, col. ii

(12.5)

20 The restoration ην εν εκτενεια follows 05. ην εκτενως (ην εκτενης is also found) is a little short, but possible.

21 γε[ινομενη] is restored (read by e.g. 03), but some manuscripts read γενομενη (*teste* Tischendorf).

21–3 The word order is best reconstructed as προς] το[ν θ(εο)ν περι αυτου] υπ[ο της εκκλησιας. 03 reads υπο της εκκλησιας περι αυτου, omitting προς τον θεον, 05* περι αυτου απο της εκκλησιας προc τον θεον, and 02* υπο της εκκλησιας προc τον θεον υπ αυτου. Although the reconstructed text is not attested elsewhere, it is of a piece with the other readings.

Fol. 3b, col. i
(**12.7**)
19–20 τ]ω [Πετρω is also read by 05 and versional evidence, notably the Peshitta and Harklean (obelized), the Middle Egyptian and it^p.
21 The space suits ελα]μψεν (επελαμψεν 05, subsequently omitting εν, present in 𝔓).
22 There is some versional support for the equivalent of απ αυτου (Harklean margin and it$^{perp\ gig}$ Lucif, the position varying). Some minuscules read επ αυτου for εν τω οικηματι. The reconstruction follows the Greek reading.
23 Point *m*. 2.

Fol. 3b, col. ii
1 νυξαc restored with 05 (cf. also it^{gig} Lucif mae). There is no space for παταξαc (cett.).
2 All other witnesses read του Πετρου; α]υτου may be intended to avoid repetition of the name.
3 All other witnesses read αυτον after ηγειρεν. Is it omitted because αυτου was used in the previous line?
5 ιδ]ου may be supported by the Middle Egyptian. και ιδου is read at the beginning of the verse (𝔓 being missing).
5–8 αι α[λυcειc ε]κ των [χειρων αυ]του [εξεπεcα]ν. The word order is otherwise unattested: 05 reads εξεπεcαν αι αλυcειc εκ των χειρων αυτου; 𝔓^{74} 01 02 03 etc. εξεπεcαν αυτου αι αλυcειc εκ των χειρων.
8 Point *m*. 2.
(**12.8**)
9 δε restored *exempli gratia*; τε (𝔓^{74} 01 02) is equally possible.
10 τω Π]ετρω: προc αυτον all other witnesses. The variant may be linked to those at lines 2 and 3.
10, 13, 15 Points *m*. 2.
12–13 υπο[δηματα: cανδαλια all other witnesses. 𝔓 substitutes the more common NT word (cανδαλιον is only found in the printed text here and Mk 6.9). υποδηcαι immediately before is an obvious cause of the reading.
13–15 κ(αι) [περιβαλ]ου τ[ο ιματιο]ν cου. This is a considerable abbreviation. 𝔓^{74} 01 02 03 05 etc. read εποιηcεν δε ουτωc και λεγει αυτω περιβαλου το ιματιον cου. it^p reads *et circumda te uestimentum tuum et sequere me. fecit autem sic*. Further down (lines 18–20) 𝔓 inserts ειπων [ακ]ολουθει μ[οι after ε]ξω.
(**12.8–9**)
16–20 και λαβο]μενος [τον Πετρον] προ[ηγαγεν ε]ξω ειπων [ακ]ολουθει μ[οι. Immediately after abbreviating a phrase, 𝔓 expands. Other witnesses read και ακολουθει μοι και εξελθων. Compare 16.30 in 05, και προηγαγεν αυτους εξω (where 𝔓 has προαγαγων αυτους εξω).
(**12.9**)
21 𝔓 builds its own version around the common word ηκολουθει, adding ο δε Πετρος before it and substituting μη ειδως ει for και ουκ ηδει οτι. Other manuscripts have little variation, except for αυτω added after ηκολουθει in 01^C and other witnesses.

Fol. 4a, col. i
(**15.29**)
Unfortunately 𝔓 resumes in the middle of this important verse, so we cannot know whether it read και πνικτων (most witnesses) or omitted it (so 05), nor whether it contained the Golden Rule (read by 05 1739 al, obelized in the Harklean Syriac).

9 πρα[ξετε. πραξατε (𝔓⁷⁴ 04 05) and πραξητε are also read. The papyrus does not share the reading of 05 that follows this word (φερομενοι εν τω αγιω πνευματι), and is alone in omitting ερρωϲθε.

(15.30)

9–12 [εν ο]λιγαιϲ [δε ημε]ραιϲ is most closely matched in 05, which reads εν ημεραιϲ ολιγαιϲ. The subsequent text is a puzzle. The wording ο[υτοι οι α]|δε[λφοι ηλθον] would fit the space. Other witnesses read οι μεν ουν απολυθεντεϲ (here 05 adds εν ημεραιϲ ολιγαιϲ) κατηλθον (ηλθον 08).

16–17 τα γραμ]ματα is otherwise unattested, but found at Acts 28.21. Other witnesses read την επιϲτολην.

17–18 ο[is evidence that the manuscript had an addition before the first word of the next verse (αναγνοντεϲ). The natural guess would be ο[ι δε αναγ]|νοντεϲ [εχαρη]ϲαν. Nu in line 18 is a possible reading, but the rest cannot be read.

Fol. 4a, col. ii

(15.34)

13–14 𝔓 resumes in the middle of a reading found in the form εδοξε δε τω Ϲειλεα επιμειναι αυτουϲ μονοϲ δε Ιουδαϲ επορευθη in 05; εδοξε ... Ϲιλα ... αυτουϲ 04 1739 (reads αυτου); 𝔓⁷⁴ 01 02 03 etc. omit it.

(15.35)

15–16 ο̣ δε Παυ[λο]ϲ̣ with 05: Παυλοϲ δε other witnesses.

21 μετα κ(αι) with most witnesses: και μετα 05*.

(15.36)

24 ειπεν δε̣ suggests that 𝔓 abbreviated the beginning of the verse. Other witnesses read μετα δε τιναϲ ημεραϲ ειπεν.

Fol. 4b, col. i

(15.38)

13, 15 Points probably m. 1.

14–15 ο̣υκ ηβο[υλε]το λεγων: ουκ εβουλετο λεγων 05: ηξιου other witnesses.

16–17 απο̣ϲτατηϲ[αν]τα with 02: αποϲτηϲαντα 05: αποϲταντα 01 03.

17 After the participle, all other witnesses have απ αυτων.

19 05 also omits αυτοιϲ after ϲυνελθοντα.

20–21 εφ ο [ε]πεμφθηϲα[ν]: ειϲ ο επεμφθηϲαν 05 (*in quo missi erant* d). No other witness contains this clause.

22–3 τουτον μη [ϲυν]ειναι αυ̣τοι[ϲ]: τουτον μη ειναι ϲυν αυτοιϲ 05: [μη] ϲυμπαραλαμβειν 𝔓⁴⁵: μη ϲυνπαραλαμβανειν τουτον 01 02 03*; μη ϲυνταραλαβειν other witnesses.

(15.39)

24 εκ τουτου appears to be a hitherto unknown version of the beginning of verse 39. Note the similar implication of the variant ουν instead of δε in 04 08.

Fol. 4b, col. ii

(15.40)

7 The reconstruction with υπο follows the majority. 05 reads απο.

(15.41)

8–9 The reconstructed Ϲυρο[φοινικη]ν is otherwise unattested, other witnesses reading την Ϲυριαν και (την) Κιλικιαν (δια c. gen. 𝔓⁴⁵). Cf. Ϲυροφοινικιϲϲα, Mk 7.26 (Φοινιϲϲα 05; Ϲυροφοινιϲϲα 032). The alternative Ϲυρο[κιλικια]ν should be rejected on historical grounds.

11–16 πα[ραδιδο]υc . . . [πρεcβ]υτερων. The addition is supported by the Harklean margin and by the Latin witnesses Codex Gigas and some Vulgate witnesses. It is partly supported by 05, which reads παραδιδουc τας εντολας των πρεcβυτερων. The wording recalls that of 16.4; see note below.

11 Point probably *m*. 1.
16 Point probably *m*. 2.

(16.1)
17 What survives agrees with 05, διελθων δε τα εθνη ταυτα κατηντηcεν. Other witnesses read κατηντηcεν δε.

Fol. 5a, col. i
2 Diaeresis *m*. 2.
All other witnesses add γυναικος after υιος (γυναικος τινος some manuscripts).

(16.2)
6 περι: υπο all other witnesses.
6–7 [Λυ]cτ[ρ]η. The singular form is also found in d (*Lystrae*). The form Λυcτροις is normal. For a parallel to the usage in 𝔓 see Tobit 6.10 A B (*Ραγη* against *Ραγοις*, the nominative, perhaps *Ραγα*, being unattested) and the form *Βεθcουρα* against *Βεθcουροις* (nominative *Βεθcουρα* or *Βεθcουραν*). See H. St J. Thackeray, *A Grammar of the Old Testament in Greek* 167 f.; Moulton–Howard, *Grammar* ii 128, 147; Blass–Debrunner–Funk–Rehkopf, *Grammatik* §57.
8 μ[αθητων: αδελφων other witnesses. Note μαθητης in the previous verse.

(16.3)
10 𝔓 is alone in omitting the article before Παυλος.
10–11 cυν]εξελθ[ειν αυτω. Space requires this change in order, otherwise unattested (cυν αυτω εξελθειν other witnesses). Compare the similar reading in 𝔓 at fol. 4b i 22–3.
12–13 λαβ[ων περ]ιετε[μεν αυτον with most witnesses. 𝔓⁴⁵ and some minuscules read ελαβεν και περιτεμων αυτον. While space allows this to be equally possible, the reconstruction follows the more common reading.
16 τω τ[οπω: τοις τοποις εκεινοις most other witnesses. Swanson reports τω τοπω εκεινω in 69 1175. (For the relationship between these two manuscripts (the former is the celebrated Leicester Codex) see K. Lake, S. New, *Six Collations of New Testament Manuscripts* (HThS 17: Cambridge, Mass. 1932) 220–43, esp. 221–5.)
At this point 𝔓 lacks a phrase found in various wordings in all other witnesses: ηδεισαν γαρ (α) παντες τον πατερα αυτου οτι Ελλην υπηρχεν 𝔓⁴⁵ 05: ηδεισαν γαρ (α)παντες οτι Ελλην ο πατηρ αυτου υπηρχεν 𝔓⁷⁴ 01 02 03 04 etc. There is no obvious cause for *parablepsis*. Did the phrase seem to contain a hint that Paul acted out of expediency?

(16.4)
16–23 δι]ερχομ[ενοι . . . ε[ντολας]. The reading of 𝔓 is similar to 05, which reads διερχομενοι δε τας πολεις εκηρυcσον και παρεδιδοσαν αυτοις μετα πασης παρρησιας τον κυριον ιησουν χριστον αμα παραδιδοντες και τας εντολας. The only difference is that 𝔓 omits και παρεδιδοσαν αυτοις, a version with better sense. The reading of 03 is ως δε διεπορευοντο τας πολεις παρεδιδοσαν αυτοις φυλασσειν τα δογματα τα κεκριμενα υπο. Much of this wording is used by 𝔓 at 15.41, perhaps leading to revision here. The development of the two versions of 𝔓 and 05 is particularly interesting in these two places.

Fol. 5b, col. ii
(16.13)
2–3 cυν[ελαλο]υν: ελαλουμεν other witnesses.

4–5 [cυνελ]ηλυθυι[αιc: cυνεληλυθυιαc 05: cυνελθουcαιc other witnesses (followed by ημιν 01* 04 08).

(16.14)

6 The restoration of [ην τι]c here and the uncertainty in line 11 seem to suggest a rather odd construction. τιc alone in line 6 is too short. Note that 08 reads και τιc γυνη . . . ητιc, with a different word order; also that ητιc appears a third time in this column at line 17.

6–11 𝔓 has a distinctive word order, with the clauses placed as follows: τιc γυνη / cεβομενη τον Θεον / ονοματι Λυδια / πορφυροπωλιc Θυατειρων. Other witnesses read τιc γυνη / ονοματι Λυδια / πορφυροπωλιc πολεωc Θυατειρων / cεβομενη τον Θεον (κυριον 05*, θεον 05*ᶜ) ἤκου(c)εν. The difficulty of reconstruction noted at line 6 may be a result of this change in order.

10 𝔓 omits πολεωc (τηc πολεωc 05), perhaps by haplography with the preceding πωλιc.

For the spelling of Θυατειρα, see the evidence of one manuscript at Rev 1.11 (Gregory–Aland 2047, copied in Rome by a German in 1543) and one at 2.18 (Gregory–Aland 2015, of the fifteenth century). (See H. C. Hoskier, *Concerning the Text of the Apocalypse: Collations of All Existing Available Greek Documents with the Standard Text of Stephen's Third Edition Together with the Testimony of Versions, Commentaries and Fathers; A Complete Conspectus of All Authorities* (London 1929) vol. ii, ad loc.) This looks like an example of assimilation to the noun θυγάτηρ occurring independently in several places (note the false word division at the line break in 𝔓). For an example of omission of gamma in θυγάτηρ, and other changes involving this letter, see Gignac, *Grammar* i 74.

11 . . .] c. The restoration is uncertain. [ητ]ιc would suit space and trace, but mars the grammar. 08 reads θυατιρων cεβομενη τον θεον ητιc ηκουεν ηc ο κυριοc διηνοιξεν την καρδιαν; could it be that 𝔓 offers an abbreviated form of something similar? Or do we have to assume an even greater corruption of θυατειρων?

Breathing on ηc m. 2.

14–16 [ινα πιcτ]ευcη [τοιc λεγ]ομε[νοιc]: προcεχειν τοιc λαλουμενοιc other witnesses (𝔓⁷⁴ places λαλουμενοιc after Παυλου). The nearest similar phrase in Acts is 8.12, οτε δε επιcτευcαν τω Φιλιππω ευαγγελιζομενω.

(16.15)

17 ητιc: ωc δε other witnesses.

18 Point m. 2.

19–21 Other witnesses read ο οικοc αυτηc παρεκαλεcεν. 𝔓 evidently had a longer reading, longer than is found in any extant manuscript, but there is no obvious restoration. Perhaps the reference to 'her and her household' was slightly expanded (see e.g. Jn 4.53).

20 The ink marks consist of a vertical stroke and two specks.

21 Point m. 2. There may be a trace of ink before it.

24–5 There is no room for τω κυριω (τω θεω 05). The words are also omitted by a few minuscules (Tischendorf cited seven). This would be an interesting example of a reading previously attested only in manuscripts of the Byzantine period being shown to be of a much earlier date.

Fol. 6a, col. i

1–3 μενετε ειc τον οικον μου: ειc τον οικον μου μενετε other witnesses (μεινατε 04 and a few minuscules).

(16.16)

The sentence has been extensively remodelled. Compare 03, which reads εγενετο δε πορευομενων ημων ειc την προcευχην. παιδιcκην τινα εχουcαν πνευμα πυθωνα υπαντηcαι ημιν ητιc εργαcιαν πολλην παρειχεν τοιc κυριοιc αυτηc· μαντευομενη.

5–6 [π]ορευομενων [δ]ε ημων: εγενετο δε πορευομενων ημων other witnesses. There is no model elsewhere in Acts which might serve for this simplification. As a consequence of this, the sentence is linked to the following one, the main verb being reconstructed as εκραζεν (line 17). Of the form as it is found in Nestle–Aland, Barrett comments 'not one of Luke's best sentences' (II 784).

6–7 εν τη προσευχη: εις την προσευχην other witnesses (την is omitted by 05 and others). 𝔓 adopts the more usual phrase. This changes the sense from a trip to a place of prayer to prayer as they were going along.

7 [[η]]τις was corrected by the scribe. The occurrence of the word in line 9 may have influenced what was first copied here (and see the two occurrences of the word in lines 11 and 17 of the previous column). παιδισκη τις is also unique, other witnesses reading the accusative after γίνομαι.

8–9 πυ[θ]ωνος, added by a corrector, is read by 𝔓45 04^C3 05^C1 08 and some minuscules. Other witnesses read πυθωνα. What was originally written consisted of three to four letters at the beginning of line 9. One may very tentatively read πο̣λυ̣.

9 For the omission of υπαντησαι ημας, see note on verse above.

9–10 πολ[λ]ην εργας[ι]αν: εργασιαν πολλην other witnesses. Both positions of πολυς with the anarthrous noun are found in Acts, the position before being more common.

12 Like 05, 𝔓 omits αυτης after κυριοις against other witnessses (including d). Like 05 also and here with d, it supplies δια τουτου (*sic* 05*, om. 05^C).

(**16.17**)

14 Point probably *m.* 2.

14 Other witnesses place αυτη before κατακολουθουσα.

15 α[υ]: the following area has lost the upper layer of fibre.

16 πολ[λα] ημων. Other witnesses read (τω) Παυλω και ημιν; πολ[λα] may be a corruption of Παυλω.

17 ε[κραζεν is restored with the majority of witnesses, but note εκραξε in a few minuscules; και εκραζον 05*.

18 𝔓 agrees with 05 in omitting ανθρωποι after οι. 𝔓45 omits δουλοι.

19 το[υ υ]ψιστ[ο]υ: του θεου του υψιστου other witnesses.

22 Both υμιν (first hand) and ημιν (corrector) are otherwise attested: υμιν 𝔓74 01 03 05 08; ημιν 02 04 𝔐.

(**16.18**)

23–4 κ(αι) τουτο. Tischendorf cites Eustathius and Origen in support of this reading; τουτο δε other witnesses.

25–6 ημεραις ικαναις: επι πολλας ημερας other witnesses. Compare 14.21, where 05 reads πολ-λους against ικανους. For ικανη with ημερα see Acts 9.23, 43; 18.18; 27.7.

Fol. 6a, col. ii

1–4 επ[ις]τρεψ[ας . . . [δ]ιαπο[νηθεις]. The word order is shared with 05; διαπονηθεις δε (ο) Παυλος και επι(ς)τρεψας τω πνευματι other witnesses.

6 τω is read by 05 and a few minuscules. Other witnesses omit.

8 εξ: απ other witnesses.

Other witnesses have more after αυτης: και ευθεως εξηλθεν (05); και αυτη[ς της ωρας εξηλθεν] (𝔓45); και εξηλθεν αυτη τη ωρα (other witnesses); *eadem hora exiit* (d).

(**16.19**)

8 Point probably *m.* 1.

8–9 [ως δε ει]δο[ν: ως δε ειδαν 05: και ιδοντες 03: ιδοντες 02*: ιδοντες δε other witnesses.

9–10 αυ]τη[ς is the reading of most manuscripts but 05, which has της παιδισκης for αυτης.

10 The ink read as ξ̣ is at the bottom extremity of a detached piece, and fits one of the horizontal strokes of this letter as well as anything else.

10–17 05 reads απεcτερηcθαι της εργαcιας αυτων ης ειχαν δι αυτης; other witnesses read εξηλθεν η ελπις της εργαcιας αυτων. 𝔓 clearly read something quite different (72 against 42 and 29 letters respectively). The first letter of line 14 is consistent with rho, but it is far from certain. What is readable is [ ]ξ[ ]θεν [c.8]αδ [c.8] της [c.8]ρ[c.20]ης[c.8] αυτης. The beginning could be restored as [ε]ξ[ηλ]θεν [η ελπις]. Or was αυτη τη ωρα from verse 18 added after εξηλθεν?

19 Cιλεαν: Cιλαν 04 05: τον Cιλαν other witnesses. For the spelling see Blass–Debrunner §53.2 'Σιλέας is not clear (A 15.34 D Σειλέα Sileae)'. 𝔓 provides important clarification. It is consistent at the subsequent occurrences: 16.25, 29; 17.10.

20 ηγα[γο]ν: εcυραν 08: ειλκυcαν other witnesses. Compare the reconstructed reading of 𝔓 at 12.8 ([και λαβο]μενος [τον Πετρον] προ[ηγαγεν]).

21 Other witnesses supply επι τους αρχοντας after αγοραν.

Point m. 2.

(16.20)

21–4 και ενεφαν[ιc]αν . . . λεγο[ντ]ες is 𝔓's variation on και προcαγαγοντες αυτους . . . ειπαν/-ον. ἐμφανίζω is used regularly of the charges brought against Paul in Chapters 23 to 25 (23.15; 24.1; 25.2, 15).

25 οι α̅ν̅[ο̅ι̅] ουτοι: ουτοι οι ανθρωποι other witnesses.

26 ταρα[cc]ουcι[ν]: εκταραccουcιν other witnesses. The compound verb only comes here and in 05 at 15.24 in the NT, while the simple form is common. Compare 17.8 (fol. 8b, col. ii 12–13), where 𝔓 reads ενεπληcαν for εταραξαν.

Fol. 6b, col. i

(16.21)

This verse shows little variation, compared to what has preceded it.

5 [εθ]η. There is insufficient room for the distinctive reading of 05, εθνη (while one might be able to squeeze in the extra letter of εθνη, there is no room for the preceding τα).

5–6 η]μιν [εξε]cτιν: εξεcτιν ημιν other witnesses (εξ. ημας 05).

6–7 One could restore either [παρ]αδε[ξα]cθα[ι with 05 or [παρ]αδε[χε]cθα[ι with other witnesses.

8–9 ὑ[παρ]χο[υcιν with 05 (used in verse 20): ουcιν other witnesses.

(16.22)

9–12 κα]ι πο[λυ]ς ο[χλο]ς επε[cτη] κ[ατ αυτ]ων [επικραζο]ντες. This separate sentence in 𝔓 is very similar to 05, πολυς οχλος cυνεπεcτηcαν κατ αυτων κραζοντες. The differences lie in the verbal compounds and the plural verb after οχλος found in 05. Note superuenerunt in d (concurrit Vg, consurrexit gig Lucif, constituit e), comparing 11.11 επεcτηcαν 05 / superuenerunt d. There is a possibility that here 𝔓 and d combine to show an older form than 05. Other witnesses read cυνεπεcτη ο οχλος κατ αυτων.

13 τοτε restored with 05*: και other witnesses.

14–15 τα ιματ]ι[α περιρηξαντες]: περιρ(ρ)ηξαντες αυτων τα ιματια other witnesses.

(16.23)

17 κα[ι π]ολλας: πολλας τε other witnesses (πολλας δε 03).

18 After επι[θε]ντ[ες] 𝔓 omits the αυτοις found in other witnesses.

24 τηρειν with other witnesses, against τηρειcθαι 05, but omitting αυτους against them all.

(16.24)

The text in 𝔓 is again distinctive.

24–5 For [ο] δε δεcμοφυ[λα]ξ other witnesses read ος; ο δε 05 may be the starting point for the reading of 𝔓. The repetition has something of the cadence of Mt 5.25.

25–col. ii 1 παρ[α]λαβ[ων α]υτους εβαλεν. 𝔓 simplifies the reading παραγγελιαν τοιαυτην λαβων and reverses εβαλεν αυτους.

Fol. 6b, col. ii

2–3 φυλακην την εcωτερω: εcωτεραν φυλακην other witnesses. The comparative of the adverb is not found elsewhere in the NT.

3, 6 Points probably m. 2.

4–5 αυτων ηcφαλιcατο with 04^C3 05^s.m. 08 (αυτων ηcφαλιcαντο 05*): ηcφαλιcατο αυτων other witnesses.

5–6 [ει]c ξυλον: εν τω ξυλω 05: εις το ξυλον other witnesses.

(**16.25**)

7 μεcην νυκτα: μεcον της νυκτος 05*: μεcονυκτιον 01: το μεcονυκτιον 05^C1 and the rest.

8 ο with 05. 04 inserts the article before Cιλας.

10 Oblique stroke m. 2.

11 Point probably m. 2.

13 δεcμωτα[ι: δεcμιοι (δεcμοι 05*) other witnesses. δεcμωται occurs at 27.1, 42 and nowhere else in the NT.

(**16.26**)

This verse has extensive revision.

13–16 The opening becomes και εξαπινης εγενετο cειcμος μεγας, instead of the usual αφνω δε (τε 04) cειcμος εγενετο μεγας. Moulton reckons that the form εξαπινης is older than εξαπινα (*Grammar* ii 311). It is not found elsewhere in the New Testament.

16 Point could be m. 1.

16–19 𝔓's κα[ι εc]αλ[ευ]θη . . . κ]αι ηνε[ωχ]θης[αν] is a simpler construction than Luke's ωcτε cαλευθηναι . . . ηνεωχθηcαν δε. The second και is similar to the text of d (*apertaquae* (scil. *-que*)), against ηνεωχθηcαν δε (05).

18 Probably restore as π[αντα], for του δεcμωτηριου. Perhaps suggested by παcαι in the following phrase.

22 The final phrase is more recognizable. 𝔓 reads ανεθη with 03 and other witnesses against ανελυθη (01* 05*).

Fol. 7a, col. i

(**16.27**)

2 παcας: της φυλακης other witnesses. Compare π[αντα in 𝔓 at 16.26. 05* reads και before cπαcαμενος.

3 𝔓 omits την before μαχαιραν, with 𝔓^74 01 02 08 and other witnesses.

4 ηθελεcε[ν]: ημελλεν other witnesses (εμελλεν 05 and some minuscules). Compare ηθελεν in minuscule 441, and Theophylact^b (*teste* Tischendorf). Compare 12.3 (fol. 3a, col. i 20), where 𝔓 supports ηθελεcεν against προcεθετο, in a similar context. θελω is quite a common word in the text of 05, appearing in its longer readings at 3.13; 4.31; 10.21; 11.2; 15.20, 29; 19.1, 14, and as a substitution at 16.7 (for πειραζω); 18.15 (for βουλομαι); 20.3 (for μελλω). Note especially this last reading.

5–6 κατακ_[ ]cαι: ανελειν 05: αναιρειν other witnesses. Restoration here is difficult. κατακε[ντη]cαι is perhaps possible, but the trace after κ is like the foot of an oblique rising from left to right (a slanting upright is another possibility). This might suggest κατακλ[α]cαι, which would fit the space, but we cannot find another passage where it would mean 'to kill oneself'.

(**16.28**)

10 αυτον Παυλος is not otherwise attested. Other witnesses omit αυτον and include μεγαλη φωνη or φωνη μεγαλη (after Παυλος 03). Most witnesses read ο Παυλος. The article is omitted by 𝔓^74 01 03 04*. For a full statement of all text forms here, see *Text und Textwert* 546–8.

11–12 μη ταραccου: μηδεν πραξης (ποιηcης 08) cεαυτω (+ τι 05) κακον other witnesses. This, with the reading επεπεcεν in line 18, may recall Lk 1.12 εταραχθη Ζαχαριας . . . φοβος επεπεcεν.

14 Point *m.* 2.
(**16.29**)
φωτα δε αιτησας with 05 (ετησας): αιτησας δε φωτα other witnesses.
16 Point *m.* 2.
17–18 υπαρχων with 04* 05: γενομενος other witnesses.
18 επιπεςων. See on lines 11–12 above. The participial form may be an error for επεπεςεν under the influence of the preceding υπαρχων, since there is no finite verb until εφη in line 24 (and note omission of και at the beginning of verse 30). 05 adds προς τους ποδας.
20 Ϲιλεα. Omission of τω with 03 04* 05. Other witnesses read τω Ϲιλα.
(**16.30**)
Other witnesses read και before προαγαγων.
προαγων 𝔓* with 01*; προηγαγεν 05; προαγαγων 𝔓ᶜ with other witnesses.
21, 23, 24 Points *m.* 2.
21–3 τους λοιπους αςφαλιςας: 05 (τους λοιπους αςφαλιςαμενος) is the only other Greek witness to include this phrase. There is versional support from the Peshitta and the Harklean (in which it is obelized text).
24 For εφη, 05 reads και ειπεν (ειπεν 05ᶜ). The remainder of the verse is very constant in the witnesses.

Fol. 7a, col. ii
(**16.31**)
2 ε[ι]πον. ειπαν is read by the old witnesses.
[αυ]τω is not otherwise attested.
3–4 επι with most witnesses: εις 08.
4 04 05 08 and most other witnesses add Χριςτον after Ιηςουν.
6 08 adds πας before ο.
Point *m.* 2.
(**16.32**)
7 αυτοις: αυτω other witnesses. Since 𝔓 omits ςυν παςιν τοις εν τη οικια αυτου after κυριου (και παςιν etc. 08), αυτοις acts as an abbreviation of the sentence.
(**16.33**)
9–11 [κα]ι εκεινη τη [ω]ρα παραλαβοντες αυτους. Other witnesses read και παραλαβων αυτους εν εκεινη τη ωρα. Apart from the change in word order, 𝔓 adopts plural forms (παραλαβοντες ... ελουςαν), following on from ελαληςαν in verse 32.
15–16 παντες οι παρ αυτου: ο οικος αυτου ολος 𝔓⁴⁵: οι αυτου απαντες 01 03: οι οικιοι αυτου παντες 02: οι αυτου παντες other witnesses. Other witnesses follow the phrase with παραχρημα. For a full statement of all text forms here, see *Text und Textwert* 548–50.
(**16.34**)
17 και remains a doubtful reading. The word is read by 05*. Other witnesses add τε (δε 04) after αναγαγων (also present in 05).
17–18, 19–20 For the plural forms ([α]ναγαγοντες, παρεθηκαν), cf. above, 9–11 n.
19 𝔓⁷⁴ 01 02 05 08 add αυτου after οικον (αυτου και 05*).
21 08 adds αυτοις before τραπεζαν. Point *m.* 2.
21–2 There is variation between ηγαλλιατο (04* 05) and ηγαλλιαςατο (04^C2 and most other witnesses).
22 05 reads ςυν τω οικω αυτου for πανοικει (08 omits). Accent *m.* 2 (wrongly).
24 επι τον θ(εο)ν with 05: τω θεω most other witnesses.

(**16.35**)

24–fol. 7b, col. i 1 γενομενης δε ημερας for ημερας δε γενομενης of other witnesses.

Fol. 7b, col. i

1–10 This is one of 𝔓's most striking long agreements with 05. They are identical, except for οι (𝔓) against οις (05 sic); του γενομενου ςειςμου against τον ςειςμον τον γεγονοτα; αποςτελλουςι against απεςτειλαν. The Harklean margin also contains this expansion. Other witnesses read απεςτειλαν οι ςτρατηγοι. For a full statement of all text forms for the variant ἀπέςτειλαν οἱ ςτρατηγοί, see *Text und Textwert* 551–2.

12 λεγοντες with the majority of the manuscripts: λεγοντας 05.

13–14 τω δεςμοφυλακι not present in other witnesses.

16–17 𝔓 omits εκεινους with 424*, present in other witnesses, and adds ους εχθες παρελαβες with 05 and the Harklean.

(**16.36**)

17–20 [ει]ςελθων δε ο δεςμοφυλαξ απ[η]γγειλεν αυτοις is more similar to 05 (και ειςελθων ο δεςμοφυλαξ απηγγειλεν) than to other witnesses (which read απηγγειλεν δε ο δεςμοφυλαξ).

20 𝔓 reads αυτοις, while 𝔓⁴⁵ 03 04 05 read τους λογους προς τον Παυλον. Other Greek witnesses and d (*hos sermones*) add τουτους after λογους.

21 απεςταλκαςιν with 05 08: απεςτειλαν 04: απεςταλκαν other witnesses.

22–4 απολυθηναι υμας: ινα απολυθητε other witnesses.

24 Point probably m.1.

24–5 απολυθητε apparently stands for the sentence νυν ουν εξελθοντες πορευςθαι εν ειρηνη found in other witnesses (εν ειρηνη: εις ειρηνην 01; om. 05). If intentional, it is an extreme example of 𝔓's tendency to abbreviate.

(**16.37**)

26–col. ii 1 προς αυτους ειπεν: εφη προς αυτους other witnesses (εφη 08).

Fol. 7b, col. ii

1–2 ακαταιτιαςτους. Compare αναιτιους 05. In 𝔓 this stands partially instead of ακατακριτους ανθρωπους Ρωμαιους υπαρχοντας after δημοςια, read by other witnesses (including 05; υπαρχοντας Ρωμαιους ανθρωπους 𝔓⁴⁵). 𝔓 reads υπαρχοντας Ρωμαιους after φυλακην (note its similarity of word order with 𝔓⁴⁵). ακαταιτιαςτους is not a known word, but cf. the well-attested ἀκαταιτίατος; it would be a regular formation from -αιτιάζειν (itself a variation of -αιτιᾶν), and would be equivalent to ακατακριτους.

1–7 ακαταιτιαςτους . . . Ρωμαιους. 𝔓 places the phrases in a unique order. Other witnesses read δειραντες ημας δημοςια ακατακριτους ανθρωπους Ρωμαιους υπαρχοντας εβαλαν εις φυλακην (with minor differences).

4 εβαλον with 𝔓⁷⁴ 01 02 08: εβαλαν other witnesses.

5 την not present in other witnesses.

8–9 εκβαλλουςιν ημας: ημας εκβαλλουςιν other witnesses (ημας παρακαλουςιν 𝔓⁷⁴).

10–11 ελθοντες ουν αυτοι is a simplification of the classical ου γαρ αλλα ελθοντες αυτοι. See also [ελθοντες αυτοι] 𝔓⁴⁵; αυτοι ημας ελθοντες 08 (bringing ημας forward).

11–12 επαγαγετωςαν ημας: ημας εξαγαγετωςαν other witnesses. The use of compound may be an error: the intended meaning is not clear.

12 Point m. 2.

(**16.38**)

12–22 For a discussion of this verse, see above, introd. (p. 14).

(16.39)

22–fol. 8a, col. i 13 𝔓 joins 05 in another longer version of the text. There are the following differences:

23 τε] om. 05
24–5 ἱκανων φιλων: φιλων πολλων 05
25 επι: εις 05

Fol. 8a, col. i

6 δικα[ιοι]: 05 adds και εξαγαγοντες παρεκαλεσαν αυτους λεγοντες.
7–8 εκ ταυτης δε πολεως: εκ της πολεως ταυτης 05
8–9 εξ[ελ]θετε: εξελθατε 05
10–11 επιστ[ρ]αφω[σιν] παλιν: παλιν συνστραφωσιν ημιν 05
11 οι om. 05

(16.40)

13–14 απολυθεντες δε abbreviates εξελθοντες δε απο (εκ 𝔓⁷⁴ 02 05 08) της φυλακης (other witnesses).
14–15 ηλθον with 05: εισηλθον other witnesses.
15 εις: προς other witnesses.
16 Point *m.* 2.
17–22 τους αδ[ε]λφους διη[γ]ησαντο οσα εποιησεν κ̄ς̄ αυτοις· και πα[ρ]εκαλεσαντες (corrected by a second hand to πα[ρ]ακαλεσαντες) αυτους. Most witnesses read παρεκαλεσαν τους αδελφους; 𝔓⁴⁵ (partially extant) and 08 read τους αδελφους παρεκαλεσαν αυτους. 05 has a very similar expansion, but 05* omits και; this was corrected to παρεκαλεσαν τε.
23 εξεησαν (scil. εξηεσαν) completes the recasting of the verse. Other witnesses read και εξηλθαν/-ον.
Point *m.* 2.

(17.1)

23–col. ii 2 και κατη⟦η⟧λθον εις Απολλωνιδα εκειθεν δε is a shorter version of the text as it is found in 05*, which reads διοδευσαντες δε την Αμφιπολιν και κατηλθον εις Απολλωνιδα κακειθεν. Other forms are:

διοδευσαντες δε την Αμφιπολιν κατηλθον εις Απολλωνιδα κακειθεν 05ᶜ
διελθοντες δε την Απολλωνιαν την Αμφιπολιν ηλθον 08
διοδευσαντες δε την Αμφιπολιν (πολιν 01*) και την Απολλωνιαν ηλθον other witnesses

𝔓 appears to have omitted the first phrase, and reads εκειθεν δε instead of κακειθεν. The clumsy construction in 05 might suggest that διοδευσαντες δε την Αμφιπολιν was a reinsertion of material found in most witnesses. But this construction is a regular feature of the manuscript (see Parker, *Codex Bezae* 253–6).

Note that 𝔓 agrees with 05 in reading Απολλωνιδα against Απολλωνιαν. The reading could hitherto have been dismissed as an error in 05 (*Apolloniam* d), but now has to be taken as a genuine variant.

Fol. 8a, col. ii

(17.1–2)

1, 3 Points *m.* 2.
3–8 The reading κατα δε το ειωθος Παυλος εισηλθεν εις την συναγωγην των Ιουδαιων is a re-ordering and abbreviation of the text as it is usually found:

οπου ην (+ η 08) συναγωγη των (των om. 𝔓⁷⁴) Ιουδαιων. κατα δε το ειωθος τω Παυλω εισηλθεν προς αυτους

05 reads

οπου ... Ιουδαιων. και (del. 05^C) κατα το εισωθος (ειωθος 05^C) ο Παυλος εισηλθεν προς αυτους

4 Accent *m*. 2.

(17.2–3)

8–13 επι ϲαββατα τρια δια[λεγο]μενος αυτοις εκ των γραφων και διανοιγων. Most witnesses read και ... διελεξατο ... διανοιγων. 05 omits και like 𝔓, but reads διελεχθη ... διανοιγων (with 08). The later tradition favours και ... διελεγετο.

11 εκ with 05: απο other witnesses.

(17.3)

17 Other witnesses add εκ νεκρων after αναστηναι.

19 Χ[(ριστο)ϲ Ι(ησου)ϲ with 𝔓^74 02 05: ο Χριστος ο Ιησους 03: Ιησους Χριστος 01: Ιησους ο Χριστος 08^L. The Byzantine form is ο Χριστος Ιησους.

(17.4)

21 αυτων (in lacuna). Other witnesses read εξ αυτων.

24–5 Most witnesses read τω Παυλω και τω Ϲιλα after προσεκληρωθησαν; 05 reads τω Παυλω και τω Ϲιλα τη διδαχη; 𝔓 reads τη διδαχη. It is tempting to conclude that 05 is a conflation of the two readings.

25–fol. 8b, col. i 1 πολλοι των ϲεβομενων is also read by 05, although 05 adds και after. Other witnesses read των τε ϲεβομενων (+ και 𝔓^74 02). In sense 𝔓 is closer to other witnesses in lacking και.

Fol. 8b, col. i

3–5 The reading [κ]αι γυναικες is shared with 05; other witnesses read γυναικων τε. This reading has attracted interest since it was noticed by E. S. Fiorenza, *In Memory of Her: A Feminist Theological Reconstruction of Christian Origins* (London 1983) 52.

(17.5)

6–11 οι δε απειθουντες Ϊουδαιο[ι ϲυν]ϲτρεψαντες τ[ι]νας ανδρ[α]ϲ τ[ων] αγοραιω[ν πολ]λους εθο[ρ]υβο[υν]. The reading is an addition to the various versions of the first part of this verse.

ζηλωσαντες δε οι Ιουδαιοι και προσλαβομενοι των αγοραιων ανδρας τινας (τινας ανδρας 01) πονηρους και οχλοποιησαντες εθορυβουν 𝔓^74 01 02 03 and the Byzantine text

οι δε απειθουντες Ιουδαιοι συνστρεψαντες τινας ανδρας των αγοραιων πονηρους εθορυβουσαν 05

ζηλωσαντες δε οι Ιουδαιοι και προσλαβομενοι των αγοραιων ανδρας τινας πονηρους απειθησαντες και οχλοποιησαντες εθορυβουν (θορυβουν *) 08

𝔓 agrees with 05 except for reading πολλους instead of πονηρους (*ex errore*?), and favouring the imperfect as 𝔓^74 01 etc. (note that d reads *turbabant*, suggesting that the reading in 05 is more recent). The restoration in line 7 includes ϲυν as in 05.

12 Point probably *m*. 2.

16 εξαγαγειν with 05; προσαγαγειν 08; προαγαγειν 𝔓^74 01 etc.

20 08 adds αλλους after τινας.

23 και λεγοντες is restored, an addition found in 05. Otherwise the text of 03 fits reasonably with the few letters visible from line 16 onwards.

Fol. 8b, col. ii

(17.6)

1 -ϲτατουντες is otherwise unattested, other witnesses reading αναϲτατωϲαντες.

2 εισιν with 05*. Other witnesses omit.

3 Point *m*. 2.

(**17.7**)

4–5 υποδε[δ]εκ[α]τος: υποδεδεκται 03 and other witnesses. The reading in 𝔓 seems to be a confusion. The reconstruction υποδε[δ]εκ[α]τος assumes that the scribe made a mistake. Perhaps he misarticulated the run of letters as δεκατος; or perhaps he omitted some letters in his exemplar, e.g. υποδεδεκ⟨ται αυ⟩τος ο Ιασων.

10 The suggested [ω]ς is otherwise unattested, other manuscripts having nothing.

10–11 λεγοντες τινα: λεγοντες ειναι ετερον 08: λεγοντες ετερον ειναι 05: ετερον λεγοντες ειναι other witnesses.

(**17.8**)

12–13 The verse begins with a different wording, ενεπλησαν τε θυμου (compare Lk 4.28 επλησθησαν παντες θυμου εν τη συναγωγη; Ac 19.28 γενομενοι πληρεις θυμου): εταραξαν δε other witnesses (και εταραξεν 05).

14–15 This is followed by a difference in word order also found in 05: τους πολιταρχας και τον οχλον; τον οχλον (πολιν 08) και τους πολιταρχας other witnesses.

16 ακουοντας with most other witnesses: ακουσαντες 05*: ακουσαντα 05^C.

(**17.9**)

17–18 For οι μεν ουν π[ολι]ταρχαι other witnesses read και. The phrase could have been suggested by a dozen passages in Acts.

18–19 ἱκανον λαβοντες: λαβοντες το ικανον other witnesses.

22 Other witnesses add αυτους after απελυσαν.

(**17.10**)

23–4 απελυον δια νυκτος is unique to 𝔓. Compare ευθεως δια νυκτος εξεπεμψαν 03; ευθεως εξεπεμψαν δια νυκτος 01; εξεπεμψαν 02; ευθεως δια της νυκτος εξεπεμψαν 08. Note απελυσαν in line 22.

25 𝔓 agrees with 05 in not reading τε after τον.

25–6 συ[ν] τω Σιλεα: και τον Σιλαν other witnesses. For the spelling Σιλεας, see on 16.19 above.

D. C. PARKER
S. R. PICKERING

II. MEDICAL AND RELATED TEXTS

The eleven papyri published in this section include a single known text, of the Hippocratic *De articulis*, with the remaining unidentified fragments preserving a range of ethical, dietetic, surgical, anatomical, and pharmacological texts. **4973** is included in the present group because of its possible veterinary content, while the document preserved on **4979** may pertain to the activity of a local doctor. The group doubles the number of papyri of medical content published previously in *The Oxyrhynchus Papyri*: III **437**, **468**, IX **1184**, XXXI **2547**, II **234**, and LII **3654** (which last appear to be written in the same hand: see I. Andorlini, in *Pap. Congr. XIX* (1992) 375–90), along with the pharmacological texts VIII **1088**, XI **1384**, LIII **3701** and LIV **3724** iii 1–6. Unedited portions of XIX **2221**v + P. Köln V 206v and IV **661**v are also reported to contain medical recipes. Other medical papyri found at Oxyrhynchus are PSI II 116, 132, XII 1275, PSI Congr. XVII 19, P. Mil. Vogl. I 15, P. Coll. Youtie I 4, and P. Med. inv. 71.77 (= M–P³ 545.2).

The following abbreviations will be used:

GMP	I. Andorlini (ed.), *Greek Medical Papyri*, vols. i (Florence 2001), ii (Florence 2009)
Andorlini, 'P. Grenf. I 52'	I. Andorlini, 'P. Grenf. I 52: note farmacologiche', *BASP* 18 (1981) 1–25
Andorlini, *Trattato*	I. Andorlini, *Trattato di medicina su papiro* (Florence 1995)
Andorlini, 'Specimina'	I. Andorlini (ed.), 'Specimina' *per il* Corpus dei papiri greci di medicina (Florence 1997)
Andorlini, *Testi*	I. Andorlini (ed.), *Testi medici su papiro* (Florence 2004)
Marganne, *Chirurgie*	M.-H. Marganne, *La Chirurgie dans l'Égypte gréco-romaine d'après les papyrus littéraires grecs* (Leiden 1998)

4969. HIPPOCRATES, *DE ARTICULIS* 57–58, 60

19 2B.76/E(a) +   fr. 1 3.5 × 1.7 cm   Second/third century
8 1B.196/G(1–3)b   fr. 2 5.2 × 4.1 cm; fr. 3 2.8 × 5.5 cm

Three fragments belonging to two consecutive leaves of a papyrus codex, found in different excavation seasons. The number of leaves per quire cannot be determined, and it cannot be ruled out that the codex was comprised of *uniones*. The pages are organised according to a sequence of the type ↓→ →↓ ('like facing like pages'), found both in *uniones*, for which it is the only possible sequence, and in quires (E. G. Turner, *The Typology of the Early Codex* (Pennsylvania 1977) 63 and n. 14). This configuration becomes common in the fourth century, but earlier examples are not unknown (*Typology* 64 ff., esp. 68). On fr. 3 → the fibres are distorted and irregular. The damage was already present, since at 4 ματαγ is written partially on the underlying vertical fibres. There is a coarse *kollesis*, with nothing unusual about its position relative to the page.

On the basis of an approximate reconstruction, the codex may have had pages of 38–40 lines with a written area of approximately 11.5 × 17.5 cm. Given that the upper margin of fr. 3 and the lateral margin of frr. 1+2 are 1.8 cm, this comes to a total for one page of 15 × 21 cm, which corresponds to Turner's Group 7 (cf. esp. PSI III 158, an astrological text, among the Aberrants 1 (*Typology* 19), assigned to the third century).

The writing is of small size, neat and careful, of the so-called 'Severe Style'. The hand is very similar to that of XLII **2999** (compare also XLII **3012** and XLVII **3321**), and may be placed between the end of the second century and the beginning of the third. The scribe sometimes writes letters smaller at line-end to maintain alignment: see frr. 1+2 ↓ 4 γαρ; 7 τον; 10 που; fr. 3 ↓ 3 the final letters of κατα. Fr. 3 ↓ preserves line ends, as seen at 1, 2, 3 as well as 5, where a line-filler appears.

Between fr. 3 → 1–2 a *diple obelismene* is found, while a simple *paragraphus* is used between 5 and 6; for their use compare P. Lond. Lit. 164, the medical treatise of the Anonymus Londinensis: in both texts the *diple obelismene* marks a stronger pause than the *paragraphus*. Elision is effected but not marked. Organic diaeresis is found at frr. 1+2 ↓ 4, inorganic at frr. 1+2 → 6. Iota adscript is not written.

This is the first papyrus witness to *De articulis* known so far, though two fragments of *De fracturis* have been published: P. Brook. 94, preserving remains of *Fract.* 1, identified by D. Hagedorn, *ZPE* 94 (1992) 47–8, and P. Aberd. 124, with remains of *Fract.* 37, identified by I. Andorlini, in *GMP* i 1. A citation of *Art.* 8 has also been recognized in an anonymous medical text on physiology of the second or third century (*GMP* i 7).

The text displays regular Ionic dialectal forms, which is generally confirmed by the older medieval manuscripts. It incorporates two Ionicisms not preserved in the manuscript tradition: at frr. 1+2 → 3, μόγις against the manuscripts' μόλις; at fr. 3 → 6, ὦν against their Attic form οὖν. The papyrus' place in the history of the textual tradition of *Art.* seems to be quite independent and cannot be related to either of the two branches of the medieval tradition. It preserves some readings in common with B (Laur. 74.4) against MV (Marc. gr. 269; Vat. gr. 276) (at frr. 1+2 → 2, 4), apparently with MV against B (at fr. 3 → 1), and includes a noteworthy variant (frr. 1+2 → 9). In addition fr. 3 ↓, which contains part of ch. 60, certainly contains a text that diverges from that preserved by the medieval manuscripts, being longer, such that the lines cannot be reconstructed. It is striking that the divergences from the medieval tradition are concentrated at this point, suggesting that the text of the exemplar was corrupt or had been interfered with here (perhaps a marginal gloss imported into the text?). Unfortunately neither Galen's commentary nor the treatise on *Art.* by Apollonius of Citium provides notes at this point on textual divergences already present in the ancient tradition.

For the collation the text of H. Kühlewein, *Hippocratis Opera quae feruntur omnia* ii (Leipzig 1902) has been used, with recourse also to those of E. Littré, *Œuvres d'Hippocrate* iv (Paris 1844), and F. Z. Ermerins, *Hippocratis et aliorum medicorum veterum reliquiae* viii (Leipzig–Paris 1864) 55–156.

frr. 1 + 2

↓
    .   .   .   .

....] τ[ο] αρ[θ]ρ[ον].[.].[§ 57 (201.10)
....] αλλ ηκιστα των [εκπαλεων ουτοι μαλλον εκτα
νουcι] και το κατα τον β[ουβωνα και το κατα την ι]γνυην αρ
θρον] προcξυνϊενα[ι μεν ουν και τοδε χρη ευχ]ρηcτον γαρ
5 ...]..υ[.] αξ[ιο]ν [εcτιν και τουc πλειcτουc λ]ηθει ο̣τι
ουδ οι υγιαινοντεc δυνανται κατα την ι]γνυη̣ν̣ ε̣
κταννειν το αρθρον ην μη cυνεκταννcω]c̣ι κ̣α̣ι̣ τ̣ο κατα τον
βουβωνα αρθρον πλην ην μη πανυ ανω αειρωcι] τον π̣[ο
δα ουτω δ αν δυναιντο ου τοινυν ουδε] c̣υν̣καμπτειν
10 δυνανται το κατα την ιγνυην αρθ]ρον ομοιωc α̣λλ̣[α]...
χαλεπωτερον ην μη cυγκαμψωc]ιν και το κατα τ̣[ον
βουβωνα αρθρον πολλα δε και αλλα κατα το cω]μ̣α τ̣[οι]α̣υ̣τ̣α̣[c
αδελφιξιαc εχει και κατα νευρων cυντα̣c̣ι̣α̣]c̣ κ̣α̣ι̣ κ̣[ατα

    .   .   .   .

→
    .   .   .   .

                    ]..[.]..[..].[
εc τουπιc[ω επι πολυ υπερεχοντω]ν υπερ του ποδ[οc τηc   § 58 (203.16)
βαcιοc κα̣ι̣ [τηc ραχιοc εc τα ιcχια ρεπ]ουcηc μογιc δε [τωι cτη
θει του ποδ[οc καθικνειται και] ουδ̣ε ουτωc ην μη [καμψηι
5 αυτοc εωυτ[ον κατα τουc βουβωναc και τωι].[
τα την ϊγ[ν]υην [επιcυγκαμψη επι δε τουτοιc αναγ
καζετ[αι ωcτε τη χειρι κατα το cιναρον cκελοc ερειδεcθαι
εc το ανω̣ τ̣ου [μηρου εφ εκαcτηι cυμβαcει αναγκαζει ουν τι
και τουτον αυτον [ωcτε καμπτεcθαι κατα τουc βου
10 βωναc εν γαρ τη [μεταλλαγη των cκελεων εν τη οδοι
πορι̣η̣ ου δυν̣α̣τ̣[αι το cωμα οχειcθαι επι του cιναρου cκελε
οc] η̣ν̣ μ̣η [προcκατερειδηται το cιναρον προc την γην

    .   .   .   .

fr. 3 →

>κεϲτον [ο]κ[οϲοιϲι δ αν εκ γενεηϲ η και αλλωϲ εν αυξηϲει εουϲιν ου   §58 (206.1–7)
τωϲ ολιϲθη [το αρθρον οπιϲω και μη εμπεϲη ην τη βιη ολι
ϲθη η[ν τ]ε [και υπο νουϲου πολλα γαρ τα τοιαυτα εξαρθρη
ματα γι[ν]ε[ται εν νουϲοιϲ οιαι δε τινεϲ αι νουϲοι
5 εν ηϲιν ε[ξαρθρειται τα τοιαυτα υϲτερον γεγραψεται ην
ων εκϲτα[ν μη εμπεϲηι του μεν μηρου το οϲτεον βρα
χυ] γινεται κ[ακουται δε και παν το ϲκελοϲ και

     .   .   .   .   .   .

↓
                    οδοιπορ]ειν ανευ ξυ   §60 (208.9–17)
λου   ] το ϲιναρον α
τε   εοντ]εϲ ουεγε κατα
                    ακαμπ]ιην ειθυγίῳ
5   ]... και ϲυ >
ρουϲι   τ]ον ποδα δε ου
                    ]. τε μη παντι
                    πτ]ερνη ουτο[ι
                    π]ρ[ο]βαιν[ειν

     .   .   .   .   .

frr. 1 + 2

↓ 1 Only the lower extremities of letters survive, but the remains are consistent with the reading] τ[ο] αρ[θ]ρ[ον].[.][, which, given the average line length, is approximately what we should expect at this point.

2 The available space between 2 and 3 suggests that it contained the word μᾶλλον, which is found in BMV, but not in PΓ or Gal. *Loc. aff.* 6.5 [viii 430–31 K.]. It is omitted by Littré and Ermerins, and athetized by Kühlewein.

3 ι]γνυην: om. Ap.

4 προϲξυνϊεναι[ι: προϲξυνειναι B.
ουν (restored) om. Gal. *Loc. aff.* viii 430 K.

5].υ[.] αξ[ιο]ν [. After upsilon, there is a small lacuna the width of a single broad or two narrow letters. The breadth and angle of the following descending diagonal suggest alpha in particular, while the slightly concave horizontal next to it suits best the upper part of xi (cf. 4), so that we should presumably read] αξ[ιο]ν [. If so, unless the preceding lacuna contained a deletion, then we have a variant reading, for the manuscripts read καὶ πολλοῦ ἄξιόν ἐϲτιν (Gal. *Loc. aff.* 6.5 adds λόγου after πολλοῦ). Not much remains of the first two letters, but πολ]λου is possible (the small trace of the first letter, high in the line, appears to be the top of a vertical, and could be consistent with lambda; it certainly does not suggest a horizontal, which speaks against λο]γου).

9 ϲυνκαμπτειν. Of first letter, foot of curve curling upwards, supporting the reading of sigma rather than the Ionic form with xi (contrast προϲξυνϊενα[ι at 4).

10].... The manuscripts have πολύ, but the damaged traces do not seem to allow for this

reading: there is a short, high horizontal, followed by a blob which would be too small for omicron, then an indeterminate trace not easily identifiable with any letter form.

→ 1 Directly above πε in 2, a small hook belonging to either epsilon or sigma is visible. A trace of ink above it would seem more likely to be part of epsilon's horizontal, but may also be that of sigma. By comparison with the transmitted text of *Art.*, the only possible candidate at this point is the epsilon of εἴη, and the sequence] ε̣ι[η] τ̣ω̣[ν] ι̣[cχιων appears to be consistent with the remaining traces.

2 On the basis of the reconstructed line, the text agrees with B in reading ἐc τοὐπίcω ἐπὶ πολύ, against MV's ἐπὶ πολὺ ἐc τοὐπίcω.

2–3 The papyrus tallies with the medieval manuscripts in the situation of the passage εἰ γὰρ πειρήcαιτο . . . ῥεπούcηc, which was transposed by Littré, followed by Ermerins, after κατὰ τὸ ἰcχίον [204.11 Kühlewein] (see the editors' comments at iv 248 n. 13 L. and iii 125.6 n. Erm.).

3 μογιc: μολιc codd. B has μόγιc against μόλιc in MV at *Art.* 1 [112.3 Kw. = iv 80.1 L.], but the manuscripts are in agreement in reading μόλιc at *Art.* 5 [117.3 Kw. = iv 86.16 L.]. There is little consistency in the distribution of these variants in the medieval tradition of the Hippocratic Corpus, as can be seen, for example, from a glance at J.-H. Kühn, U. Fleischer, *Index Hippocraticus* (Göttingen 1986) s. vv. μόγιc and μόλιc.

4 ην with B (adopted by Littré and Kühlewein): ει MV.

9 τουτον αυτον: τουτο αυτο codd. The reading should not simply be regarded as an error, and it is unlikely that it represents a vulgarism, otherwise attested in Ptolemaic papyri (cf. E. Mayser, *Grammatik der griechischen Papyri aus der Ptolemäerzeit* i2.2 67). On the other hand, it cannot be explained as a dialectal variant, since neuter pronominal forms in -ον are attested, for αὐτόc alone, in Attic more than in Ionic, but are in any case present in both (E. Schwyzer, *Griechische Grammatik* i 610). The reading can perhaps be interpreted as a form of the masculine accusative, referring to the patient, who is the logical subject of the whole passage. If so, it parallels a usage of αὐτόc attested elsewhere in the surgical treatises, in which it is used with reference to patients even when they have not been named in what precedes: cf. *Art.* 37 [158.13 Kw. = iv 166.6 L], 38 [159.14 Kw. = iv 168.4 L.], but the passage has a difficult structure.

10 After cκελεων (restored), B adds και.

fr. 3

→ 1 [ο]κ̣[οcοιcι. What remains of the putative kappa is the top of an upright with left-facing serif, which is sometimes found in kappa, but not in iota; this suggests reading οκοcοιcι with MV, but excludes B's οιcι. The adoption of the manuscripts' text results in a longer than average line, pointing to an omission or variant in the papyrus: και before αλλωc is omitted in B and Ap., but it is doubtful whether such an omission alone could account for the discrepancy.

1–2 ου]τωc with MV: ουτω B.

2 οπιcω (restored) om. Ap.

3 τα (restored) om. B.

5 ηcιν with BV: ηcι (cι sscr.) M.

6 ων: οὖν codd. The form ὦν, about which P. Chantraine, *Dictionnaire étymologique de la langue grecque* s.v. οὖν, expressed doubts, is considered Ionic by F. Bechtel, *Die griechische Dialekte* iii 239, who cites some examples from the Hippocratic Corpus, even if the tradition is often divided. For instances of variants among the manuscripts, cf. e.g. *Vict.* 4.87 [vi 642 L. = p. 98.10 Joly] οἱ δ' οὖν [M: ὦν θ: om. Littré] οὐ διδάcκουcιν]; perhaps also a trace in *V. M.* 7.1 [i 584.7 L. = p. 126.3 Jouanna]: οὖν M, but οὖν in A has ου deleted by A². In any case the form is regularly attested in the Herodotean tradition.

↓ 1 οδοιπορ]ειν. The manuscripts transmit the hyper-Ionic οδοιπορεειν, whose presence in the papyrus cannot be excluded.

2–3 A reconstruction of the lines on the basis of Kühlewein's text results in a shorter-than-average line length: ὁδοιπορ]εῖν ἄνευ ξύ[λου καὶ πάνυ μέντοι εὐθέες ἐπί γε] τὸ cιναρὸν ἅ[τε οὔτε . . .

3 ουεγε. (Nothing remains of the top horizontal of the putative gamma, but it cannot be iota, since the latter does not normally descend below the line). Perhaps a corruption of οὐδέ γε, and thus a variant (elsewhere unattested) of οὔτε in the codices, corresponding to the previous οὔτε.

Alpha at line end is written smaller and above the line.

3 ff. Reconstruction on the basis of Kühlewein's text repeatedly yields shorter-than-average lines. The text of the passage concerned, with the corresponding portions of the papyrus highlighted, is as follows (ch. 60 [p. 208.10–17 Kw. = iv 256.14–20 L.]): οὔτε κατὰ τὸν βουβῶνα εὔκαμπτοι ἐόντες **οὔτε κατὰ** τὴν ἰγνύην. διὰ οὖν τοῦ βουβῶνος τὴν ἀκαμπ**ίην εὐθυτέρωι** ὅλωι τῶι cκέλει ἐν τῆι ὁδοιπορίηι χρέωνται ἢ ὅτε ὑγιαῖνον. **καὶ cύ**ρουcι δὲ ἐνίοτε πρὸc τὴν γῆν **τὸν πόδα, ἅτε οὐ** ῥηιδίωc cυγκάμπτοντες τὰ ἄνω ἄρθρα καὶ **ἅτε παντὶ** βαίνοντες τῶι ποδί· οὐδὲν γὰρ ἧccον τῆι π**τέρνηι οὗτοι** βαίνουcιν ἢ τὸ ἔμπροcθεν· εἰ δέ γε ἠδύναντο μέγα π**ροβαίνειν** . . .

4 ειθυγιω : εὐθυτέρωι codd. It is possible that the corrupt text has arisen from a mistaken reading of a damaged exemplar.

5 Of the first three letters, an upright with trace of ligature joining the next, another upright and a small round trace. Of sigma, the upper right extremity is visible, joined to the following letter; the trace could be consistent also with ϵ. The traces are so uncertain that it is impossible to identify the text, but the initial traces do not accord well with the manuscripts' ὑγιαῖνον before καὶ cύ|[ρουcι.

6 τ]ον ποδα δε ου. Unless we wish to regard πόδα δὲ οὐ as the result of a false reading of πόδα ἅτε οὐ in the codices through simplification and assimilation, we are confronted with an interesting variant, which presupposes a different syntactical structure.

7] . τε μη παντι. In this case it is difficult to account for the text as the result of a mechanical error: the presence of the negative before παντί implies a contradictory text, according to which those affected by an untreated hip dislocation do not put their weight on the whole sole of the foot as they walk. This must also have consequences for the following phrase (according to Littré's translation, *en effet, ils ne marchent pas moins avec le talon qu'avec la partie anterieure*).

D. MANETTI / D. LEITH

4970. Prose mentioning the Hippocratic *Oath*

112/38   17 × 6.4 cm   Second century
Plate I

An excerpted text copied against the fibres on the back of a land register. The papyrus has been cut from a much larger roll to accommodate only the six lines of text preserved, and all edges are intact except the right. At their deepest, the upper margin measures 1.7 cm, the lower 1.1 cm. At left, the incision bisects the first letter of the last line, suggesting that the papyrus was cut, or at least trimmed, after the excerpt was written. At right, two strips of the underlying layer of papyrus project some 2 cm opposite 3–4 and 6. The upper strip in particular terminates in a clean edge, 1 cm in breadth, which lines up precisely with the much narrower extremity of the less intact lower strip. It is possible that these edges preserve the original incision at the right, indicating that perhaps only a piece 2 cm in width of the upper surface of the papyrus has been lost. This would be consistent with the restorations that have suggested themselves, especially at 3, 4 and 5, but there are textual difficulties at 2 which cannot be satisfactorily resolved according to this reconstruction (see 2), and the text breaks off mid-sentence at 6. I am inclined to accept the reconstruction as presented below, on the grounds of improbability that such an intelligible text could result at 3–5 if it were wrong, but it cannot perhaps be ruled out that there were more substantial losses at right.

The text is written in a somewhat ill-formed rounded hand. Sharp, right-facing hooks are found often at the bottom of descenders. It is characterized by rounded ϵ with cross-stroke sometimes touching the upper arc; θ with midstroke projecting to the right and often touching the following letter; c with relatively straight top-stroke; V-shaped γ. It displays general affinities with the third hand of *GMAW*² 68 (later ii, assigned) and *GMAW*² 22 (ii, assigned), and may likewise be assigned a date in the second century.

There is a single instance of itacism (3). Inorganic diaeresis is employed at 1 and 6.

The text appears to derive from the prooemium of a medical treatise (see 1 and 2 nn.), its explicitly pedagogical content suggesting that this may have been some form of introductory manual. The author affirms the ethical importance of the Hippocratic *Oath* as the initial subject of study for the student of medicine.

PSI XII 1275, also from Oxyrhynchus and assigned to the second century, offers some interesting points of comparison. Its text occupies a relatively small space on the back of the final sheet of a roll which contained *Iliad* 23, with some additional marginal scribblings and a short passage copied on the other side. It is certainly excerpted from the prooemium of a medical manual, and names the book's addressee, Demosthenes. There are obvious parallels with **4970** in its introductory formula (see 2 n.). Most interestingly, it offers an opposing view on where medical education should begin, instead emphasising the basic necessity of learning the names of the parts of the body, a subject to which the treatise was apparently devoted. It thus seems plausible that both texts were deliberately excerpted by certain physicians in second-century Oxyrhynchus with a direct interest in medical education.

The text of **4970**, on the other hand, is closely paralleled by Scribonius Largus, *Compositiones* pref. 5 (composed in 47/8), who asserts that 'Hippocrates, the founder of our profession, has handed down that the beginning of learning should be from the *Oath* (*initia disciplinae ab iureiurando tradidit*), . . . for a long time moulding the minds of students towards humanity.' From late antiquity, within the context of the more formal Alexandrian medical curricula, recommendations for the beginning student to read and learn the Hippocratic *Oath* first are made by Stephanus of Athens, *In Hip. Aph.* pref. [*CMG* XI 1.3.1 p. 30.25–6 Westerink], and ps.-Oribasius,

In Hip. Aph. pref. [ed. J. G. von Andernach (Basel 1535) 9]: *etenim qui initiantur arti, primo legant sacramentum ipsius Hippocratis, inde librum praeceptorum, tertio librum hunc, in quo totius artis speculatio continetur* (on ps.-Oribasius' treatise, see P. Kibre, *Hippocrates latinus* (New York 1985) 19–23). Gregory of Nazianzus' statement that his Christian brother had no ethical need for the *Oath* during his Alexandrian medical education (*Or.* 7.10) is perhaps to be understood as alluding to a corresponding initial stage.

By contrast, Rufus of Ephesus, *De corporis humani appellationibus* pref. 6–7 [134.3–7 Daremberg–Ruelle], agrees with the author of the PSI text in prioritizing anatomical nomenclature in medical education. A variety of views on this topic, however, is attested in the Roman period. The utility of definitions in general relevant to the medical art, especially for the student, is emphasised by the ps.-Galenic author of *Def. med.* pref. [XIX 346 K.], while the author of a text preserved in BKT III 22–26, laments that students of surgery are taught merely about the history and theory of their art, and lack the basic knowledge necessary for its practice. Some also advocated different Hippocratic treatises as the initial subjects of study for medical students, such as *Off.* (Gal. *In Hip. Off.* pref. [XVIII/B 632 K.]) and *Aph.* (Gal. *In Hip. Aph.* 1 [XVII/B 351 K.]), both containing prefaces that were interpreted as introductory to the whole of medicine. In the context of what appears to have been a much wider debate concerning the proper foundation of medical learning, this excerpt emphasizes the importance of ethics to the medical profession, and of the authority of the Hippocratic *Oath* in this connection.

Along with the third-century papyri XXXI **2547**, preserving a text of the *Oath*, and III **437**, containing indirect references to two of the *Oath*'s prohibitions, apparently in a surgical context, this fragment offers additional testimony for the uses made of the Hippocratic *Oath* in Oxyrhynchus. In particular, it suggests a plausible connection with medical teaching in the metropolis, which is paralleled by the inclusion of the *Oath* in the Alexandrian medical curricula attested by later sources. It may be remarked too, in this regard, that there is no evidence that the *Oath* was ever sworn in the post-Classical period, or that it was regarded as more than an authoritative text for ethical reflection in medicine. It is noteworthy that in the (admittedly late) passages cited above, Stephanus of Athens urges students to learn (ἐκμανθάνειν) the *Oath*, ps.-Oribasius to read (*legere*) it.

```
    τῶν νέων τοῖ[c κ]ατὰ λόγον εἰc τὴν ἰατρικὴν [ε]ἰcα[γ]ομέν[οιc,
    θεωρήματα, π[ρο]cῆκόν ἐcτιν, ὡc ἔγωγαι διαλαμβάνω, [
    ἐν πρώτοιc ἀπὸ τοῦ Ἱπποκρατίου ὅρκου τὴν ἀρχὴν τῆc [
    μαθήcεωc ποιε[ῖ]cθαι, ὥcπερ νόμου δικαιοτάτου κα[ὶ
5   cφόδρα βιωφελο[ῦ]c καθεcτῶτοc. τοῖc γὰρ διὰ τοῦτο μ[υ-
    cταγωγηθεῖc⟨ι⟩ ἄ[π]ταιcτον ἅμα τὸν ἐν τῷ ἰατρεύειν [
```

1 ἰατρικήν   2 l. ἔγωγε   3 l. Ἱπποκρατείου   5 τοιϲ: ϲ corr. from γ   l. τούτου?
6 ἰατρεύειν

'For those young men who are being introduced in a systematic way to medicine . . . it is proper, as I see it at least, in the first place to make the beginning of learning from the Hippocratic Oath, since it was established as a most just law and extremely useful for life. For to those who have been initiated through it (?), . . . in medicine . . . at once unerring . . .'

1 At line beginning, there appears to be a short horizontal to the left of tau's crossbar; it may however belong to the tau, whose crossbar in this hand generally extends slightly further to the left of the upright than it does to its right.

Formulae such as this, which describe beginning students of medicine, recur in various prooemia to introductory medical manuals. Cf. e.g. ps.-Gal. *Def. med.* pref. [XIX 346 K.]; Galen's later addition of the subscription 'τοῖϲ εἰϲαγομένοιϲ' to the titles of some of his early works, viz. e.g. *De sect.*, *De oss.*, *De puls.* (see *De libr. propr.* 1 [Scr. min. II 93–4 Mueller]); and PSI XII 1275.1–2, quoted below, 2 n. This excerpt would seem to sit most easily in such a context.

τοῖ[ϲ κ]ατὰ λόγον. The formulation lends support to M. Manfredi's suggested emendation to τοῖϲ κατὰ λόγον at PSI XII 1275.1, where the papyrus reads τοιϲκαταλογοιϲ. The construal τοῖϲ καταλόγοιϲ, however, is defended by G. Azzarello in Andorlini, *Testi* 239–40 n. 5. The phrase seems to isolate a particular form of medical education, one that was systematic or governed by reason, and apparently distinguishable from other, less stringent, ways of gaining medical knowledge. These papyrus texts clearly imply a notion, or at least an ideal, of a formal, systematically structured medical training associated in particular with young people. The texts discussed above that offer alternative views on where to begin medical education attest to the fluidity of such an ideal in the Roman period and the controversies over what such training should consist in.

2 θεωρήματα. This word is extraneous to the syntax of the sentence as reconstructed. The term does, however, surface in discussions of the utility of practical as opposed to theoretical knowledge for the student of medicine (cf. e.g. ps.-Gal. *Def. med.* pref. [XIX 346 K.]; BKT III 22–26 ii 20–25), which might be thought to bear some relevance to our author's concerns. This could of course be an indication that the lacuna at right was more extensive, with θεωρήματα representing the object of a lost infinitive construed with π[ρο]ϲῆκον, or indeed that the beginning of the sentence is missing. The possibility of emending εγωγαι at 2 to ε⟨ἰϲα⟩γωγαί, followed by the infinitive διαλαμβάνε[ιν, is suggested by Professor Andorlini, but it is unclear precisely what this would mean or how it would be reconcilable with the rest of the sentence. On the other hand, the subsequent reconstruction of the text makes excellent sense, with ποιε[ῖ]ϲθαι in 4 modifying π[ρο]ϲῆκον. I have considered whether the text up to and including θεωρήματα may represent a heading, but it is not presented as such, and it is difficult to see how the *Oath* itself or the subsequent text might be classified as medical theorems. It might alternatively be suggested that θεωρήματα could be accounted for as a corruption of the name of the work's addressee (e.g. Θέωρε). The close similarity in expression and syntax of this introductory clause with that found at PSI 1275.1–3, where the addressee's name appears in a corresponding position in the sentence, may support this hypothesis (τῶν νέων τοῖϲ κατὰ λόγον εἰϲ τὸ ἰατρεύειν προϲάγουϲιν, ὦ Δημόϲθενεϲ), though the putative corruption remains difficult to account for.

3 τῆϲ [. A curved descender survives, as of the back of ε, θ, ο, ϲ. A genitive is surely called for after ἀρχήν, and the likelihood that τῆϲ is the article of μαθήϲεωϲ in 4 seems overwhelming, especially in light of the parallel which this phrase finds in Scribonius' *initia disciplinae* (see above).

4–5 It seems unavoidable to read the two genitive phrases as parts of the same genitive absolute completed by καθεϲτῶτοϲ in 5, and thus to restore κα[ί at 4.

5 διὰ τοῦτο. It is unclear to what τοῦτο could logically refer in the context (the fact that the

4970. *PROSE MENTIONING THE HIPPOCRATIC* OATH

beginning of learning should be made from the *Oath*; that it was established as a most just law), and it seems preferable to emend to τούτου, i.e. the *Oath* itself. διά + gen. is regular with μυcταγωγέω.

5–6 μ[υ]cταγωγηθεῖc⟨ι⟩. The article τοῖc at 5 seems to demand the emendation to the dative plural participle. There is nothing with which a feminine participle μυcταγωγηθεῖcα[might agree in what remains, and there seems no way to make sense of the subsequent sequence except by reading ἄ[π]ταιcτον. The metaphor of religious initiation is used in the context of medical education most famously at Hp. *Law* 5, a text which may lurk somewhere in the background of this fragment (note the description of the *Oath* as a νόμος in 4). Cf. also, e.g., Gal. *UP* 12.6 [II 196 Helmreich]. The use of the term μυcταγωγέω need imply nothing about the *Oath*'s being sworn as such.

6 ἄ[π]ταιcτον. The final sentence of this excerpt is incomplete, and breaks off abruptly at the end of the line, perhaps indicating that the copyist was primarily interested in the first sentence. Considering the ethical content, we might expect a reference to the 'unerring' or 'infallible' conduct in medical practice produced in the student by his adherence to the Oath, as e.g. ἄ[π]ταιcτον ἅμα τὸν ἐν τῷ ἰατρεύειν | βίον, with a subsequent impersonal verb governing the dative (for βίος in a broadly similar sense, cf. *Oath* ἁγνῶς δὲ καὶ ὁcίως διατηρήcω βίον ἐμὸν καὶ τέχνην ἐμήν). Scribonius Largus, *Compositiones* pref. 5 focuses on the *Oath*'s prohibition of abortives, and envisages the positive effect this will have on the student's respect for human life: 'to those who consider it a crime to injure the uncertain hope of a person [i.e. the foetus], how much more wicked will they judge it to harm a person fully-formed?' If, as suggested, this sentence went on to emphasize the resulting faultlessness of the doctor's conduct, it is perhaps more likely that the author had in mind not only the *Oath*'s prohibitions concerning therapeutic practice, but also those regarding the doctor's more general relations with his patients.

D. LEITH

4971. MEDICAL TREATISE

101/43(d)   7 × 14.5 cm   First/second century
Plate I

Damaged remains of a single column of 21 extant lines, of which a fairly generous upper margin survives, extending to 4 cm at its deepest, as well as small portions of the left and right margins. The back is blank. This is a finely produced copy, and its hand is a fair-sized informal round hand adhering to strict bilinearity, with в extending above the line, ϕ above and below. ᴀ is sometimes found in older capital form with horizontal cross-bar (e.g. 2, 13, 14); ɛ is round, often with high midstroke touched by upper arc, and once written in a single movement (15); м is deep and curved; н has high cross-bar; ʏ is generally Y-shaped with wide shallow curve, though more cursively written at 12; ω is written in two separate strokes (cf. esp. 2, 17). Descenders are often adorned with small finials. It may be assigned to the late first or perhaps early second century, comparable with *GLH* 11b (94) and P. Lond. Lit. 22 (Kenyon, *Pal. Gr. Pap.* pp. 97–8 and pl. xix) (first or second century, assigned). There are notable similarities to LXV **4453** (first century, assigned) and LXII **4307** (second century, assigned). The content of the text itself suggests a *terminus post quem* for its composition of the mid first century.

Paragraphus is found below 1, accompanied by a high dot, to mark section end. No space between letters was made for the high dot, and it may have been added subsequently, though there is no obvious difference in the ink used. Iota adscript is recorded (see 5).

The fragment focuses on the important and recurrent question in therapeutic literature as to the correct time to give food in illness (cf. e.g. Celsus 3.4.6–10), and apparently in universal terms rather than in connection with a specific disease (cf. plural πάθη at 3 and 10). The author states that food should generally be given on the more serious day, the use of the comparative indicating that he has in mind one of two days, and further confirmed by the further specification that it should be given after the paroxysm, which according to this author occurs for the most part every third day, i.e. counting inclusively every other day (διὰ τρίτης, 2–3). Thus food is to be prescribed first on the third day of an illness and every other day until its abatement, and after the paroxysm that will fall on those days.

This simple scheme coincides precisely with what is known of the therapeutic system of the *diatritus*, developed by the Methodist physician Thessalus of Tralles, whose successful career at Rome overlapped with the reign of Nero (see D. Leith, 'The Diatritus and Therapy in Graeco–Roman Medicine', *CQ* 58 (2008) 581–600). The *diatritus* represents the recurrent third day of an illness (the third, fifth, seventh days, etc.), and according to its system, which also governed the use of most forms of dietetic therapy, food is to be prescribed cyclically on these days, in exactly the manner specified on **4971**. The patient was also fed on these days only after the paroxysm had occurred. The notion, certainly not shared by all ancient physicians, that an illness's paroxysm would for the most part occur on the third day is associated in our sources with the Methodists generally and with the *diatritus* in particular (e.g. Sext. Emp. *PH* 2.237–8; Stephanus of Athens, *Comm. in prior. Gal. Ther. ad Glauc.* 7 [ed. K. Dickson, *Stephanus the Philosopher and Physician* (1998) 48.4–7]). This system, with its fixation on the recurrent third day alone, is not adopted by Celsus, for example, or the pre-Thessalian doctors whose opinions he summarises at *De med.* 3.4.6–7. It is anathema to Galen, who could attack it on the grounds that the paroxysm also often occurs every day or every three days, as in quotidian or quartan fever (e.g. *Meth. med.* 8.3 [x 561.7–11 K.]), and furthermore that food at times ought to be given before the paroxysm (e.g. *Meth. med.* 10.3 [x 678.11–14 K.]).

This fragment thus appears to preserve a general account of the mechanics of the *diatritus* system by an adherent. It would as such be unique, for the remaining evidence consists generally of open criticism, or of isolated mentions found in therapeutic recommendations for specific diseases. This new testimony offers further confirmation of the importance attached to the occurrence of the paroxysm in the system of the *diatritus*.

The *diatritus* is elsewhere mentioned on papyrus at PSI inv. CNR 85/86[1] ii 43–44 (late first or early second century) [ed. partim I. Andorlini, in Andorlini,

4971. MEDICAL TREATISE

'Specimina' 153–68], and most likely on the Greek medical fragment P. Golenischeff (third century), at ii 11 (see *GMP* II 15). Works by Thessalus are known to have been circulating in Egypt by the third century. P. Vars. 5.23 [= R. Otranto, *Antiche liste di libri su papiro* (Rome 2000) no. 17] mentions Thessalus, along with his Methodist predecessor Themison at 26b, in a list of books. P. Horak 2, a title tag with the inscription Θεσσαλοῦ περὶ τοῦ φιλιατρεῖν τοὺς εὐςχήμονας ἄνδρας, is also very likely to refer to the Methodist. See too LII **3654** 8 n. for Thessalus' possible influence. Methodists were certainly well established in Alexandria by the mid second century, in particular Julian of Alexandria and possibly therefore his teacher Apollonides of Cyprus (cf. Gal. *Meth. med.* 1.7 [x 53–5 K.]; *Adv. Jul.* 1.1 [XVIII/1 248 K.]). According to Suda Σ 851, Soranus of Ephesus also spent time there, perhaps at the end of the first century. The author of the present text, if not Thessalus himself, would seem to have been at least influenced by his doctrine. Although the *diatritus* was adopted unsystematically by apparently non-Methodist physicians, such as the so-called Anonymus Parisinus, author of *On Acute and Chronic Diseases*, the detailed discussion found on the papyrus suggests a direct engagement with Methodist doctrine.

```
     τοιςκαιροιςδιδοντα·ε [           τοῖς καιροῖς διδόντα. ε [
     επειδιατριτηςωςταπο[            ἐπεὶ διὰ τρίτης ὡς τὰ πο[λλὰ
     παροξυνεται ταπαθητ[            παροξύνεται τὰ πάθη, τ[ὴν
     τροφηνκατατοπλειςτ[             τροφὴν κατὰ τὸ πλεῖςτ[ον
5    εντηιβαρυτερ_ _τακτεον[         ἐν τῆι βαρυτέραι τακτέον
     ]πο_εξαμε_ουςτονπα[             ἀ]ποδεξαμένους τὸν πα-
     ]ξυςμοντηνμεντοι_[              ρο]ξυςμόν. τὴν μέντοι π[α-
     ...]ειςινπεφυλαγμενη_[           ράθ]εςιν πεφυλαγμένην
     ...]ειςθαιδειμεχριτης            τηρ]εῖςθαι δεῖ μέχρι τῆς
10   ..]_κμηςτωνπαθωνο               παρ]ακμῆς τῶν παθῶν ο-
     .....]_ιδονταςεανμητρο[         .....] διδόντας, ἐὰν μὴ τρο-
     .....]ηταιιςχυραπεριτα[          πὴ γίν]ηται ἰςχυρὰ περὶ τα[ύ-
     .....]_ςςωμαςινηαποςτ[           την το]ῖς ςώμαςιν ἢ ἀποςτ[
     .....]_ουςααςθενεια             .....]ηςουςα ἀςθένεια
15   .....]ωδειςεπυςειςε             .....]ώδεις επυςειςε
     .....]_οτινοςαλληςς[            .....]πό τινος ἄλλης [
     .....]_αλυωνταιδιατα[           .... κα]ταλύωνται διὰ τα[
     .....]δυν_μειςαπερεν[           .....] δυνάμεις ἅπερ ἐν [
     .....]ω[.]_υμβαινειτο[           .....]ω[ι] ςυμβαίνει το[
20   ...........]ινοςαπαν
     ...........]γκα[.]ουκ[
```

1 .[, ε's crossbar meets damaged vertical, apparently at top   5 ερ, upper arc, as of ε, c; the remaining portion of the letter has become dislodged, but is consistent with the crossbar of ε touching small loop high in line, as of ρ   .., indistinct traces   6 ., traces would admit of ⲁ, ⲇ, or λ   ., upright   7]ξ, extremes of horizontals above and below   .[, vertical with finial below, topped by a trait projecting slightly to left, apparently horizontal, as of π, but diagonal of ɴ cannot be excluded   8]ε, remains consistent with extremes of ε's crossbar and lower arc   .[, vertical topped by trait projecting to left, followed by lower extreme of vertical, as of ɴ, π   10].., extreme of diagonal touching subsequent letter at foot   11].., downward tending diagonal, with descender touching near top, as of ⲁ, ⲇ, λ   ο[, left part of circle, with no evidence of crossbar, most resembling ο, but c possible   12]η, vertical, with very faint trace of horizontal to left at two-thirds height   ι, trace of vertical's foot; available space seems to demand ι   ạ[, small trait projected above τ's crossbar, with foot of steep diagonal tending to left   13 τ[, beginning of horizontal high in line   14].., lower part of vertical   15 π̣, ΓI also possible   16].., upright leaning to right   ι, fibres twisted, but vertical visible, curving to right at the foot   ç, remains of curve visible to left of break, and end of descending stroke high in line to right   17].., end of horizontal touching subsequent letter high in line, as of c or τ   18]δ̣, extremes of diagonal and horizontal meeting low in line, and touching foot of ʏ   ., extreme of diagonal touching ᴍ's foot   19].., trace of extreme of horizontal low in line   20]γ, end of horizontal touching subsequent letter high in line   ạ, diagonal rising from foot of previous letter, then descender

'... giving ... the stages .... [Then?], since the affections reach a paroxysm in most cases every third day, one must prescribe food generally on the heavier (day), having received the paroxysm. It is necessary to make sure that the prescription is maintained until the abatement of the affections, giving (food) [in the same way?], unless a strong change happens to the bodies around this (day) or weakness ... some other ... their strength is destroyed, which happens ...'

1 Masculine plural participles refer to the physician at 6 and 11, which seems to preclude the possibility that διδόντα here does likewise. It is impossible to say what the participle may agree with, whether masculine singular or neuter plural, or indeed whether it governs the dative καιροῖς. The καιροί meant here are the stages of a disease (beginning, increase, crisis and abatement—either of the whole disease from start to finish or of its partial phases marked by consecutive paroxysms), employed as an important framework for assigning therapies to their correct times by many ancient physicians, including the Methodists.

ε.[. A small fragment, detached, but which belongs here, may preserve the intersection between midstroke of epsilon and top of vertical (cf. πλεις-, 4), suggesting εἶ[τα.

5 βαρυτέρᾳ. There is space for iota adscript, though the damaged traces preclude a certain reading. The 'heavier' day refers to the more severe presentation of a disease, and thus the day on which the paroxysm falls. Cf. e.g. Gal. *De diebus decr.* 3.8 [IX 927 K.]; ps.-Gal. *Def. med.* 203 [XIX 402 K.]; Celsus 3.4.13, with *gravior* in the same sense.

9 τηρ]εῖσθαι. Alternatively perhaps ποι]εῖσθαι.

10–11 ὁ|[μοίως] seems the most likely supplement. ὁ|[λίγην] or ὁ|[μοίαν] (sc. τροφήν) might be considered. There is, however, no reference to quantity or quality of food in the preceding sentence, but merely guidance as to the time at which food is to be administered. A further reference to the need to continue the same procedures here would seem more appropriate.

11–13 ἰςχυρά in this context seems to demand the restoration of τροπή rather than τροφή: cf. e.g. Herodotus med. *apud* Aët. *Iatr.* 5.133 [*CMG* VIII 2.109.10–11 Olivieri], where ἰςχυρὰ τροπή is used to describe a dramatic downturn in the patient's humoral constitution which can occur after the paroxysm of a certain form of fever. Together with the weakness referred to at 14, this concessive conditional appears to describe the possibility of a more serious collapse in the patient's health, to be distinguished from the paroxysm, which demands that the normal prescription of food according to the *diatritus* (7–11) be abandoned.

13–14 ἀποcτ[| . . . .]ηcουcα ἀcθένεια. A plausible supplement is perhaps ἀποcτ[ε|νοχωρ]ήcουcα, i.e. 'weakness that will cause narrowing'. This particular compound is attested in a medical work only at ps.-Gal., *Def. med.* 219 [XIX 408 K.], to describe the narrowing of the artery in an anomalous pulse. If a Methodist context is accepted for this text, then the notion of 'narrowing' might well refer to the alteration of the 'pores' (πόροι) in the body which underlies the concepts of the 'constricted' and 'lax' commonalities, deriving ultimately from the corpuscular theory of Asclepiades of Bithynia. Concerning food in particular, one might compare Plut. *Quaest. conv.* 687B–E, where a physician Philo, perhaps identifiable with the Methodist of that name (cf. M. Tecusan, *The Fragments of the Methodists* (2004) fr. 269 and p. 52), directly attributes thirst and hunger to an alteration in the constitution of the pores. Perhaps cf. also BKT III 19–21.5–11, which Kalbfleisch speculated may have been a Methodist work, in which the physician, should he judge it the right time to cause narrowing in the treatment of constipation (εἰ cτενοχωροίμε|[θα π]ερὶ τὴν εὐκαιρίαν), will postpone giving food, and other treatments, until the next day. The therapeutic principle of *metasyncrisis*, also associated by Galen with Thessalus (cf., e.g., *Meth. med.* [X 268 K.]), involves the deliberate alteration of the pores, but is designed only for the treatment of chronic diseases during periods of remission, and cannot be related to this immediate context.

15 επυcειcε. The sequence presents considerable difficulties. The traces of the second letter are consistent with pi, if not a perfectly formed one, with two clear verticals topped by a horizontal which does not project beyond them on either side. Indeed, the horizontal does not appear quite to touch the second vertical, which would suggest rather ΓΙ, but some slight damage to the surface of the papyrus at this point could well account for this. The overall impression is also somewhat distorted by the very wide bowl of upsilon following, which touches the second vertical above. We would most naturally expect a plural noun after an adjective ending]ώδειc, but there seem to be no satisfactory possibilities; the reading γρ can be excluded (as in ἐγρύcειc, reading ἐκρύcειc; for internal γ > κ, see Gignac, *Grammar* i 79). επυcει might alternatively be read as the future indicative ἐποίcει (cf. Gignac, *Grammar* i 197–8), but cε- at the end of the line is difficult to account for (the blank gap after epsilon seems to be sufficient to indicate that it is the last letter of the line). Unfortunately no other plausible explanations have presented themselves.

16–19 At 16, the vertical stroke at the break would be consistent with pi, to give presumably either ὑ]πό or ἀ]πό τινοc ἄλληc. At the beginning of 17, the remains of a high horizontal touching alpha's oblique are consistent with sigma or tau. While ἀλύω is attested in the Hippocratic Corpus, it is rare; καταλύω is much more common in medical literature, and, given the reference to weakness in disease in this fragment, apparently much more desirable in sense. κα]ταλύωνται, then, construed as passive, suggests ὑ]πό τινοc ἄλληc in the previous line, and some such word as αἰτίαc might just fit at the beginning of 17. If we take ὑ]πό τινοc ἄλληc as referring to the agent in this way, then διά at 17 is presumably not used in its causal sense: perhaps διὰ τα[ύ|τηc], i.e., 'on this day'? In view of the neuter plural relative ἅπερ at 18, δυνάμειc should be taken either as the subject of κα]ταλύωνται (αἱ] δυνάμειc) or as an accusative of respect (τὰc] δυνάμειc), the subject then being the patients themselves. Given the subject matter of the fragment, perhaps ἅπερ ἐν | [διατρίτ]ω[ι] cυμβαίνει should be restored ('. . . which happens in the *diatritus* . . .'), as suggested by Professor Andorlini.

21 ἀνα]γκα[ῖ]ον κ[?

D. LEITH

4972. Division of Surgery

50 4B.24/K(3–4)   5.5 × 19.5 cm   Second/third century
Plate VIII

Remains of a single column containing 43 lines, written on the back of a letter. Parts survive of the right margin only.

The text is copied in a small-sized, informal hand with little attempt at bilinearity, the lines themselves often tapering downwards as they proceed in the middle portion of the column. ε often leans to the right, with midstroke at times extended to meet the following letter; η has a high horizontal joining the top of its second vertical; μ appears somewhat flattened with curved diagonal obliques; ω is particularly broad and written in a single fluid movement, barely rising in the middle. It would seem to admit of a second-century dating (cf. LII **3654**, LI **3643**, *GLH* 15c, the first hand of XXXI **2536** = *GMAW*² 61), but the apostrophe used to separate double consonants (28, 29, 35, 36) may well point to a date in the early third century (cf. *GMAW*² p. 11).

The text is organized into sections by headings in the form of a question. For medical papyri in question-and-answer format, see esp. I. Andorlini, 'Testi medici per la scuola: raccolte di definizioni e questionari nei papiri', in A. Garzya, J. Jouanna (eds.), *Les Textes médicaux grecs: Tradition et ecdotique* (Naples 1999) 7–15; more recently published examples are *GMP* I 6 (see also A. E. Hanson, 'Text and Context in Papyrus Catechisms on Afflictions of the Head', in A. Garzya, J. Jouanna (eds.), *Trasmissione e ecdotica dei testi medici greci* (Naples 2004) 199–217), P. Strasb. gr. inv. 849 (ed. C. Magdelaine, in Andorlini, *Testi* 63–77), and P. Oslo inv. 1576 (ed. A. Maravela-Solbakk, D. Leith, in *Pap. Congr. XXIV* (2007) ii 637–50).

The question-headings (21–3, 26–7, 33–4) are in *eisthesis*; whether they were also accompanied by *paragraphus* or *diple*, as e.g. on P. Aberd. 11 and PSI III 252 respectively, is impossible to determine, given the loss of line beginnings. Horizontal traits are employed to mark the ends of answers at 20 and 32. Itacism is prevalent, with ει almost everywhere represented by ι. There are two *hapax legomena*, τομικός (7–8) and ἐγκατατομικός (16–17).

The text preserves a systematic exposition of surgery, unparalleled in scope and complexity, consisting in divisions firstly into its 'forms' (cχήματα, cf. 7), which may be understood as the forms or categories of knowledge that surgery encompasses, and secondly into different classes of surgical operations distinguished primarily by their therapeutic or cosmetic aims. The text can thus be divided into two sections, at 1–20 and 21–42 respectively.

Some idea of the bewildering array of highly complex divisions of the parts of medicine in circulation in the second century can be gleaned from such tracts as Gal. *De partibus artis medicativae* (ed. Schöne *CMG Suppl. Or.* II) (for a general discussion of ancient divisions of medicine, see H. von Staden, *Herophilus: The Art of Medicine in Early Alexandria* (Cambridge 1989) 89–108). Conscious systematizations of the parts of medicine are attested from the Classical and early Hellenistic periods on, and a variety of schemes are attributed e.g. to Mnesitheus of Athens (frr. 10–11 Bertier), Herophilus (T42–49 von Staden) and Erasistratus (fr. 32 Garofalo). Cels. *De med. pref.* 9 outlines the tripartite division of medicine that became standard, into dietetics, pharmacology, and surgery (already implied in Hp. *Oath* 2–3, 5), but more often this tripartite division is encountered as one of therapeutics, itself a branch of medicine along with various others, differently attested, but including e.g. physiology, pathology, and hygiene (cf. ps.-Gal. *Def. med.* 11 [XIX 351–2 K.]; ps.-Gal. *Intro.* 7 [XIV 689–90 K.]; Gal. *Part. art. med.* 1 [*CMG Suppl. or.* II 119–20 Schöne]). The Empiricist sect also developed its own peculiar division constructed around its epistemological doctrine, in which surgery represented a subdivision of therapeutics, itself a part of the so-called 'perfective' branch of medicine (see K. Deichgräber, *Die griechische Empirikerschule*[2] (Berlin & Zurich 1965) 288–91).

Extant divisions of surgery are limited either to bipartite divisions (cf. ps.-Sor. *Quaest. med.* 39 [ed. V. Rose, *Anecdota graeca et graeco-latina* (1870) ii 252], based on the natural vs. accidental causes of conditions; and ps.-Gal. *Intro.* 19 [XIV 781 K.], based on operations that aim at synthesis or separation), or to simple lists of various surgical procedures (cf. *Chirurgia Eliodori* [ed. H. E. Sigerist, *Archiv für Geschichte der Medizin* 12 (1920) 1–9]). The Methodists' surgical 'commonalities' may also be regarded as a further division (ps.-Gal. *Intro.* 3 [XIV 681 K.]). On papyrus, P. Gen. inv. 111 preserves a list of definitions of various surgical terms, incorporating parallels with the *Chirurgia Eliodori* (see Marganne, *Chirurgie* 85–95).

The divisions of surgery presented on the papyrus may have formed part of a broader division of medicine as a whole, and it is possible that the present text thus derives from some form of introductory handbook on medicine in general. Given the complexity of the divisions involved, however, which far exceeds those attested in surviving medical handbooks, it is perhaps more likely that we are faced with an introductory section of a treatise specifically on surgery, which provided a systematic, structural analysis of the discipline (cf. e.g. Sor. *Gyn.* 1.1–2, where a discussion of the divisions of gynaecology serves as a preface to, and determines the structure of, the treatise as a whole; note that the text of the *Gynaecia* is also regularly articulated by question-headings). For other examples of surgical texts on preliminary topics, one might compare the discussion of the fundamentals of surgical knowledge found in BKT III 22–26, as well as III **437** (ed. alt. A. Wouters, *Philologus* 121 (1977) 146–9), which offers a description of the best surgeon, a subject that would likewise find a suitable home in the introduction to a surgical treatise (as at Cels. *De med.* 7.4, in the preface to the surgical books; cf. also Sor. *Gyn.* 1.4, with its question-heading τίς ἀρίστη μαῖα;).

].[.]..[
μεθο]δικὸν δὲ τό τ[ινος] με̣θόδ[ου·
τὸ δὲ] cχηματικόν ἐcτιν τὸ τῶ[ν
ἐπιτη]δίων cχημάτων ὥcπερ
ὅταν] λέγωμεν ἀνάροπον ἢ
κατάρ]οπον cχηματίζιν τὸν
κάμν]οντα· τὸ δὲ cχῆμα τὸ το-
μικόν] ἐcτιν τὸ τῶν ἐπιτηδίων
τμημ]άτων ὥcπερ ὅταν λέ-
γωμε]ν πλαγιοτομῖν ἢ λοξ[ο-
τομῖν·] τὸ δὲ καιρικόν ἐcτιν
καθ' ὃ δ]ηλοῦνται αἱ μετὰ τὴν
χειρου]ργίαν θεραπίαι· τὸ δὲ
cημιω]τικόν ἐcτιν καθ' ὃ μετὰ
τὴν cη]μίωcιν προλέγωμεν
ἂν περ]ὶ τῶν ὄντων· ἐνκατα̣-
τομι]κ̣ὸν δὲ τὸ τῆc λεγομένηc
ἐμβρυ]οτομίαc· τὰ δὲ ἄλλα ἀπ̣[
.....]ν ὀνομάτων γνωριζό-
μενα] τυνχάνει. ⸺
κατὰ πόcουc τρόπουc
τὰ ἐν χειρουργίᾳ πάθη
μεθορεύει;
κατὰ] μὲν ἁπλοῦc τρόπουc
β̄, κατ]ὰ δὲ ἐπιμίκτουc β̄.
ποῖοί εἰcιν οἱ ἁπλοῖ
τρόποι;
οἱ ἐνι]κ̣ὴν ἔχοντεc ἐπαγγελίαν. ἐ]παγγέλλεται γὰρ ἢ εὐ-
πρέπι]αν ἢ ἀπρέπιαν καὶ πάλιν ἢ κα]λῶc ζῆν ἢ κακῶc ει
.....]ερ αὐτοῦ τοῦ ζῆν. ⸺[
ποῖο[ί] εἰcιν οἱ {αι} ἐπί-
μικ[τ]οι τρόποι;
οἱ διc]cὴν ἔχοντε̣c ἀπαγγε-
λίαν. ἐ]παγγέλλεται γὰρ ἡ χε[ι-
ρουργί]α̣ ἐπὶ τῶν κατὰ τοὺc ἐ-

πιμίκ]τουc τρόπουc καὶ ἐπὶ
τῶν δι]ccὴν ἐχόν[τ]ων cωτη-
40   .... π]ροcαγεται [..].[.]...
   .....]ωc ζῆν ἢ κ[....] ευπρε[
   .....]   (vac.)
          ].....[   ]..η[

4 l. ἐπιτηδείων   5 ρο corr. from ρα   l. ἀνάρροπον   6 l. cχηματίζειν   8 l. ἐπιτηδείων   10–11 l. πλαγιοτομεῖν ἢ λοξοτομεῖν   13 l. θεραπεῖαι   15 l. cημείωcιν
16–17 l. ἐγκατατομικὸν   20 l. τυγχάνει   25 l. ἐπιμείκτουc   28 επαγ᾽γε   29,
36 ε]παγ᾽γελλεται   29–30 l. εὐπρέπειαν ἢ ἀπρέπειαν   33–4 l. ἐπίμεικτοι   35 απαγ᾽γε-
l. ἐπαγγε-   37–8 l. ἐπιμείκτουc

'... The methodic is that concerned with a particular method. The position-based is that concerned with appropriate positions, as when we speak of positioning the patient tilted up or tilted down. The incision-based form is that concerned with appropriate incisions, as when we speak of cutting obliquely or at an angle. The stage-based is that by which the treatments after surgery are indicated. The semiotic is that by which, after inferring from the signs, we may talk about the present circumstances (sc. of the condition) without being told. The obstetric surgical (sc. form) is that concerned with what is known as embryotomy. The rest happen to be recognizable from the names [themselves?].

'In how many ways are the affections in surgery [treated]? In two (?) simple and two compound ways.

'What are the simple ways? Those that have a single promise. For (sc. surgery) promises either attractiveness or unattractiveness or else a good or bad quality of life, [if it does not concern?] living itself.

'What are the compound ways? Those that have a double promise (?). For surgery, in those cases according to the mixed ways and in those that have a double (sc. promise), promises preservation (?).... is added...'

1–20 That further unnamed forms are referred to at 18–20 indicates that they were listed before each was explained individually in the surviving passage. To judge from parallel formulations, a total number of forms may also have been given at the beginning, and we can infer that this total would have come to at least nine: the first (lost) being introduced in an initial 'μέν' clause; the six named in the text; and at least two represented by τὰ δὲ ἄλλα at 18. We can only speculate on what these lost forms may have been. There may, however, be an indirect reference to a comparable division of surgery at ps.-Gal. Def. med. 469 [XIX 460 K.], where τὸ ὀργανικόν is attested as a part of surgery, encompassing the resetting of fractures (and the instruments used for this purpose). Other possibilities might include bandaging, reduction of dislocations, etc. The introductory question may thus have been something like πόcα τὰ cχήματα τῆc χειρουργίαc;

The first four forms listed here broadly parallel extant accounts of surgical operations, which regularly address in order the appropriate procedure to be selected for a given condition, the position of the patient which this demands, the appropriate type of incision, and the post-operative measures to be taken depending on the type of operation (as a representative example, cf. Heliodorus/Antyllus ap. Orib. Coll. med. 50.3.5–9 [CMG VI 2.2.57 Raeder]).

2 μεθο]δικόν. Restoration is clearly suggested by μεθόδ[ου at the end of the line. See 16–18 for a parallel construction. This would presumably refer to the selection of a suitable surgical procedure upon examination of the patient. For μέθοδος in a comparable sense, cf. e.g. Paul. Aeg. 6.77.4 [CMG IX 2.120 Heiberg].

3–7 Placing the patient in the correct position for a given operation was naturally an important preliminary for surgery. Various positions are named in the literature, such as the 'seated' (καθέδριον, Aët. Iatr. 15.5 [ed. Zervos, Athena 21 (1909) 19]) or the 'Alexandrian' (P. Ryl. III 529r ii 66–76, on which see Marganne, Chirurgie 129 and n. 29). For the terms used here, cf. Gal. MM 6.4 [x 415 K.], cχῆμα δ' ἐπιτήδειον τῷ κάμνοντι πρὸς μὲν τοῖς κάτω μέρεςι τῆς τρώςεως γεγενημένης τὸ ἀνάρροπον, πρὸς δὲ τοῖς ἄνω τὸ κατάρροπον. These apparently refer to positions in which the patient is lying back on a sloped surface with either the head (ἀνάρροπον) or the feet (κατάρροπον) raised higher.

4 ἐπιτη]δίων. Between 3 and 4, there is a trace of an ascending diagonal above delta, but apparently too high to form part of a letter.

7 κάμν]οντα or πάςχ]οντα.

7–11 Different types of incision were deemed appropriate for different parts of the body and anatomical structures: cf. e.g. Antyllus *ap.* Aët. Iatr. 15.5 [ed. Zervos, Athena 21 (1909) 19], ἀνεπιτήδειος γὰρ ἡ πλαγιοτομία τραχήλῳ, ὅτι τὰ ἀγγεῖα κατ' εὐθὺ τέτακται καὶ τὰ νεῦρα. Antyllus describes three forms of incision at Aët. Iatr. 3.15 [CMG VIII 1.274 Olivieri], that at right angles (presumably relative to an underlying blood vessel), the straight (or parallel), and the angled: cχήματα δὲ τρία διαιρέςεως· τὸ μὲν ἐπικάρςιον, τὸ δὲ εὐθὺ οὐχὶ κεῖρον, ἀλλὰ cχίζον τὴν φλέβα κατ' εὐθύ, τὸ δὲ μεταξὺ τούτων προcαγορευόμενον λοξόν. It is thus difficult to determine precisely the nature of the contrast between πλαγιοτομεῖν and λοξοτομεῖν (cutting obliquely / at an angle) mentioned on the papyrus, unless of course they are meant as synonyms.

11–16 The following two 'forms' appear to be concerned with more abstract aspects of the surgeon's knowledge. Broadly speaking, καιρός in medical literature refers to the stage reached in the course of an affection, or the 'opportunity' or 'correct time' to offer a particular treatment appropriate to this stage. The *kairikon* form described here is said to indicate the post-operative treatments, and may simply designate the surgeon's general awareness of the identifiable stages of a condition and their importance in determining particular forms of treatment. Semiotics, the art of predicting the past, present, and future development of a condition, was widely recognized as a fundamental aspect of ancient therapeutics in general, as well as of surgery in particular (cf. e.g. ps.-Gal. Intro. 8 [XIV 693–4 K.]), and especially with a view to establishing the doctor's authority in a clinical context (cf. esp. Hp. Progn. 1). It is unsurprising to find it attested here specifically as an important part of surgical expertise.

16–18 Interestingly, obstetric surgery is singled out here, presumably reflecting more general tendencies to isolate gynaecology as a particular field within medicine (cf. e.g. Sor. Gyn. 3.1–5). See Hp. Foet. exsect. 1.1 for use of the verb ἐγκατατέμνω in an obstetric context. Various operations using surgical instruments to remove the foetus in cases of dystocia, referred to under the headings of ἐμβρυοτομία and ἐμβρυουλκία, are described in detail at Cels. De med. 7.29 and Sor. Gyn. 4.9–12.

18–19 There is insufficient space for both the article, which seems necessary, and another word before ὀνομάτων, and I suggest that ἀπ' | [αὐτῶ]ν ⟨τῶν⟩ ὀνομάτων should be restored, though no doubt there are other possibilities.

21–42 The author in this section sets out a separate division of surgery based on distinctions between the aims of different categories of surgical operation, expressed as what surgery 'promises' (ἐπαγγέλλεται). The primary division is into simple and compound ways (τρόποι) of treating, which are each further divided into two kinds. It is clear that the two simple ways, described at 26–32, are defined by their each having a single aim, thus encompassing operations that are principally concerned either with a patient's appearance (promising εὐπρέπεια or ἀπρέπεια) or with the resulting quality of life, presumably referring to physical ability (καλῶc or κακῶc ζῆν). Though in a non-surgical context, a comparable division into four simple and four compound ways of curing (ἁπλοῖ and cύνθετοι τρόποι τῆc ἰάcεωc) can be found at Gal. *MM* [x 103–4 K.], each aiming to counteract an excessively hot, cold, moist, or dry condition of the body, or the four possible combinations of these elemental qualities.

The discussion of the compound ways at 33–42 is rather more difficult to interpret from the remains. Firstly, the fact that there are two compound ways of treating precludes the possibility that they involve merely a combination of the two simple ways. Rather the distinction between the compound ways appears to parallel that between the simple ways, so that one additional factor is added (προcάγεται, 40) to each of the latter. The mention of what must be cωτη|[ρία at 39–40 would seem to suggest that this additional factor or aim concerns the preservation of the patient's life, when this is under threat, suggesting that the final clause or sentence of the previous section on the simple ways (31–2) should be interpreted as specifying that these are not concerned with life-or-death situations. Thus at 40–42, where the second indicative π]ροcάγεται suggests a new sentence, we should have the statement that preservation of life (cωτηρία) is added to or combined with the distinguishing aims of the simple ways of surgical treatment (i.e. either a good quality of life or attractiveness). There will thus be four ways of treating surgically, according to their aims or objectives: (i) will be directed primarily at leaving the patient physically able; (ii) will be primarily cosmetic; (iii) will involve saving the patient's life, when this is threatened, and will leave the patient physically able (at the expense of appearance); and (iv) will save the patient's life and leave a pleasing appearance (at the expense of physical ability). An obvious objection to this scheme would be that a pleasing appearance and good quality of life are not mutually exclusive outcomes of surgery, but the distinction may only pertain to the primary aim of the procedure. See below 35–42 n. for a possible reconstruction of this section.

23 μεθορεύει. This unattested verb, which could mean something like 'to share boundaries with', I assume to be an error. An emendation to μεθοδεύει ('treats/cures') is the simplest solution palaeographically, but we are left without an obvious subject. The passive μεθοδεύεται would give the most satisfactory sense, i.e., 'In how many ways are the affections in surgery treated?', and thus seems preferable, though the error is more difficult to explain.

25 The restoration of the number $\overline{β}$ in lacuna is required by the two separate outcomes of the simple ways of treatment set out at 29–31, each being described by a positive and a negative alternative.

26–32 That surgical procedures were indeed distinguished according to their primarily cosmetic or corrective outcomes emerges from such texts as P. Fuad Univ. App. I 1 9–13 [ed. alt. M.-H. Marganne, *L'ophtalmologie dans l'Égypte gréco-romaine d'après les papyrus littéraires grecs* (Leiden 1994) 147–72], where the relative merits of two types of *periscythismus* operation are discussed (the one μᾶλλον τοῦ ἀποτελέcματοc ἔχεται, the other is εὐπρεπέcτεροc); cf. also the similar distinctions between operations made at Aët. *Iatr.* 7.94; Paul. Aeg. 6.19, 53, 54.

31–2 Given my interpretation of the nature of the compound ways, I think it most likely that this clause indicates that the simple ways of treatment are not relevant under circumstances in which the patient's life is in danger: they are directed only towards the patient's appearance or quality of life, not life itself. I thus suggest as a possible restoration εἰ | [μὴ ὑπ]ὲρ αὐτοῦ τοῦ ζῆν ('. . . if it does not concern/is not for the sake of living itself').

35–42 The precise meaning of this passage on the compound ways remains somewhat obscure. I offer the following tentative reconstruction of the whole section:

35 οἱ διc]cὴν ἔχοντεc ἀπαγγε-
    λίαν. ἐ]παγγέλλεται γὰρ ἡ χε[ι-
    ρουργί]α ἐπὶ τῶν κατὰ τοὺc ἐ-

πιμίκ]τους τρόπους καὶ ἐπὶ
τῶν δι]ccὴν ἐχόν[τ]ων cωτη-
40 ρίαν· π]ροcάγεται [..].[.]...
τῷ καλ]ῶc ζῆν ἢ κ[αὶ τῇ] εὐπρε-
πία]   (vac.)

35 l. ἐπαγγε-   41–2 l. εὐπρε|[πεία]

'Those that have a double promise. For surgery, in those cases according to the mixed ways and in those that have a double (sc. promise), promises preservation. [For this?] is added to a [good quality] of life or [even] to attractiveness.'

I suggest that cωτηρίαν at 39–40 should be taken as the object of ἐπαγγέλλεται. Although it would seem unnatural to separate it from διccήν in this way at 39, the phrase τῶν διccὴν ἐχόντων can be read as referring back to 35–6, with ἐπαγγελίαν subsequently left understood. At the end of 40, the traces might admit of a reading such as [α]ὕτῃ, giving perhaps e.g. π]ροcάγεται [γὰ]ρ [α]ὕτῃ, but this is very unclear. This schematization of course appears somewhat contrived, and doubtless other interpretations are possible.

D. LEITH

4973. Veterinary or Physiognomical Text

62 6B.75/B(1–5)a   15.8 × 13.3 cm   Second century

Remains of three columns written against the fibres, on the back of a register of landholdings and taxes assignable to the second century. Column i contains only the final letters of each line. The passage in column ii is preserved almost intact, while column iii offers the beginnings of 15 lines. The papyrus is of poor quality, the handwriting an upright cursive, heavily written, and giving a somewhat relaxed impression: cf. P. Lond. I 110 = *GLH* 18a, a horoscope of 138, and PSI 240 (re-ed. in PSI Corr. I pp. 7–10, with plate), assigned to the first or second century. **4973** may also be assigned to the second century.

One notices immediately the presence of a number of anatomical terms. The text appears to constitute an anatomical description, in the form of a list, articulated by participles and in asyndeton. It is not easy to identify the subject to which the terms refer, whether a person or an animal, since they are applicable to either and any passages that would illuminate the context are lost. Nor is it clear whether a normal or a pathological state is described. The text at ii 3–4 seems to suggest an abnormal state, followed by an explanation of the passage articulated by participles and in asyndeton. It is difficult to determine what these terms refer to (ii 4), and they are apparently followed by a description of symptoms. On the other hand, the nature of the parts described (e.g. eyes, teeth) may point instead to a description of a normal state. Additionally, the observation at ii 8–9, οἱονεὶ φλεκτιδώδη (l. φλυ-) διάθεcιν, seems to indicate that a pathological condition has been described. The difficulties in interpretation are also due to the fact that no clear syntactical structure is in evidence. In col. ii, which at certain points preserves an almost complete text, one notes in particular a sequence of terms in the accusative. Many lexical difficulties remain, in that individual words are either not attested or apparently used in an anomalous sense in the context: cf. e.g. ii 4 transitive πληθύω; ii 7–8 intransitive ὑποκάμπτω; ii 9 φλεκτιδώδη (φλυκτιδώδη is probably to be read, likewise unattested).

Parallels can be found in physiognomical texts, in which many anatomical features are considered significant, but it is nevertheless not entirely certain that we have a text of this genre. There are a number of differences. All references, for example, to the significance of the anatomical characteristics described on the papyrus are lacking, and descriptions of teeth (see ii 12) are entirely absent in physiognomical texts. It can otherwise be excluded that the text represents a description of a person's physical characteristics for the purposes of identification.

The text appears to correspond better to a description of an animal. The *Hippiatrica* literature and the *Cynegetica* do not provide decisive parallels, but Philumenus' treatise *De venenatis animalibus* of the first century offers more suggestive terminology for comparison with **4973**: there are interesting correspondences (though it should be noted that the text has reached us only as an epitome) both in individual details (see the notes below) and in the fact that both texts present a similar syntactical structure, in the form of a list of terms in the accusative (cf. e.g. *CMG* x 1.1.34.8 ff. Wellmann). Note that in these contexts the description of jaws and teeth is an important element: cf. e.g. p. 36.7 ff. (shrew); p. 28.19–20. There are further parallels in the description of the crocodile in Hdt. 2.68. In view of the quality of the material, it cannot be ruled out that this is an *ad hoc* composition rather than a copy of a text.

Col. i

```
     ] . . .
     ]ναι
     ]ων
     ]υ
5    ] . φ . .
     ]ατο
     ]ων
     ] . . .
     ] . .
10   ] . ι
     ] .
```

3 vertical strokes before lacuna   6 alternatively ϲτο   8 the traces may admit of πα̣ι̣, τῳ̣ι̣ or τῳ̣ν̣   9 vertical extending below the line: ρ or φ (ι also sometimes extends below the line)

Col. ii

      .   .   .   .
      ]. [
      ]δ[
τεταραγμ[. . . . .]ο̣[ ]χλω-
ρον ἢ ὅτι τὰϲ φ[. . . . .] πληθύ-
5 ον. καὶ τὸ μὲν ἄν̣ω βλέφαρον ἐπηρμένον, τὸ δὲ ὑπο-
κάτω παρειμένον καὶ ὑπο-
κάμπτον ἐπιφαῖν[ο]ν οἱ-
ονεὶ φλεκτιδώδη διάθεϲιν,
10 τὰϲ δὲ παρειὰϲ [.]υτώδειϲ καὶ
παρειμέν[αϲ] τὰϲ γνάθο[υ]ϲ,
γομφίουϲ πλ[α]τεῖϲ ἀ⟨ρ⟩ρύθμουϲ,
ὦτα μεγάλα τοῖϲ λοβοῖϲ,
ὀγκώδη ῥώθωνα παχύν·
15 πρὸϲ δὲ τῷ μετώπῳ τὰ π .
   .[. . .]. .[
     ]. .[
     ]. .[

Col. iii

    .   .   .
. . . . .[
αρθρωτοι δὲ [
χοι ὄνυχεϲ .[
μέϲα τῶν .[
5 πεφυκότεϲ [
βαρεῖϲ ω[
τῶν ποδῶ[ν
ε . ων ευο̣υ̣[
ροι τὸ δὲ μ .[
10 τηϲ τοῦ ϲω[
ἔχοντεϲ [
περιπλε .[
τω[. .]. [

.ελε[
15   ].[
         .   .   .

'... mottled ... greenish/yellowish, or because it is full [in the veins / in the mind?]. And the upper eyelid raised, the lower relaxed and folded downwards, with the appearance of a pustulous condition, the cheeks ... and relaxed at the jaws, molars broad and irregular, ears with large lobes, nose swollen and thick. Alongside the forehead, the ...

'... articulated ... nails ... in the middle of ... by nature ... heavy ... of the feet ... of the [body?] ... having ...'

Col. ii

3 τα is somewhat obscured by a partially detached and twisted fibre, on which traces of two preceding lines are visible; the piece on which ταρ is written has been moved below its original position. The participle τεταραγμένος is used to describe a 'mottled' complexion or eye colour at Arist. Phgn. 812a 17 (οἱ δὲ ἔνωχροι καὶ τεταραγμένοι τὸ χρῶμα δειλοί) and 812b 8 (οἱ ὠχρόμματοι ἐντεταραγμένους ἔχοντες τοὺς ὀφθαλμοὺς δειλοί), as noted by Dr Leith. At the end of the line, there may or may not be space for a narrow letter between omicron and chi, allowing perhaps for ὑπ]όχλω|ρον, used to describe skin colour at Physiogn. [I 387.2 Foerster]. This suggests as a possible restoration τεταραγμ[ένον ἢ ὑπ]όχλω|ρον ('... mottled or pale'), with the noun which these terms qualify being perhaps the skin (τὸ δέρμα), or the face (τὸ πρόσωπον), etc. Like all the descriptive elements that follow, this is non-specific by itself and can be found in multiple contexts, as for example in the description of an animal: cf. Philum. pp. 34.21, 36.7 ff.

4 φ before lacuna is uncertain, and may alternatively be ρ: only a vertical extending below the line is visible.

ἢ ὅτι τὰς φ[λέβας] or φ[ρένας] πληθύ|ον. Both restorations, offered *exempli gratia*, fit the space. The presence of ἢ ὅτι suggests that the previous lines referred to the cause of a pathological state. πληθύω is standardly intransitive, but there are some instances of the transitive (Soph. fr. 718 Radt). The noun may however be taken as accusative of respect.

5 ν and κ seem to overlap, and a small piece of papyrus, where κα is read, is situated towards the left: in fact they touch the traces of ι next to them, but on the image there appears to be a lacuna the width of one letter.

5–7 The eyelids are a recurrent element in physiognomical descriptions: cf. Arist. Phgn. 807b 29, βλέφαρα παχέα; Physiogn. [I 30.14 Foerster], βλέφαρα ... παχέα; [I 636.6 ff.], ὀφθαλμοὶ μειδιῶντες, ἅμα ὑγρότητι, βλέφαρα ἀνειμένα ... τὰ ἀμφὶ βλέφαρα λαγαρά; [I 413.2], β. ἀναπεπετασμένα παχέα; [I 415.2], β. ἀνατεταμένα. For βλέφαρα ἐπηρμένα, cf. Gal. In Hp. Epid. III [XVII/A 540.14 K.] and ps.-Gal. Intro. [XIV 768.13 K.].

8–9 φλεκτιδώδης does not exist and is meaningless. It is probably an error for φλυκτιδώδης, an unattested adjective that could be derived from φλυκτίς, 'pustule': for an analogous error in the *Hippiatrica* tradition, see Hippiatr. 2.218.23, φλυκτίδας v. l. φλεκτίδας. The adjective is parallel to φλυκταινοειδής and φλυκταινώδης, both attested in medical literature. φλυκτίς and φλύκταινα are equivalent: cf., e.g., Aët. 7.31 [CMG VIII 1.277.20 Olivieri], although they are distinguished in Suda 4.476. The adjective can plausibly refer to the eyelids, even if οἱονεί specifies that a pustule-like appearance is meant rather than pustules themselves.

9 ςιν, ς ligatured to ι in a curve descending to right to shorten the line.

10 The cheeks are also an important element in physiognomical texts (cf. Physiogn. [I 348.14 Foerster]), and are associated with the jaws, as mentioned here immediately afterwards (cf. ibid.

[1 378.7 ff.]). The adjective that qualifies them presents a difficulty: there are traces before τωδεις, but space only for two letters, and the traces of the second letter suit γ well. Thus the possibilities seem restricted to αὐτώδης and φυτώδης, neither of which fits the context. If, however, we suppose that there was a scribal error as in the previous line, [ῥ]υτώδεις might be restored, and emended to [ῥ]υτ⟨ιδ⟩ώδεις. The adjective is attested in Hp. *Prorrh.* 2.23, Arist. *HA* 604a 28, *Phgn.* 807b 4, 808a 8, 18, 28, etc., and is suited to the context. Wrinkled cheeks are noted in physiognomical texts: cf. *Physiogn.* [II 227.13 Foerster], παρειαὶ ἐρρυτιδωμέναι. γνάθος can refer to the jaws of humans or animals.

12 Attention is naturally paid to the characteristics of the teeth in the *Hippiatrica* literature (cf. e.g. I 320.25 ff.; I 325.7–9), though not in physiognomical texts.

13 The ears can of course refer to humans and animals, but ears with large lobes suggest in particular an animal. Even in this case parallels can be drawn both in physiognomical texts (ὦτα μεγάλα at I 380.7 ff., I 424.5) and in the *Hippiatrica*. In the latter case, however, attention is paid above all to the movement and posture of the ears rather than their size.

14 ῥώθων, 'nose', but found most often in the plural in the sense of 'nostrils': cf. Poll. 2.72; Hsch. s.vv. μύξα and ῥώθωνες; Ruf. Eph. [137.7 Daremberg]. The term is naturally found in the *Hippiatrica*, but in the plural. On the other hand, cf. *Physiogn.* [II 324.24 Foerster], with reference to a species of bull, ῥώθωνι παχεῖ.

Col. iii

2 ἀρθρωτοί or more likely a compound adjective of the form (ἀ)διάρθρωτοι.

3 Perhaps [δολι]]χοὶ ὄνυχες?

5 ff. We have evidently arrived at the end of the description, which included some comment on nature (πεφυκότες) and weight (βαρεῖς), with the mention of the feet or legs. All these final elements are found in close proximity in Arist. *Phgn.* 810a 15 ff., ὅσοις οἱ πόδες εὐφυεῖς τε καὶ μεγάλοι, διηρθρωμένοι τε καὶ νευρώδεις . . . ὅσοι δὲ τοὺς πόδας μικροὺς στενοὺς ἀνάρθρους ἔχουσιν . . . οἷς τῶν ποδῶν οἱ δάκτυλοι καμπύλοι, ἀναιδεῖς καὶ ὅσοις ὄνυχες καμπύλαι.

8 The second letter is difficult to interpret: ⲁ, λ, or, less likely, malformed ρ.

ευογ[. Perhaps a form of εὔογκος (in phonetic spelling), suggested by Dr Leith.

10 Perhaps τοῦ cώ[ματος.

11 Initial ε apparently corrected to λ or accidentally malformed.

D. MANETTI
(translated from the Italian by D. Leith)

4974. OSTEOLOGICAL FRAGMENT

16 2B.45/C(c)   5.5 × 4 cm   Second or third century

A small, rectangular piece containing remains of five lines of text written against the fibres. Only the upper margin survives, to a height of just under 1 cm. The other side contains no writing, but there is a patch of smudged ink that appears to have been partially wiped off.

The text is written in a medium sized, semi-cursive with little attempt at bilinearity. The letters are generally upright, some tending slightly to the right. μ is wide, curved, and shallow; ν's diagonal meets the second, often curved, hasta at two-thirds height; υ is small and V-shaped, with a pronounced hook to right; ω is small and barely rises in the middle. Similar hands can be found in XXXI **2533** and *GMAW*² 17a, both assigned to the second century.

The presence of the terms γόμφωcιc and cύμφυcιc, and the association of the former with the teeth, indicates that the text drew on ancient classifications of the various forms of joint in the body. The preface to Galen's early work *De ossibus ad Tirones* [II 732–39 K.] constitutes the fullest extant account of such a classification, while ch. 12 of the ps.-Galenic *Introductio sive Medicus* [XIV 720–25 K.] offers a much less complex scheme, with some variation in the usage of certain terms. The systematic classification of joint types appears to have been a development of the Hellenistic period: while some of the specific technical terms employed find parallels in the Hippocratic and Aristotelian Corpora, there is little indication that they formed part of a comprehensive taxonomy, though the beginnings of one can be clearly identified at *PA* 2.9.654a 32–b 22 (see also 2 and 3 n.). There is scant evidence of direct osteological research associated with Alexandrian anatomy. One might otherwise think of the work Περὶ cκελετῶν by the Peripatetic Clearchus of Soli (see frr. 106–10 Wehrli) as a possible source of such classifications: cf. fr. 108, recording Clearchus' assertion that there are 26 bones in the hand; and Galen's comment at *AA* 1.2 [II 220 K.] that some people gave a similar title to his own osteological handbook *De ossibus*. The earliest references to the technical terms for these joint types are found in P. Lond. Lit. 167 [ed. alt. M.-H. Marganne, *BASP* 24 (1987) 23–34], of the first century BC or AD; in PUG II 51 [ed. alt. I. Andorlini, in V. Boudon-Millot et al. (eds.), *Ecdotica e ricezione dei testi medici greci* (Naples 2006) 83–91], of the first century AD; and in ps.-Gal. *Def. Med.* 470 and 474–5 [XIX 460–61 K.], thought to date from the later first century. They were also employed in the 20-book treatise on anatomy by Galen's predecessor Marinus, in the early second century (cf. Gal. *Libr. propr.* 4.15 [XIX 26 K. = *Scr. min.* II 105 Müller]). Galen further tells us that certain terms, such as ἐνάρθρωcιc, ἀρθρωδία, and cυγχόνδρωcιc, were coined by the 'more recent' anatomists, and were not used by the ancients, implying a continuing development of these classifications (*Oss.* pref. [II 735, 738 K.]).

Beyond its general osteological content, there is little discernible thematic continuity in what survives, and there may have been a fairly extensive loss of text. The repetition of κατὰ δέ at 2 and 4 perhaps indicates that the text offered a list of the various joint types, illustrated by examples. A similar construction is used in ps.-Gal. *Intro.* 12 [XIV 720–22] (see 2 n.). The instance of κατά at 5 might thus be read as introducing a further type, though in this case it is possible that the preposition refers simply to the location of the anatomical feature under discussion.

```
       ]ι νευροχοντρώδη cώ[ματα
     κατ]ὰ δὲ γόμφωcιν οἱ ὀδόντ̣[εc
       ]η ἁπλοῖ τῆc cυμφύcε[ωc
       ]ιcιν οὗτοι· κατὰ δὲ το[
5      ]ν ὀcτέον κεῖται κατα[
            .     .     .
```

1 l. νευροχονδρώδη

1 ἐcτ]ι or κα]ί?

νευροχοντρώδη. For δ > τ after ν, see Gignac, *Grammar* i 76–7, 81. The anatomical term νευροχονδρώδηc ('neuro-cartilaginous') is not attested before Galen and the ps.-Galenic author of the *Intro.*, and is thus notably absent in Rufus of Ephesus. There is no indication as to which part of the body it describes here. It is generally used of a particularly hard and dense kind of ligament (cύνδεcμοc: cf. Gal. *De temp.* [I 602–3 K.], attributing the term to 'the anatomists'; *PHP* 1.9.5 [*CMG* V 4.1.2 I 94 de Lacy]), and is associated especially with those ligaments that bind a joint from within, such as the *ligamentum teres* in the hip, as opposed to those that surround the joint (cf. Gal. *AA* 2.9 [II 328–9 K.], 2.10 [II 332 K.]). Galen refers to such 'neuro-cartilaginous' ligaments also in the knee-joint (*AA* 2.10 [II 329 K.]), between the carpal bones (*Oss.* 15 [II 770 K.]), and variously in the joints at the ankle, heel and metatarsals (*AA* 2.10 [II 333–4 K.]; *Oss.* 25 [II 777 K.]). He also describes the bone in the heart as a 'neuro-cartilaginous' body (*UP* 6.19 [I 366 Helmreich]; *AA* 7.10 [II 619 K.]). By contrast, it is also used to describe the nature of the sphincter muscle in P. Lund I 7.7–11 [ed. alt. M.-H. Marganne, *CE* 62 (1987) 189–200].

2 κατ]ὰ δὲ γόμφωcιν. At the break, a small trace of a descending diagonal survives, consistent with alpha. The phrase is closely paralleled by ps.-Gal. *Intro.* [XIV 722 K.]: κατὰ γόμφωcιν δὲ cύγκεινται οἱ ὀδόντεc, ἐγγεγόμφωνται γὰρ τοῖc φατνίοιc. The ps.-Galenic author sets out each of the three types of joint he discusses in the same manner: κατὰ ῥαφὴν μὲν οὖν cύγκεινται τὰ ἐκ τῆc κεφαλῆc ὀcτᾶ [XIV 720 K.]; κατὰ δὲ cύμφυcιν τὰ τῆc ἄνω γνάθου ὀcτᾶ cύγκειται [XIV 721 K.]. The papyrus may have employed a similar structure, though it would have incorporated much less intervening material than the ps.-Galenic text.

Galen likewise illustrates joints κατὰ γόμφωcιν solely with reference to the teeth (*Oss.* pref. [II 738 K.]). But see ps.-Gal. *Def. med.* 474 [XIX 461 K.] (διακίνημά ἐcτι τῶν κατὰ γόμφωcιν ἢ καθ' ἁρμονίαν cυγκειμένων ὀcτῶν ἐν τῷ αὐτῷ τόπῳ εἰc τὸν παρὰ φύcιν τόπον ἔκcταcιc· ὥcπερ ἐκ ταρcοῦ ὀcταρίων ῥαγέντων ἢ cπονδύλων εἴωθε γίγνεcθαι), which appears to associate joints κατὰ γόμφωcιν with those of the upper foot and vertebrae. A possible precursor may be found in Aristotle, who twice compares the hock-joint of quadrupeds with a γόμφοc, or peg, in the context of describing the actions of particular joints (*PA* 2.9.654b.19–22, 4.10.690a.12–14). Aristotle's use of the term, borrowed from carpentry, is clearly illustrative rather than classificatory here, but may have had an influence on later osteological terminology.

3 ἁπλοῖ. Of the second letter, two straight verticals, with a missing fibre at top that could have contained a thin cross-bar; the traces do not suit eta. It seems possible that this refers to a distinction between teeth that have a single or multiple roots, as enummerated by Galen at *Oss.* pref. [II 753 K.], though he does not use this term.

cυμφύcε[ωc. According to Gal. *Oss.* pref. [II 734 K.], the type of joint κατὰ cύμφυcιν is characterized by a sort of 'natural union' that in some way combines two bones effectively into a single unit. A favoured example of such a joint is the connection (non-existent in humans) in the centre of the lower jaw at the chin (ibid. [II 733 K.]), but the joining of the fingernail to the finger is also so described (*AA* 2.11 [II 336–7 K.]). In the Hippocratic Corpus, the term cύμφυcιc is apparently used in a looser sense, denoting simply a natural connection or point of contact between two bones: it is likewise used of the joint in the lower jaw at *Art.* 34 [IV 154 L.], as well as of the joints of the vertebrae (*Art.* 46 [IV 196 L.]) and of the fingers and toes (*Art.* 67 [IV 278 L.]; cf. also *Fract.* 37 [III 542–3 L.] and *Mochl.* 41 [IV 390 L.]). Galen's usage would seem to owe more to the Aristotelian conception of cύμφυcιc as a type of connection that goes beyond mere contact, and in which the parts at some point come to share in the same material (cf. *Metaph.* 5.4.1014b.22, 11.12.1069a.12; *Ph.* 4.5.213a.9). Aristotle refers to such a connection between the bones of the forehead (*HA* 3.12.518b.8). On the other hand, at ps.-Gal. *Intro.* 12 [XIV 721], in contrast to Galen's terminology, cύμφυcιc is used to describe straight-edged joints, such as those of the face, for which the Galenic term is ἁρμονία (Gal. *Oss.* pref. [II 737–8 K.]).

It is unclear how the reference to cύμφυcιc here is related to the discussion of γόμφωcιc, but it is suggestive that Galen explicitly compares the two types of joint at *Oss.* pref. [II 738 K.]: ἡ δὲ γόμφωcιc cυνάρθρωcίc ἐcτι κατ' ἔμπηξιν. ἐπαμφοτερίζει δέ πωc ἤδη τοῦτο καὶ πληcίον ἐcτὶ τῆc cυμφύcεωc, ὥcθ', ὅταν ἀκριβῶc ἐγγομφωθῇ τι, μηδὲ βραχυτάτην αὐτῷ κίνηcιν ἀπολείπεcθαι, καθάπερ ἐπὶ τῶν ὀδόντων ἔχει. ἀλλ' ὅτι γε οὐ cυμπεφύκαcιν οὗτοι τοῖc φατνίοιc, οἱ ἐξαιρούμενοί τε καὶ αὐτομάτωc ἐκπίπτοντεc δηλοῦcιν. A similar analogy may be at work here, cύμφυcιc perhaps having been discussed previously.

5]ν ὀcτέον. There are many possible restorations, and the context offers no obvious means of reducing them.

D. LEITH

4975. Pharmacological Manual

| 31 4B.10/C(4–6)a | fr. 1 14 × 13 cm, | Second century |
| | fr. 2 4 × 4.5 cm, fr. 3 1.5 × 3.5 cm | Plate VI |

Three fragments, and two insignificant scraps, written on the back of a document. Fr. 1 preserves the upper, left, and right margins of a single column, and fr. 2 a portion of the right margin. There are four vertical folds at approximately 2.5 cm intervals in fr. 1, the first appearing 2.5 cm from the left edge, evidenced by breaks in the fibres and various symmetrical holes at either side. The scribe seems deliberately to have left spaces in the text to avoid areas of poor quality on the surface of the papyrus, especially at the third fold some 8.5 cm from the left edge, indicating that they were present when the pharmacological text was copied.

The hand resembles an official cursive, roughly bilinear, with φ especially extending far above and below, ɜ, ρ, and τ below. The letters are in general considerably broader than they are tall. Noteworthy are its large ε with extended midstroke sometimes touching its upper arc; θ with midstroke projecting some distance to either side; small, deep, curved μ; broad horizontals in π, τ; ω with high centre. There are variations in the formation of certain letters: note capital and cursive forms of β (fr. 1.1, 8); large, wedge-shaped α with left trait dipping below the notional lower line and its smaller, looped form (e.g. in -δια παιδιων, fr. 1.8); ν in both its standard form and with diagonal meeting its second vertical near top, occasionally with a loop (e.g. beginning of fr. 1.6). The hand may be assigned to the second century, most probably the second half. Similar hands may be found on BGU V 1210, *Gnomon of the Idios Logos* (= Seider, *Pal. d. gr. Pap.* i 37; mid second century), *GLH* 14 (mid second century, assigned), and P. Turner 8 (second century, assigned).

I have been unable to join the fragments. Supplementation for frr. 1 and 2, as well as a comparison of their interlinear spacing, render it unlikely that they can be closely associated. The mention of liquid measures at fr. 1.17–19, and of dry measures at fr. 2.4–5, suggests that these lines do not correspond. More generally, as Professor Andorlini remarks, the specification of quantities in drachmas in fr. 2 and perhaps fr. 3, in contrast to the layout of the recipes in fr. 1, suggests that the fragments may come from different columns.

The fragments preserve sections of a pharmacological manual that contained multiple columns of recipes, each written out in continuous prose line by line. Among the best examples of such manuals on papyrus rolls are P. Ryl. III 531, VIII **1088**, and PSI X 1180 (for which see also Andorlini, *Testi* 81–118). Comparable formatting is to be found in these papyri, with recipes separated by *paragraphus*, followed by a title in ekthesis. A wide column also seems to be favoured in the examples mentioned, as well as generally more professional or practised hands when compared with medical recipes found on smaller, single pieces of papyrus. The recipes seem to have been arranged to a limited degree according to the affected part which they are intended to treat. Thus 3–12, and perhaps also 1–2, contain prescriptions for conditions in the area of the groin, while the immediately following recipes are for difficulty in breathing, thereby also overturning the more general *a capite ad calcem* arrangement sometimes employed in pharmacological compilations.

fr. 1

ἄλ(λο)· cταφίδα γλυκεῖαν β[. . . . . .]νω τρείψας μετὰ
μέλ[ι]τος κατάπλαcον. [vac.   ]
πρὸς αἰδοίων πόνον· εν[. . .] . νια κατακαύcας ξηρὰ
τῇ cποδῷ χρῶ.
5   ὄρχεων πόνον κα[ὶ] φλεγμονάς· πηγάνου καὶ δάφνης φύλλα μετὰ μέλιτος λείοις· κατάπλαcον.
πρὸς παραμήρια· cπόδιον μετὰ νάρδου λεῖον ἐνφύcα.
πρὸς ἐντεροκηλείδια παιδίων· λαβὼν κυπάριccον
χλωρὰν λέανον μετ' οἴνου Αἰγυπτίου καὶ ποιήcας
10 cφαῖραν προcτίθει καὶ ἐπίδηcον καὶ μὴ λύε ἐφ' ἡμέρα[
πρὸς τὰ τεθηριωμέ[να] αἰδοῖα καὶ αἱμορροοῦντα· ὀθόνιον
κατακαύcας καὶ τ[ρεί]ψας ἐπίπαccε.
ὀρθόπν[ο]ιαν αὐθημερεὶ cτῆcαι· καρδάμου [c.9   ὑοc-
κυάμου cπέρματος πεπέρεως λευκ[οῦ

4975. PHARMACOLOGICAL MANUAL

15 τρείψας ἀναπλάςας ἐν μέλιτι ἢ κικίν[ῳ ἡλίκον κύαμον Αἰγύπτιον ἐν μέλιτι καὶ οἴνῳ δί[δου
ἄλ(λο) ὑςςώπου ἀκόπου ὀξύβαφον [
ἀπόβρεχε ἐν κοτύλης τρίτ[ῳ μορίῳ   τῇ
]ἐχομ[έ]νῃ ἀφέψει εἰς κοτύλην [
20   ] αν ἀβρυτάνο[υ
        ].[   ]δα[ ].[

1 α^λ   l. τρίψας   7 l. ἐμφύςα   8 l. ἐντεροκηλίδια   11 l. αἱμορροοῦντα
12 l. τ[ρί]ψας   15 l. τρίψας   17 α^λ

fr. 2

          ]χ[
       ] ποιή[ςα]ς [
       ]παντο ν
       ] δαύκους (δρ.) δ
5   ]νθου (δρ.) δ ὑος-
κυάμου ςπέρματος   ].[.]. αναπ.[
               ].ταν.[
               ].[

4, 5 ⟩ = δραχμαί

fr. 3

       ]τ[
       ]πος.[
       ]β λε[
       ]ν προς[
5   ]οξως[
       ].[

fr. 1
'Another: having pounded a sweet raisin in [. . . wine?], apply with honey as a plaster.
'Against pain in the genitals: having burnt [some?] dry [pieces of linen?], use the ashes.
'Pain and inflammation of the testicles: you grind rue leaves and bay leaves with honey. Apply as a plaster.

'Against (sc. inflamed?) inner thighs: blow on (zinc?) oxide ground with nard.

'Against little inguinal hernias in children: take green cypress, crush with Egyptian wine and having made a ball, apply, bind it, and do not untie for [?] day(s).

'Against inflamed and bleeding genitals: having burnt a piece of linen and pounded it, sprinkle it over.

'To stop difficult breathing immediately: having pounded [equal amounts?] of nose-smart, ..., seed of henbane, white pepper, ..., and having shaped [into the size of] an Egyptian bean in honey or castor-oil, give [to drink?] in honey and wine.

'Another: soak an oxybaphon of unground hyssop ... in a third of a kotyl ... on the following day decoct ... to a kotyl ... of southernwood ...'

fr. 1

1 cταφίδα γλυκεῖαν. Gal. *De alim. fac.* [VI 581–4 K.] discusses the various types of raisin and their medicinal properties, stating that many raisins, as here, are sweet, a few sour, but most a mixture of the two [VI 581 K.]. The sweet raisin in particular possesses moderate cleansing properties [VI 582 K.], as Oribasius also attests, at *Coll. med.* 3.13.10 [*CMG* VI.1.1 p. 75 Raeder] and 3.24.1 [p. 83 Raeder]. The affliction which this recipe is to treat is lost, but the following five recipes deal with various afflictions in the area of the groin, and it is possible that some skin condition in this area, requiring cleaning, was referred to in the previous column.

β[. . . . . .]νω. Professor Andorlini notes that we expect the ingredient with which the raisin is to be pounded, suggesting perhaps β[ραχεῖ οἴ]νῳ, 'with a little wine'.

3 ἐν[. . .]νια. Perhaps ἔν[ια ὀθ]όνια, 'some pieces of linen'? Of the first letter after the break, only a faint trace survives high in the line; of the putative alpha, the beginning of a rising diagonal. Linen is mentioned below at 11–12 as the object of κατακαύcας in a recipe for a complaint also affecting the genitals. There, the ashes from the linen are presumably intended to soothe the affected area, and it is possible that this entry describes a comparable recipe.

5–6 Paralleled at Dsc. 3.45.3 [II 58 W.], under the entry for πήγανον, or rue (*Ruta graveolens* L.): τὰς δὲ τῶν διδύμων φλεγμονὰς cὺν δάφνης φύλλοις καταπλαcθὲν ὠφελεῖ. Bay leaves when externally applied are also described as beneficial for all kinds of inflammation at Dsc. 1.78.1 [I 78 W.].

λε̣ι̣οῖc. We expect an aorist participle before the imperative, such as λαβών, but the sequence οιc seems certain. Of the preceding traces, a curving descender is visible, followed by faint marks which would be consistent with the end of a horizontal meeting a vertical mid-line. The use of the second person singular in such contexts is rare but attested: cf. e.g. P. Acad. inv. 4r.9–14 [ed. alt. J.-L. Fournet, in Andorlini, *Testi* 185–7].

7 πρὸc παραμήρια. If the inner thighs are meant, the condition affecting them may be left understood, e.g. αἱμορροοῦντα (cf. 11). Alternatively, παρὰ μηρία, 'in the area of the thighs', could be read, in which case the affliction may be that mentioned in the previous recipe, i.e. πόνοc καὶ φλεγμοναί. The extended final trait of λ serves to distinguish the recipe proper from its application.

While cποδόc at 4 clearly refers to the ashes from the burnt material mentioned, cπόδιον here probably designates a metal oxide, perhaps of zinc: cf. e.g. this sense of cποδόc at Dsc. 5.75 [III 40–45 W.].

8–10 Cf. Dsc. 1.74.1–2 [I 74 W.], under the entry for κυπάριccοc, cypress (*Cypressus sempervirens* L.): τὰ δὲ χλωρὰ cφαιρία κοπέντα καὶ cὺν οἴνῳ πινόμενα ἁρμόζει πρὸc αἵματοc ἀναγωγὴν καὶ δυcεντερίαν καὶ κοιλίαc ῥευματιcμόν, ὀρθόπνοιαν, βῆχαc· . . . cτέλλει δὲ καὶ ἐντεροκήλαc καταπλαcθέντα, καὶ τὰ φύλλα δὲ τὰ αὐτὰ ποιεῖ.

8 The diminutive ἐντεροκηλίδιον, little inguinal hernia, is a *hapax*.

10 ἐφ' ἡμέρα[ν or ἐφ' ἡμέρα[c n.

11–12 The medicinal use of burnt linen ashes is also attested, for example, at ps.-Gal. *De remediis parabilibus* [XIV 535 K.] (for burns), and ps.-Dsc. *De simpl. med.* 1.179 [III 220 W.] (for lesions).

12 τ[ρεί]ψας. The restoration seems unavoidable. Of the first letter, only a small trace remains high in the line; after the break, the extreme of a horizontal, rising slightly, almost touches alpha above mid-height, and would appear to be consistent only with epsilon or psi.

13 ὀρθόπν[ο]ιαν: difficulty in breathing or shortness of breath, which is eased by sitting up straight; cf. e.g. Gal. *De diff. resp.* [VII 923 K.].

αὐθημερεί. An extremely rare form of the adverb, found in inscriptions (cf. Inscr. Prien. 28.17; IG 2.471.71; and IG 3.73.24–5).

13–14 ὑος]|κυάμου cπέρματος. The mention of seed indicates that ὑοςκύαμος was referred to, rather than the bean (κυάμου), which is often also found with the ethnic Αἰγύπτιος in the medical papyri. Seed of henbane (*Hyascyamos niger* L.) is common in pharmacological literature (on papyrus, cf. P. Strasb. inv. gr. 90; Andorlini, *Trattato* fr. B 37.4; P. Rein. I 4 + BKT III 33–4 fr. B i 16; as also apparently here, below at fr. 2.5–6), and was added to such recipes as an analgesic: cf. also Dsc.4.68 [II 224–7 W.]; Gal. *Simpl. med. temp. ac fac.* [XII 147–8 K.].

14 πεπέρεως λευκ[οῦ. The effectiveness of pepper for chest complaints is noted at Dsc. 2.159.3 [I 225 W.].

The absence of quantities provided for the individual ingredients listed here suggests the supplementation of a word such as ἴca in the lacuna at the end of this line, i.e. 'equal amounts of . . .'.

15–16 For the preparation and administering of this recipe, cf. e.g. VIII **1088** ii 41–5 (in this case for quartan fever) ἀναπλάcας μεθ' ὕδατος κολλύρια ποεῖ ἡλίκον Αἰγύπτιον κύαμον, εἶτα ἐν τῇ cκιᾷ ξηράνας ταῦτα νήςτῃ δίδου πιεῖν τρίψας ἐν γλυκέως ἡμικοτυλίῳ; also Gal. *De comp. med. sec. loc.* [XIII 68, 293 K.].

κικίν[ῳ. Castor oil was used for a variety of cosmetic and medicinal purposes. Dsc. 1.32.2 [I 37 W.] states that when mixed into plasters it increases their effectiveness.

16 δί[δου. Presumably δί[δου πίνειν, a common formula used in medical recipes for orally ingested medicaments, and apparently warranted here by the direction to give the prepared drug 'in honey and wine'.

17 ff. This recipe for ὀρθόπνοια involved soaking a small amount of hyssop (*Hyssopus officinalis* L.) and decocting it on the following day, though the precise details of the directions given remain obscure. The decoction may have been intended to be ingested orally. The liquid in which the hyssop was to be soaked was presumably specified at the end of 18, and therefore another ingredient may have been mentioned at the end of 17. A parallel may identifiable in Dsc. 3.25.1 [II 35–6 W.], which prescribes a drink of hyssop with figs and rue decocted in water and honey for a range of chest conditions, including ὀρθόπνοια: ἀφεψηθεῖcα δὲ [sc. ὕccωπος] μετὰ cύκων καὶ ὕδατος καὶ μέλιτος καὶ πηγάνου καὶ πινομένη ἀρήγει περιπνευμονικοῖς, ἀcθματικοῖς, βηχὶ χρονίᾳ, κατάρρῳ, ὀρθοπνοίᾳ. Cf. also Aët. *Iatr.* 8.74 [*CMG* VIII 2.540.1–3 Olivieri] and *Cyranides* 5.20.

20 ἀβρυτάνο[υ. Southernwood (*Artemisia abrotonum* L.). ἀβρότονον is the standard spelling, but that found here appears to be a genuine variant among the papyri, attested also at VIII **1088** iii 68 (the *ed. pr.* has αβρυανου, but I have checked the papyrus [= British Library Pap. 2055], and ἀβρυτάνο(υ) should be read) and PSI X 1180 fr. A ii 8 (ἀβρυτ[ό]ν[ο]υ) [Andorlini, *Testi* 81–118]. Cf. also BGU IV 1132.11, where the proper name Ἀβρυτάνου is recorded, a form not found in an online LGPN search. To my knowledge, the form ἀβρότονον is not attested on papyrus. At Dsc. 3.24.2 [II 34–5 W.], ὀρθόπνοια is found first in a list of conditions for which the fruit of southernwood is effective, either when boiled in water or crushed raw and drunk, which might suggest that this line forms part of the recipe begun at 17, or that it comes at the beginning of a third recipe for the same condition.

fr. 2

4 δαύκους. A plant of the Umbelliferae family, with general warming properties (cf. Dsc. 3.72 [II 83–4 W.]). The genitive form δαύκους is also attested at VIII **1088** iii 50 and 53, while the third

reference to the plant at iii 65 (*ed. pr.* δαύκου cπέρμα(τοc)) may conceal an instance of haplography, i.e. reading δαύκουc ⟨c⟩πέρμα(τοc). This points to a fluctuation of declension, and the variant neuter form τὸ δαῦκοc (τὸ δαῦκον is attested in Thphr, *HP* 9.15.5, etc.; see Gignac, *Grammar* ii 98–9 for the comparable case of ὁ γάροc / τὸ γάροc). See also P. Lund I 66 3 [= Andorlini, *Trattato* vii 52], which reads τὸ δαυ[(note that Andorlini also suggests supplementation of the plant name at vii 60–61). BKT III 32–3 i 11–12, however, reads δαύκου | φύλλου, though this parchment codex is of the fifth or sixth century, and thus considerably later.

5 χαλκά]νθου (a product of copper from the furnace) or τερεβί]νθου (turpentine)?

fr. 3

3 A small blank space after β here suggests that it is a numeral, specifying a quantity, followed perhaps by a form of λεαίνω, λειόω or λεῖοc.

D. LEITH

4976. Medical Recipe

103/217(d)   6 × 6.5 cm   Second or third century

This piece preserves seven short lines of text written against the fibres. The front contains scant remains of two columns of a document. The papyrus was pre-cut to accommodate the text on the back, and appears to retain the original dimensions: the upper margin is greater than the interlinear spaces, and the writing has been compressed towards the right margin to ensure that it would fit. It is possible that the text is complete. The piece had been folded vertically in three, approximately equally, resulting in various symmetrical holes in the papyrus.

The text is copied in a somewhat angular informal hand leaning to the right. ρ especially extends far below the line, and to a lesser degree ι and τ. Among its characteristic forms are α with hooked oblique reaching high in the line; narrow θ with its cross-stroke projecting to the right; υ curved and always V-shaped, often hooked to the left in its first movement. The hand would seem to belong to the late second or third century, and can be broadly paralleled in the second hand of *GMAW*² 68 (later second century, assigned), in 65 (third century, assigned), and in 66 (second or third century, assigned).

Alternative quantities have been added below 1 and 2, perhaps by a second hand (see nn.). There are two *paragraphi*, the first between lines 3 and 4, and the second on a level with line 5, presumably to distinguish the fourth ingredient, which is the first to occupy two lines.

The text preserves a single medical recipe, unusually lacking a title or any indication as to its application (other examples include SB XIV 12074, *GMP* I 14 = P. Sijp. 6, *GMP* ii 11 = P. Eleph. Wagner 4, and P. Vindob. Worp 20). The presence of alternative quantities in medical recipes is even rarer on papyrus: P. Princ. III 155 is the only other example published to date, but there the alternatives are certainly recorded by the same hand. It may be that the papyrus was given or sent by one doctor or druggist to another, and that the recipient subsequently adapted the recipe with his alternative quantities (cf. P. Merton I 12 for an exchange of recipes between doctors and the sorts of correspondence which this could generate). The details of the recipe's application and preparation might thus have been communicated independently, perhaps orally or in a covering letter.

The recipe itself would have produced a highly acrid compound, and the closest parallels among surviving pharmacological compilations suggest that it may have been intended for the treatment of intestinal worms in general, or for the tapeworm (πλατεῖα ἕλμινc) in particular (cf. Paul. Aeg. 4.57.13 [*CMG* IX 1.386 Heiberg]; ps.-Dsc. *Eup.* 2.68.2 [III 279 W.] (especially if the transmitted πεπέρεωc is emended to πτέρεωc, often confused in the mss.)). πτερίc, μελάνθιον, and κάρδαμον are each widely attested as being individually effective as a vermifuge, and all ingredients are found in various compound recipes against these parasites. Doubtless the compound drug was to be ingested orally, though μελάνθιον was also applied externally to the area of the stomach in order to expel intestinal worms (cf. Dsc. 3.79.2 [II 93 W.]; ps.-Dsc. *Eup.* 2.69.3 [III 280 W.]).

```
       πτερίδ[ο]c (δρ.) η
1a     (δρ.) δ                    (m. 2?)
       δακρυδίου (τριώβολον)
2a     (δρ.) α (τριώβολον)        (m. 2?)
       μελανθείου (δρ.) β̄
       καρδάμου cπέρ-
5      — ματοc (δρ.) β
       νίτρου Ἑλληνι-
       κ[οῦ] (δρ.) β
```

$ = δραχμαί Γ = τριώβολον   3 l. μελανθίου

'Male fern, 8 drachmas (4 drachmas); scammony, ½ drachma (1 ½ drachmas); nigella, 2 drachmas; seed of garden cress, 2 drachmas; Greek natron, 2 drachmas'

1 πτερίδ[ο]c. Male fern (*Nephrodium filix-mas* L.). This variant genitive form, more commonly attested as πτέρεωc, is used also in Theophrastus and Dioscorides.

2 δακρυδίου. Scammony (*Convulvulus scammonia* L.). Its use in this recipe may have been as a purgative (cf. Dsc. 4. 170. 3–4 [II 319 W.]), to expel the remaining acrid ingredients before they could cause harm. The term δακρύδιον is relatively rare. It is used by Alexander Trallianus in his *Therapeutica*, *De febribus*, and *De oculis*, but is otherwise found only three times, in each case simply noting it as an alternative name for cκαμμωνία: (i) the later (pre-fifth-century AD) interpolations to Dsc. *MM* that record additional alternative plant-names preserve it under the entry for cκαμμωνία (4. 170 [II 318 W.]); (ii) a herbal lexicon falsely attributed to Galen [ed. A. Delatte, *Anecdota Atheniensia et alia* ii 385–93], has at p. 388 the entry δακρύδιν ἤτοι cκαμωναία; and (iii) P. Ryl. I 29(a)1 13, where both names seem to be recorded together.

1a, 2a The alternative amounts here are written small, squeezed between the lines. The abbreviation for τριώβολον curves sharply downwards at its end, in marked contrast to the upwardly curving final movement in the example at 2. Delta is also somewhat differently formed. These discrepancies can perhaps be explained by the more confined space, and there is no discernible difference in the colour of the ink, but it seems quite possible that a second hand was responsible. It should also be noted that these are indeed alternatives, since no attempt has been made to delete the originals, and their placement below the line does not suggest an intention to correct. They were presumably meant to offer a version or versions of varying potency, perhaps to be tailored to different levels in the severity of the condition. Note that the alternatives are proportionally based on the original amounts, in the first case dividing by two, in the second multiplying by three.

3 μελανθείου. Nigella (*Nigella sativa* L.).

4–5 καρδάμου cπέρ|ματοc. Seed of garden cress (*Lepidium sativum* L.). Bitterness or sharpness (δριμύτης), one of the most commonly recognised properties of this plant, of nigella and of the male fern, was considered active in expelling intestinal worms (cf. e.g. Gal. *Simpl. med. temp. ac fac.* [XII 42 K.]).

6–7 νίτρου Ἑλληνι|κ[οῦ]. The medicinal use of natron, sodium carbonate, is well attested, but the form of the mineral qualified by the adjective Ἑλληνικόν is very rare. Its only attestations are in two other papyri: PUG II 62.11 (a loan of money of 98 from Oxyrhynchus, for which a 24-artabas amount of Greek natron, along with four talents of 'other' natron, is the guarantee—its specification as 'Greek', and the fact that it is listed first and in smaller quantity, suggests that it was more valuable; cf. also the editor's n. ad loc.); and P. Ct.YBR inv. 1443 fr. C 4 and 6 (a recipe list; fr. A ed. A. E. Hanson in *Pap. Congr. XXIV* (2007) i 427–33). Other forms of νίτρον found in a medical context include νίτρον Ἀλεξανδρινόν and νίτρον Βερενικάριον, each denoting an Egyptian origin. There were three sources of natron in ancient Egypt (cf. R. J. Forbes, *Studies in Ancient Technology* iii (1955) 174–9): the Wadi Natrum, the oasis in the Western desert; a site near Naucratis; and five spots near El Kab in Upper Egypt. Pliny, however, at *HN* 31.107, in the course of a long passage on *nitrum* in general, cites a location in Macedonia as producing a finer and purer form of *nitrum*, which is better than the Egyptian varieties. This would seem to be a plausible source of the 'Greek natron', so named from an Egyptian perspective, and mentioned only in the papyri. This particular 'Greek' type may have been specified here because it was considered of higher quality, as Pliny tells us and PUG II 62 suggests, and therefore of more potent therapeutic effect.

D. LEITH

4977. Medical Recipes

69/14(b)   9 × 8.5 cm   Late second or third century
Plate VI

This fragment contains on the front a single column, with a short text in the same hand copied in its left margin, at right angles to the main text. Only the right margin is intact, and the incised edge is relatively undamaged. The papyrus was folded twice from left to right. On the other side of the fragment, five lines of unclear traces in a second, cursive hand can be discerned, written with the fibres. This hardly legible text seems to have been written on the papyrus after it had been folded, for it is found only on the back of the portion of the recto bounded by the right-hand edge and the fold nearest to it.

The papyrus has been cut to accommodate at least three medical recipes. The surviving main text on the front totals 13 lines, while the marginal text preserves a further three. The main column is divided into two sections (comprising 1–2 and 3–13 respectively) by a rather meandering horizontal line. The text at 2 is written up against the right margin, and appears to have been added after the text at 3 had already begun to be written. The horizontal line and immediately subsequent text thus slope downwards markedly to accommodate it.

The first line of the second section (3) is in ekthesis. There are two instances of itacism (8, 12), and two of inorganic diaeresis (1, 10). Abbreviations are employed at 3, 4, and 8. The monograms ⳍ for χρ(ῶ) and ℼ for πρ(όc) are found at 1 and 9 respectively, both used in other pharmacological papyri (e.g. PSI X 1180 fr. A ii 4, iv 14 *et passim* [ed. partim Andorlini, *Testi* 81–118]; see also K. McNamee, *Abbreviations in Greek Literary Papyri and Ostraca* (BASP Suppl. 3: 1981) s. vv.). The last two letters of ὕδωρ at 1 are also written as a monogram, but this does not involve an abbreviation.

The well preserved recipe at 3–13 is for a collyrium (as may have been the preceding; see 1–2 n.), a form of eye salve very commonly found among the papyri, apparently named after the 'cakes' or 'sticks' into which the ingredients were initially formed and stored before being mixed again with a liquid in order to be applied. The recipe here is described as 'that made with eggs', a title attested at Alexander Trallianus, Περὶ θεραπείαc ὀφθαλμῶν [II 65 Putschmann], where the collyrium itself offers few points of comparison; cf. also the collyrium stamp CIL XIII 3.2, *Signacula medicorum oculariorum* 10021 no. 28, *L. Caemi Paterni authemer(um) len(e) ex o(vo) acr(e) ex aq(ua)*. Much closer parallels, however, can be found with collyria described, as here at 10, as 'mild' (τρυφερόν, or in Latin *lene*): see esp. Scrib. Larg. *Comp.* 19–27; Gal. *Comp. med. sec. loc.* 4.7 [XII 757.6–10 K.]; ibid. [XII 758.3–8 K.]; ibid. [XII 758.15–759.3 K.]; ibid. [XII 769.11–17 K.]; Aët. *Iatr.* 7.108 [*CMG* VIII 2. 374–5 Olivieri]; and Alex. Trall. Περὶ θεραπείαc ὀφθαλμῶν [II 9 Putschmann]. These are likewise often given another title, such as 'Dioclean', 'apple-coloured' or 'parrot-coloured'. Each contains two metal ingredients, most commonly, as here, καδμεία (zinc oxide) and ψιμύθιον (white lead). To these a further three or four plant-derived ingredients are added, of which ὄπιον, poppy juice, is common to all, its analgesic properties presumably having contributed to its milder effect. Most also include κόμμι, gum arabic, but this was an important ingredient in most collyria (see 4–5 n.). In contrast to the papyrus, these recipes do not include eggs among the main ingredients, whereas water and egg is to be added in all of them to form the paste when the collyrium was ready to be applied.

These mild collyria are prescribed for a range of eye conditions, including περιωδυνία (excessive pain), φλύκταιναι (pustules), ὑπόπνοι ὀφθαλμοί (suppurating eyes), ἕλκη (sores), ἐπικαύματα (spots on the cornea), χημώcειc (inflammation). The papyrus mentions διαθέcειc (established conditions; see 9 n.) and ἐπιφορά (constant discharge from the eye; 11 n.). Note that the author draws a connection between

82   MEDICAL TEXTS

the mild nature of the collyrium and its effectiveness against these established conditions (τρυφερὸν γάρ ἐςτιν, 10). In the descriptions of the mild collyria listed, it is repeatedly stressed that they are suitable for those whose complaints render them unable to bear any additional pain. Such mild collyria thus seem to have been tailored in particular to patients suffering from painful, serious and chronic eye diseases, and may be viewed as an alternative to the apparently much harsher type of collyrium known as the ἀχάριςτον, or 'thankless' (see also 9 n.).

   .   .   .
  κόμεως (δρ.) ᾱ, ὕδωρ. χρ(ῶ)
    μεθ' ὕδατος.
  ‾‾‾‾‾‾‾‾‾‾‾‾‾‾‾‾‾‾

  κολ(λύριον) τὸ διὰ τῶν ᾠῶν· καδμείας (δρ.) δ̄, ψιμιθίο(υ) (δρ.) ᾱ, κό-
5 μεως (δρ.) β̄, κρόκου (δρ.) ᾱ (τριώβολον),
  ὀπίου (δρ.) ᾱ (τριώβολον), ᾠῶν δ̄. τὸ
  ὑγρὸν ἐπίβαλε καὶ
  τρεῖβε καὶ ἀναλάμβαν(ε).
  ποιεῖ δὲ πρ(ὸς) διαθέςεις.
10 τρυφερὸν γάρ ἐςτιν. ἱςτᾷ
  δὲ καὶ ἐπιφορὰν μετ' ᾠοῦ
  μέςῃ κράςῃ ι παχυτέ-
  ρᾳ].[
   .   .   .

In the left margin, across the fibres:
  . . . . ξ . . . ρ . [
15 πεπέρεως (δρ.) ᾱ, ε . [
   κόμεως (δρ.) ⸗ [
   .   .   .

1, 4, 5, 6 ⸋ = δραχμαί   1 l. κόμμεως   ϋδϕ ✱   3 κο^λ   4 ψιμιθι°   l. ψιμυθίο(υ)
4–5 l. κόμμεως   5, 6 ⸌ = τριώβολον   8 l. τρῖβε   αναλαμβα^υ   9 ⸆   10 ϊςτα
12–13 l. κράςει ἢ παχυτέ|[ρᾳ   16 l. κόμμεως

(1–13) '. . . 1 drachma of gum arabic, water. Apply with water.
 Collyrium, made with eggs: 4 drachmas of calamine, 1 drachma of white lead, 2 drachmas of gum arabic, 1 ½ drachmas of saffron crocus, 1 ½ drachmas of poppy juice, 4 eggs. Add liquid, grind down and apply. It works against established conditions, for it is mild. It also stops constant discharge of tears with egg in a medium or rather thick consistency . . .'
 (14–16) '. . . 1 drachma of pepper, . . . , . . . drachmas of gum arabic, . . .'

1 κόμεως. Cf. 4–5. Regularly written in ostraca and papyri with a single mu (e.g. O. Bodl. II 2182.8, 2185.6; P. Grenf. I 52r.5; *GMP* I 13.9). Gum arabic, procured from the acacia tree, was an important ingredient in collyria: cf. Cels. *De med.* 6.6.3, 'although *cummi* has certain other properties, this stands out most, that when collyria are mixed and then dried, they are glued together and do not crumble' (*cummi cum quasdam alias facultates habeat, hoc maxime praestare, ut, ubi collyria facta inaruerunt, glutinata sint neque frientur*). Dsc. 1.101.3 [I 93 W.] also attests to its alleviating effect when combined with harsh drugs (δύναμιν δὲ ἔχει . . . ἀμβλυντικὴν δριμέων φαρμάκων).

1–2 The repeated mention of water, once as an ingredient in the recipe proper, and again in preparation for application, suggests that this recipe, like the following, was a collyrium. The use of κόμμι, gum arabic, further supports this suggestion (see 1 n., 4–5 n.).

3 τὸ διὰ τῶν ᾠῶν. It was a common practice for collyria to be named after a distinguishing ingredient, as e.g. δι' ἐρείκης or ἐρικηρόν (Aët. *Iatr.* 7.104 [*CMG* VIII 2.364 Olivieri]; O. Bodl. II 2185.1), διὰ λιβάνου (Gal. *Comp. med. sec. loc.* 4.7 [XII 758 K.]; O. Bodl. II 2184.1–2).

3–4 καδμείας. Calamine, a zinc oxide, very common in collyria.

4 ψιμιθίο(υ). White lead. ψιμίθιον is the standard spelling of ψιμύθιον in the papyri: see L. C. Youtie, *P. Mich. XVII: The Michigan Medical Codex* (Atlanta 1996) 8 n. to l. 10, who observes that of eleven occurrences of the word in published papyri, only one, MPER XIII 6.9, can be shown to have used the form ψιμύθιον; see now also PSI X 1180 fr. A ii 33, iii 12, fr. C ii 27, retaining the form ψιμίθιον in each case.

4–5 κόμεως. The alleviating effect of gum arabic, as attested by Dioscorides (see 1 n.), will have been especially desirable in this 'mild' collyrium.

5 κρόκου. Saffron crocus, the stigmas of the crocus flower. Dsc. 1.26 [I 29–31 W.] recognises its emollient properties, and notes its use in the treatment of rheum in the eyes. Cf. **4979** 4 n.

6 ᾠῶν. Apart from the binding properties of eggs, Cels. *De med.* 6.6.8B recognises the benefits of egg white and breast milk in making collyria milder, and the use of such recipes for more serious inflammations of the eyes: 'the more serious the inflammation, the more soothing must be the drug through the addition of egg white or breast milk' (*quo gravior vero quaeque inflammatio est, eo magis leniri medicamentum debet adiecto vel albo ovi vel muliebri lacte*). The purely therapeutic prescription of eggs in the recipe here should be distinguished from their additional use in softening the collyrium for application in the case of ἐπιφορά, as described at 10–13.

9 πρ(ός). Three verticals close together, topped by a horizontal. There are faint traces of what must have been the loop of rho high in the line above pi's crossbar.

διαθέσεις. διάθεσις is regularly used in a medical context to denote an underlying condition or state of the body, often pathological. In the context of ophthalmological recipes, however, the term is often contrasted with recent or incipient eye complaints (e.g. ps.-Gal. *Intro.* 15 [XIV 765 K.], πρὸς ἀρχομένας ὀφθαλμίας . . . πρὸς τὰς διαθέσεις), suggesting that it refers specifically to established or chronic conditions. ἀχάριστα collyria were apparently regarded by some as unsuitable for such established eye conditions: Gal. *Comp. med. sec. loc.* 4.7 [XII 749–50 K.], for example, referring to an ἀχάριστον recipe, notes that ὅπου δέ ἐστι περὶ τοὺς ὀφθαλμοὺς διάθεσις, ἀπέχεσθαι δεῖ τοῦ κολλυρίου. On ἀχάριστα, cf. esp. Andorlini, 'P. Grenf. I 52'. Note that this type of collyrium has as its mixing agents water, wine or wine-vinegar, never egg or milk as we find in its 'mild' counterpart.

10 ἱστᾷ. ἱστάω is a rare alternative to ἵστημι in medical literature, but cf. e.g. Gal. *AA* [II 460 K.], and Meletius, *Nat. hom.* 30 [p. 136.30 Cramer].

11 ἐπιφοράν. Chronic discharge of fluid from the eyes, mentioned specifically in other recipes for 'mild' collyria at Scrib. Larg. *Comp.* 27 and Gal. *Comp. med. sec. loc.* 4.7 [XII 758 K.]. It is also a condition for which ἀχάριστα collyria were considered suitable: cf. Andorlini, 'P. Grenf. I 52' 8.

12 κράσῃ ι. This appears to be a phonetic error (cf. Gignac, *Grammar* i 235–42), though perhaps

affected by μέcη preceding. That κράcει ἤ should be read is suggested by Aët. *Iatr.* 7.117 [*CMG* VIII 2.394.5–6 Olivieri], χρῶ μετ' ᾠοῦ ἢ γάλακτος ἢ ὕδατος μέcη κράcει ἢ παχυτέρᾳ.

14 The surface of the papyrus is badly damaged throughout the line, with many dislodged fibres. Of the second letter, there is a trace perhaps of a horizontal mid-line; of the fourth, a steep diagonal rises from left to right high in the line, perhaps of upsilon; of the eighth, a curving movement rises then descends, with a diagonal oblique projecting from its lower extreme, apparently of upsilon; of the last letter or letters, the feet of two verticals survive.

D. LEITH

4978. Medical Recipes

75/65(a)   7 × 7.5 cm   Second or third century

A single column, copied with the fibres, of which the lower margin alone is lost. The back is blank. The papyrus has been cut to size, and the original edges survive at top and right, and presumably also at left in its lower portion, though it is badly damaged.

The hand is medium-sized, upright, informal and rounded. Characteristic letters are ⲁ and ⲗ with high obliques, often touching the following letter near top; large, rounded ⲉ; large ⲍ ending in a broad flourish; small ⲙ with deep centre; ⲱ rising to full height in the middle. There are broad similarities to *GMAW*² 86 (later second century, assigned), and *GLH* 20c (mid third century); cf. also **LVI 3836** (second century, assigned). I would be more inclined to assign the hand to the later second century, but a third century dating should not be excluded.

The text preserves three complete medical recipes of varied application, each begun on a new line in ekthesis. No punctuation or lectional signs are in evidence. Measures are abbreviated. There is a single instance of itacism (5).

   ἀρ]αιωτικόν· μήκω-
   νο]ς cπέρμα καὶ μυ-
   ῶν] ἀφόδευμα ἴca
   μείξ]ac μετὰ μύρου
5 ἐπί]χρειε τὸ μέτωπον.
   ἐμε]τικόν· cίλφιον ὕ-
   δατ]ι ζέcac πότιcον.
   καθαρτικόν· ἅλατος
   κύ(αθον) ᾱ, μέλιτος κύ(αθον) ᾱ,
10 ὄξους κύ(αθον) ᾱ, ὕδατος
   κυ(άθους) ζ̄ ὁμοῦ μείξας

κίρνα κατὰ κύαθον καὶ
πίε νήςτης.

. . . .

5 l. ἐπίχριε   9–11 κυ = κύαθον

'Rarefying drug: having mixed poppy seed and mouse droppings in equal amounts with scented oil, anoint the forehead.

'[Emetic]: having boiled silphium in water, give to drink.

'Purgative: having blended together 1 kyathos of salt, 1 kyathos of honey, 1 kyathos of vinegar, 7 kyathoi of water, mix by the kyathos and drink on an empty stomach.'

1 ἀρ]αιωτικόν. At the break, the end of a horizontal meets a vertical at mid-point. It is too low for τι, and most resembles ΑΙ or ΕΙ.]Ν seems to be excluded, though Professor Andorlini suggests ὑπ]νωτικόν, which would be very tempting, especially in view of the inclusion of poppy seed in the recipe (cf. VIII **1088** 66). The traces and available space, however, seem to guarantee ἀρ]αιωτικόν. Galen describes ἀραιωτικά drugs as those which open up the pores of the skin (*Simpl. med. temp. ac fac.* [XI 749 K.]), and refers to their general warming properties (ibid. [XI 753, 754 K.]). The application of this recipe to the forehead, and its use of poppy seed, might suggest that its purpose was to relieve some sort of perceived blockage or congestion in the head, perhaps associated with pain.

1–2 μήκω|[νο]ς cπέρμα. Poppy seed is used in a wide variety of remedies, but principally exploited for its cooling and narcotic properties (Dsc. 4.64.2 [II 219 W.]; Gal. *Simpl. med. temp. ac fac.* [XII 72–4 K.]). Dsc. 4.64.3 recommends its application to the forehead and temples in order to promote sleep, but it was used also for headache (cf. the selection of recipes for headache using poppy seed at Gal. *Comp. med. sec. loc.* [XII 556–8 K.]).

2–3 μυ|[ῶν] ἀφόδευμα. Mouse droppings, when applied externally, are almost exclusively associated in surviving literature with the treatment of *alopecia*, a condition involving greying of the hair with subsequent hair loss (cf. ps.-Gal. *Def. med.* 314 [XIX 431 K.]; ps.-Gal. *Remediis parabilibus* [XIV 325 K.]). This application goes back at least to Asclepiades of Bithynia (fl. later second century BC): cf. Gal. *Comp. med. sec. loc.* [XII 414.2–3 K.]. It is also found in Dioscorides (2.80.5 [I 163 W.]), while Pliny, *NH* 29.106, names Varro as his source for this treatment, and it continues to be repeated by subsequent writers. On the other hand, mouse droppings are attested as having a 'dispersing' (διαφορητική) quality (cf. Zopyrus *ap.* Orib. *Coll. med.* 14.62.1 [*CMG* VI 1.2.231 Raeder], preserving a long list of simples under the heading ὅcα διαφορεῖ, in which ἄφοδος μυῶν appears at 231.18 Raeder). Such a property was considered active in the relief of certain kinds of pain in the head (cf. Gal. *Comp. med. sec. loc.* [XII 548–9 K.]), and it may be related to the rarefying action referred to in the recipe's title.

4 μετὰ μύρου. The presence of perfumed oil in this recipe would presumably also have gone some way towards counteracting the unwelcome odour of the mouse droppings, but such unguents were commonly used as mixing agents for the preparation of ointments and plasters, and their warming and soothing properties are often noted. When applied to the head in the form of an ointment, as here, perfumed oils were widely considered effective for headaches (cf. e.g. Dsc. 1.43.4 [I 43 W.], on the effectiveness of rose–oil for headaches; Archigenes *ap.* Gal. *Comp. med. sec. loc.* [XII 541–3 K.], describing the use of many kinds of scented oil for pains in the head).

5 ἐπί]χριε. Of compounds of -χρίω, by far the most frequent in medical writers are ἐπιχρίω and καταχρίω. κατά]χριε seems too long for the space. Another possibility is the much rarer διά]χριε, used at Orib. *Syn. ad Eust.* 8.17.6 [*CMG* VI 3.255 Raeder] of rubbing an ointment, as here, into the forehead.

6 ἐμε]τικόν. End of horizontal meeting iota near top, as of tau or gamma. There is space for perhaps three letters at the beginning of the line here, and the attested purgative properties of silphium (see below) suggest ἐμε]τικόν as the most likely supplement.

cίλφιον. Silphium (*Ferula tingitana*) was used for a very wide variety of ailments (cf. e.g. Plin. *NH* 22.100–106). When administered orally in liquid form, Dioscorides, at 3. 80. 5 [II 96 W.], describes its effectiveness against poisons, bites or stings and poisoned weapons, chills, convulsive tension, sudden spasms and ruptures, as well as its ability to promote menstruation. He also describes its purgative properties when administered alone, paralleled at Gal. *Simpl. med. temp. ac fac.* 8. 16 [XII 123 K.] and Plin. *NH* 19.43. Silphium swallowed with a liquid is also attested specifically as an emetic at Gal. *De antidotis* [XIV 143 K.], for those who have drunk bull's blood.

6–7 ὔ[δατ]ι. Of the final letter, the upper part of a vertical survives. The context calls for a liquid in which the silphium is to be boiled, leaving little alternative but a reference to water.

8–13 Salt and vinegar were widely used in purgatives. While honey may have been intended to sweeten the mixture, Dioscorides also refers to its diuretic effects (2.82.3 [I 166 W.]). We may note that the four ingredients found here are also those used in the preparation of oxymel as described at Dsc. 5. 14 [III 15–16 W.]. This is clearly a purgative of the most basic kind.

9–11 In these lines κύαθον is abbreviated simply to κυ, without any further marker.

12 κίρνα. κιρνάω in medical literature is used of mixing or tempering liquids: cf. e.g. Dsc. 3.22.4 [I 29 W.]; Gal. *De ther. ad Pis.* [XIV 250 K.]; Herodotus *ap.* Orib. *Coll. med.* 5.30.36, 38 [*CMG* VI 1.1.150 Raeder]. Directions to mix the ingredients, however, have already been given (11). The sense required here is of dividing or portioning out the liquid in certain amounts ('by the *kyathos*') once it has been mixed, but I have found no parallel for such a usage of κιρνάω.

D. LEITH

4979. List of Items

104/82(c)   4.5 × 4 cm   Second or third century

A piece of thick, poor quality papyrus, originally with a horizontal fold in the centre. The text is written against the fibres, while the other side is blank, and all margins save the upper survive. The lines exhibit a marked downward slope. The semi-cursive hand is very small, written with a relatively thick nib. A similar impression is given by *GMAW*² 65 (third century, assigned), but most letter forms can be broadly paralleled in *GMAW*² 82 and 86 (both second century, assigned); cf. also LV **3799** (second or third century, assigned) and LXVI **4503** (third century, assigned).

The text is a simple list, with each item recorded in the nominative singular on a new line. The fact that all the terms found here can refer to objects or substances attested as having some therapeutic purpose might point to a broadly medical context, and it may be that the list represents some sort of inventory or 'shopping list' associated with a doctor's surgery (ἰατρεῖον). Cf. perhaps P. Michael. 36 for a list of medicaments that was not compiled for medical purposes, though it is clearly of a quite different form and nature from the present text, recording also quantities and values. If the items listed are linked by their medical application, they cannot be more closely associated through a common therapeutic purpose: in particular, the πιλίον in a medical context was most likely for treating ailments of the head, the γλωccόκομον for fractured limbs (see 2 and 3 nn.). On the other hand, the πιλίον and γλωccόκομον more commonly refer to everyday items of personal property, while the other three recorded items also have non-medical uses, such that the medical aspect should perhaps not be pressed.

```
    . . .
      ].
   πιλίον
   γλωζόκομον
   κρόκοc
5  cανδαράκη
   ἀρcενικόν
```

3 l. γλωccόκομον

'. . . ; cap?; chest?; saffron; realgar; orpiment.'

2 The πιλίον, diminutive of πῖλοc, generally designates an article of clothing made of felt, most commonly used of a cap worn on the head. It is mentioned as such an article of personal clothing in P. Cairo Zen. IV 59659.23, P. Tebt. I 230, XXXI **2598** 5 and P. Ryl. IV 627v.212. In his edition of **2598**, J. W. B. Barns suggested that the πιλίον requested there by a charioteer from his trainer may be identified with the yellow caps worn by the Antinoë charioteers [*GMAW*^{2} 81; *ed. pr.* S. J. Gasiorowski, *JEA* 17 (1931) 1–9; *ed. alt.* E. G. Turner, *JHS* (1973) 192–5, the cap being described there as a 'crash-helmet']. The connotations of protectiveness implicit in the charioteer's cap are perhaps further highlighted by the use of cognate terms in several sources for certain kinds of medical covering for the head. Pl. *Resp.* 406d, for example, refers to certain πιλίδια placed on the head by doctors, apparently as a means of applying medicaments. Leonides *ap.* Aët. *Iatr.* 6.1 [*CMG* VIII 2.124 Olivieri] recommends that the head be protected by a πιλάριον after a surgical procedure to drain fluid in cases of hydrocephalus (καὶ πιλαρίῳ cκεπάcθω τὸ κεφάλαιον). At Sor. *De fasciis* 2 [*CMG* IV.159 Ilberg], the πιλίον represents a particular method of bandaging the head, whereby a strip of linen was drawn in a sort of zig-zag pattern from one side of the head to the other (an illustration survives in cod. Laur. LXXIV 7 [pl. 1.2 Ilberg]). The term πιλάριον is also attested, however, as a type of eye-salve (cf. Aët. *Iatr.* 7.103 [*CMG* VIII 2.360 Olivieri]; Paul. Aeg. 7.6.11 [*CMG* IX 2.337 Heiberg]) or as a plaster used against abrasions (Orib. *Ecl. med.* 89.23 [*CMG* VI 2.2.269 Raeder]): see generally S. Russo, *Le calzature nei papiri di età greco-romana* (Florence 2004) 94–6, on the meanings of these terms, and PSI XV 1541.2 for a further attestation in a private letter. The item referred to in the papyrus was presumably an object, and if it had a medical purpose, then it is perhaps most likely that it was some form of protective head covering such as Leonides' πιλάριον, or indeed Plato's πιλίδιον.

3 γλωζόκομον. For interchange of c and ζ, see Gignac, *Grammar* i 123. A variety of spellings of γλωccόκομον is attested on papyrus: cf. P. Tebt. II 414.21, γλωcόκομον; P. Mil. II 76.21, κλωccοκόμ[ῳ]; PGM XIII 1009, κλοcόκομον; SB VIII 9834b.46, γολοcόκμον.

The γλωccόκομον, with such variants as γλωccοκομεῖον, standardly refers to a chest or case for the storage of valuables, generally made of wood (see esp. H. C. Youtie, *Scriptiunculae* (1973)

442–4, for discussion of its derivation and meanings). It could be of varying size: cf. P. Tebt. II 414.21, γλωσόκομον τὸ μέγα, with LIX **4005** 6, μικρὸν δὲ γλωσοκωμῖον. In a surgical context, the γλωσσόκομον refers to a box-splint, open at both ends and placed over a fractured leg to prevent movement. Galen offers a description at *In Hip. Fract.* 2.64 [XVIII/2 501–5 K.], stating that the medical variety must be longer and narrower than ordinary γλωσσόκομα, since it must not be thicker than the leg if it is to prevent further injury to the fracture. It is made of wood and rectangular in shape, and is thus to be distinguished from the cylindrical splint called the σωλήν (Paul. Aeg. 6.106 [*CMG* IX 2.159 Heiberg] specifies that the σωλήν is sometimes made of wood, sometimes of clay). Neither splint is associated with any part of the body other than the leg, and it may encase either the whole leg or only the calf if the fracture is located there (Gal. ibid. [XVIII/2 504 K.]). Bandages and woollen padding were placed inside the splints to limit lateral movement and minimise articulation at the knee, and Galen adds that some doctors placed a straight piece of wood under the sole of the foot to prevent the splint from sliding upwards. A so-called 'mechanical' (ὀργανικόν) γλωσσόκομον was also developed, which employed a system of ropes, axles and pulleys built into the splint's structure, designed to enable the broken bone to be extended and reset (Gal. ibid. [XVIII/2 505–6 K.]; Orib. *Coll. med.* 46.1.76–88 [*CMG* VI 2.1.207–8 Raeder] and 49. 7 [*CMG* VI 2.2.12–13 Raeder]). Galen further observes that he knows of physicians who keep in reserve several σωλῆνες in a range of different shapes and sizes for potential patients (*In Hip. Fract.* 2.64 [XVIII/2 504–5 K.]), and it may be that box-splints in general, including γλωσσόκομα, were regularly stored by doctors in their ἰατρεῖα in case of emergency. The standard meaning of the term as a chest, however, may on the other hand point to an inventory list, the other items found here perhaps having been contained in the chest, although its position in the list would then be more difficult to explain: cf. e.g. SB XX 14403.1–2, λό(γος) ἀ[να]λώμ(ατος) γλωσσοκόμου | χωρίου Εἰρήνης; P. Dryton 37.3 and 42.12, with p. 283; P. Worp 14 ii 44.

4 κρόκος. Saffron crocus, the dried stigmas of the crocus flower, was widely used in a range of medical recipes, in particular for eye-salves, and is very commonly attested in medical papyri and ostraca spanning the third century BC to the sixth century AD (cf. V. Gazza, 'Prescrizioni mediche nei papiri dell'Egitto greco-romano', *Aegyptus* 36 (1956) 86; also O. Bodl. II 2185.2; P. Amst. inv. 148.4; P. Ant. II 66r i 4; P. Ant. III 134.4; P. Athen. Univ. inv. 2780 i 20; P. Berl. Möller 13 ii 1; P. Mich. inv. 482 ii 24; P. Mich. inv. 3243.9; P. Strasb. inv. gr. 90 fr. 1 A 4; P. Tebt. II 273 iv; P. Tebt. II 677 fr. A 12; P. Vindob. Worp 20.3; P. Corn. inv. 47.4; P. Acad. inv. 4.10). Medical writers ascribe to it warming, digestive, soothing, astringent, and diuretic properties (Dsc. 1.26 [I 29–31 W.]; Gal. *Simpl. med. temp. ac fac.* 7.10 [XII 48 K.]). Saffron was also used, for example, as a dye to produce a yellow colouration in textiles.

5–6 σανδαράκη (realgar) and ἀρσενικόν (orpiment) are both natural sulphides of arsenic, the former of a more orange or red hue, the latter more yellow. They were likewise widely employed in medical recipes, often for the same purposes, but they are also found as discrete ingredients in the same recipe (e.g. Gal. *Comp. med. sec. loc.* [XIII 295–301 K.]). Their general caustic and cleansing properties are attested (Dsc. 5.104–5 [III 74–5 W.]; Gal. *Simpl. med. temp. ac fac.* [XII 212, 235 K.]). Among Greek medical papyri, σανδαράκη is mentioned in P. Ryl. III 531 recto ii 16 and verso ii 48, and along with κρόκος in SB XX 14501 frr. 1+2 ii 4 and 10; ἀρσενικόν in VIII **1088** ii 28 and PUG I 15.3. Both ἀρσενικόν and σανδαράκη are found in P. Horak 15 fr. 4 ii 25–6. They were also used as ingredients in the manufacture of pigments (cf. e.g. the presence of ἀρσενικόν in lists of pigments at MPER XIII 13.4 and P. Horak 63.6).

D. LEITH

III. DOCUMENTARY TEXTS

4980–4999. Documents addressed to Authorities

4980. Census Declaration

75/77(a)   11 × 23 cm   7 March 34

Only the concluding part of the document survives, with the oath and the date clause. A plurality of persons were declared (12), and these included women (6). The text uses a formula not attested elsewhere, which cannot be restored in full (5–8). The absence of a subscription (contrast II **254**, **4981**, P. Oxy. Hels. 10) may suggest that this is a copy. The back is blank.

Other Oxyrhynchite declarations for the census of 33/4 are P. Oxy. Hels. 10, which dates from the same month as **4980**, **4981**, and perhaps II **254** (it could also come from the previous census) and **256** (date uncertain). There are two other declarations from the same census, both Arsinoite (SB I 5661, X 10759).

A descriptive catalogue of census declarations is given in R. S. Bagnall, B. W. Frier, *The Demography of Roman Egypt* (1994, repr. 2006) [hereafter: *Demography*] 179–312, updated on pp. 314–25 of the reprint, and by J. M. S. Cowey, D. Kah, *ZPE* 163 (2007) 179–82; add now LXXIII **4956–7**, and those published in this volume.

```
       .   .   .   .   .
       Καίcαρα [ c.16
       Cεβαcτὸν [Αὐτοκράτορα θεοῦ
       Cεβαcτοῦ [υἱὸν ἦ μὴν ἐξ ὑγιοῦc
       καὶ ἐπ' ἀλη[θείαc ἐπιδεδωκέναι
  5    τὴν προ[κ(ειμένην) c.4 ] . . . . αν . . . .
       γυναικ(ῶν) τ[ c.5 ] τῶν παρ' ἐμοὶ
       οἰκοῦντ[ων c.3 ] ᾗ παράκειται ἡ ἑ-
       κάcτου . . [ c.3 καὶ] μηδένα ἕτερον
       μήτε Ῥωμ[αῖον μ]ηδὲ ἀπελεύθ(ερον)
 10    μηδὲ Ἀλ[εξαν]δρέα μηδὲ ἐπίξε-
       νον μηδ' [ἄλλο]ν μηδένα τῷ κα-
       θόλου παρὲξ τῶν προγεγρα(μμένων) οἰκεῖ-
       ν παρ' ἐ̣μ̣ο̣ί̣. εὐορκοῦντι μέν μοι εὖ εἴη,
       ἐπιορκοῦντι δὲ τὰ ἐναντία.
 15       (ἔτουc) κ Τιβερίου Καίcαροc Cεβαcτοῦ,
           Φαμ(ενωθ) ιᾱ.
```

6 γυναι^κ   9 απελευ^θ   12 προγεγρ^α   13 ἐμοί: ε corr. from α   15 L
16 φα^μ

'... Caesar ... Augustus Imperator, son of the divine Augustus, that I have indeed honestly and truthfully submitted the above (return?) of ... women ... who live with me ..., to which everyone's ... is annexed, and that no one else, neither Roman nor freedman nor Alexandrian nor alien nor anyone else at all lives with me except for the above-written. If I observe the oath, may it be well with me, but if I swear falsely, the reverse.

'Year 20 of Tiberius Caesar Augustus, Phamenoth 11.'

1 ff. For the oath clause, see P. Oxy. Hels. 10.15 n.

1–3 The oaths by Tiberius display slight variations in the description of the emperor; see the listing in P. Sijp. pp. 117–18; also CPR XXIII 1.13–16 n. There are three other examples from this year, P. Oxy. Hels. 10 and the Arsinoite P. Sijp. 19, which have ὀμνύω Τιβέριον Καίсαρα Ϲεβαϲτὸν Αὐτοκράτορα θεοῦ Ϲεβαϲτοῦ υἱόν; and **4981** 3–6 ὀ[μνύω Τιβέριον] Καίϲαρα [Νέον Ϲεβαϲτὸν] Αὐτοκρ[άτορα θεοῦ Ϲεβαϲτοῦ] υἱόν (restorations suggested by space). It is unclear what stood in the break in line 1. One could reckon with a dittography, Ϲεβαϲτὸν Αὐτοκράτορα written twice, but this seems rather long for the space.

5–8 This papyrus and **4981** 7–9 offer a novel version of the formula, previously known in simpler form: P. Oxy. Hels. 10.18–19 τ[ὴν γρ]αφ[ὴν] | τῶν παρ' ἐμοὶ οἰκούντω[ν]; II **255** = W. Chr. 201.17–18 τὴ[ν π]ροκειμένην | γ[ρα]φὴν τῶν παρ' ἐμοὶ [ο]ἰκούν[των] (ἀ[πο]|γ[ρα]φήν BL VIII 234, but the on-line image indicates that nothing is written after π]ροκειμένην in 17).

5] . . . . αν . . . . . In view of γυναικ(ῶν) in 6, one would expect γραφὴν τῶν ἀνδρῶν καί (with abbreviations), but I cannot read it in the remains. γραφ]ήν would be possible, but the upright before alpha is hard to explain. The semi-horizontal after the putative nu could conceivably be part of delta, but what follows, the lower part of a descending oblique, is not part of rho, and the potential delta is not raised in the line to indicate an abbreviation.

7–8] ᾗ παράκειται ἡ ἑκάϲτου . . [. ᾗ probably refers to the putative γραφήν, which may well have stood in 5. What would have been added next to each person declared is their age, perhaps accompanied by physical characteristics and occupational details, but I am not aware of a suitable technical term. The only word that would match what is visible after ἑκάϲτου is ἑϲ[τία, but this does not have the expected sense (ϲ could be read instead of ε, and then ο, but I cannot think of a plausible reconstruction).

11–12 τῷ καθόλου. The addition of this element to the formula is new.

12–13 οἰκεῖ|ν. The word division is odd. Over nu and intersecting the theta that starts the previous line, there is a right-facing arc or sigma; I do not see what it meant.

16 The date falls in the year of the census; cf. **4981**, **4982**.

N. GONIS

4981. Census Declaration

1 1B.115/G(h)   8.9 × 12.7 cm   26(?) April 34

Like **4980**, this fragment too comes from the lower part of declaration for the census of 33/4. The declarant was a man, and a plurality of persons (8), perhaps including an one-year-old child (1), lived in his house, which he seems to have shared with his brother (9). The subscription (18) is in the same hand as the rest of the text.

The back is blank.

. . . . .

    ἐνιαύϲι[οϲ(?)
    Ἀπολλ[
    ὁ προγεγρα(μμένοϲ) ὀ[μνύω Τιβέριον
    Καίϲαρα [Νέον Ϲεβαϲτὸν
5   Αὐτοκρ[άτορα θεοῦ Ϲεβαϲτοῦ
    υἱὸν εἶ μ[ὴν ἐξ ὑγιοῦϲ καὶ ἐπ' ἀλη-
    θίαϲ ἐπεδεδ[ωκέναι τὴν γραφὴν τῶν
    ἀνδρῶν κ[αὶ γυναικῶν τῶν παρ' ἐμοὶ
    καὶ τῷ ἀδελ[φῷ οἰκούντων
10 καὶ μηδένα ἕτερον μήτε Ῥωμαῖο[ν
    μηδ' ἀπελεύθερον μηδ' Ἀλεξα(νδρέα)
    μηδ' ἄλλον μηδένα παρὲξ τῶν
    προγεγρα(μμένων) οἰκῖν παρ' ἐμοὶ καὶ τῷ ἀδελφ(ῷ)
    καὶ μηδὲν διεψεῦϲθαι. εὐορκοῦν-
15 τι μέν μοι εὖ εἴη, ἐπιορκοῦντι δὲ τὰ
    ἐναντία. (ἔτουϲ) κ Τιβερίου Καίϲαροϲ,
        Ϲεβαϲτοῦ, Παχ . .
    Ἀπολλ[
    . . [

. . . . .

3, 13 προγεγρ^α   6 l. ᾖ   7 l. -θείαϲ ἐπιδε-   11 αλεξ^α   13 l. οἰκεῖν αδελφ^φ
16 L

'. . . one-year old(?) . . . I, Apoll— . . . the above-written, swear by Tiberius Caesar Novus Augustus Imperator, son of the divine Augustus, that I have indeed honestly and truthfully submitted the return of the men and women who live with me and with my brother, and that no one else, neither Roman nor freedman nor Alexandrian nor anyone else lives with me and with my brother except for the above-written, and that I have not lied in any respect. If I observe the oath, may it be well with me, but if I swear falsely, the reverse. Year 20 of Tiberius Caesar Augustus, Pachon (1?).

'I, Apoll— . . .'

1 ἐνιαύϲι[οϲ. The scribe first wrote something else (an oblique linked to alpha is clearly visible), and then penned upsilon partly over it. The word should mean that the person declared is one year old; it has occurred in one other census return, SB VI 9572.18–19 (61/2), as re-edited by R. A. Coles, *JEA* 52 (1966) 135–7 (p. 137 for comment). Cf. also P. Strasb. VIII 768.18 (174/5 or later), an extract from a census return, though the context is different.

7–9 For the formula, see **4980** 5–8 n. Line 9 is short as restored; there may have been some additional textual loss at the end of the line.

17 Παχ.. After chi, what seems to be alpha, followed by an oblique stroke. Even though chi is not superscript, we could reckon with an abbreviation: Παχ(ων) α̣. But the oblique that follows is not a numerical marker at this time.

N. GONIS

4982. Census Declaration

27 3B.39/D(1–3)a   6 × 22 cm   28 May 62
Plate VII

What survives is the lower part of the document, blank on the back. The part lost would have contained the prescript and the names of the persons declared. The declarant and his family resided in the house of the declarant's wife, in the village of Phoboou. None of the persons mentioned in this text is known from elsewhere. The text uses a formula otherwise attested in Arsinoite declarations (see 2–4 n.), but other formulas are typical of Oxyrhynchus (see 5 n., 13–15 n.).

This is the second Oxyrhynchite return for the census of 61/2 to be published, after SB XII 10788B, which dates from the same day as **4982**. The only other published declaration for this census is the Arsinoite SB VI 9572 (re-ed. *JEA* 52 (1966) 135–7).

```
              .   .   .   .
                ].[
         κατ]αγινόμεθα δὲ ἐν
         τῇ τ]ῆς γυναικός μου Ταποντ(ῶτος)
         τῆς] Ἀπολλωνίου οἰκίας
   5     ἐν κ]ώμῃ Φοβῳ̣ου τῆς α(ὐτῆς) τοπ(αρχίας).
         κ]αὶ ὀμνύω Νέρωνα Κλαύδιον
         Καίςαρα Cεβαςτὸν Γερμανικὸν
         Αὐτοκράτορα ἐξ ὑγιοῦς καὶ
         ἐπ' ἀληθ(είας) ἐπιδεδωκέναι
   10    τ]ὴν γραφήν. εὐορκοῦντι
         μ]έν μοι εὖ εἴη{ι}, ἐπιορκοῦντι
         δ]ὲ τὰ ἐναντία.
         Ἱέρ]αξ Ζωΐλου ἐπιδέδωκα
         κ]αὶ ὀμώμεκα τὸν προγεγρα(μμένον)
   15    ὅ]ρκο[ν]. Πλουτίων Ἡρακλείδ(ου)
         ἔ]γραψα ὑπὲρ αὐτοῦ μὴ
         εἰ]δότος γράμματα. (ἔτους) η
```

4982. CENSUS DECLARATION

Νέρωνος Κλαυδίου Καίϲαροϲ
Ϲ]εβαϲτοῦ Γερμανικοῦ Αὐτοκράτ(οροϲ),
20   Πα(υνι) γ̄.

2 κατ]αγινόμεθα: ε corr. from αι   3 ταπον^τ   4 l. οἰκίᾳ   5 ᾱτο⸍   9 αλη^θ
14 l. ὀμώμοκα   προγεγρ^α   15 ηρακλει^δ   17 L   19 αυτοκρα^τ   20 πᾱ

'. . . And we reside in the house of my wife Tapontos daughter of Apollonius in the village of Phoboou of the same toparchy. And I swear by Nero Claudius Caesar Augustus Germanicus Imperator that I have honestly and truthfully submitted the return. If I observe the oath, may it be well with me, but if I swear falsely, the reverse. I, Hierax son of Zoilus, have submitted (the return) and have sworn the above-written oath. I, Ploution son of Heraclides, wrote on his behalf because he does not know letters. Year 8 of Nero Claudius Caesar Augustus Germanicus Imperator, Payni 3.'

2–4 κατ]αγινόμεθα δὲ ἐν κτλ. Examples of this formulation are listed by J. M. S. Cowey, D. Kah, *ZPE* 163 (2007) 176 n. 155. It comes after the statement that one is registered for a given 'house-by-house registration', and is usually (not in P. Berl. Leihg. I 16) followed by a listing of the persons declared.

5 Φοβῳου. The reading is not easy, but I doubt that any other toponym was intended. I have assumed that the part between phi and upsilon is very quickly written, as if in *Verschleifung*, so that not all letters can be made out individually. Phoboou was a village in the Eastern toparchy.

τῆϲ α(ὐτῆϲ) τοπ(αρχίαϲ) implies that the toparchy was mentioned earlier in the text. This could have been mentioned with reference to the *topogrammateus* (cf. **4983** 4), the *origo* of the declarant, or to property owned by the declarant in a village of this same toparchy. This reference to a toparchy in a text of this date suits an Oxyrhynchite provenance.

10 τ]ὴν γραφήν. This is the latest example of the use of this term in this context instead of ἀπογραφή; cf. P. Oxy. Hels. 10.18 n.

13–15 ἐπιδέδωκα [κ]αὶ ὀμώμεκα τὸν προγεγρα(μμένον) [ὅ]ρκο[ν]. This formulation is characteristic of Oxyrhynchite documents. P. Palau Rib. 10 and P. Wisc. I 16, which attest it and are said to be of unknown provenance, are likely to be Oxyrhynchite.

20 Πα(υνι). A short horizontal stroke over alpha is better interpreted as a degenerated upsilon than an abbreviation marker that would allow any letter to be supplied, as in later times; i.e., I do not think that Pachon was meant.

N. GONIS

4983. Census Declaration

46 5B.51/E(4–5)b   8.1 × 15.4 cm   c.76
                                              Plate VII

The upper part of a declaration addressed to the strategus (probably new; see 22–3 n.) and royal scribe of the Oxyrhynchite nome, the *topogrammateus* of the Upper toparchy, and the *komogrammateus* and *laographoi* of Cercemunis. The declarant is a woman who registers her share of a vacant house in the village of Cercemunis. The text does not mention her place of residence, for which she may have submitted another declaration (cf. Bagnall–Frier, *Demography* 15); this could have been in a different locality, possibly in Oxyrhynchus, the place of her origin. There are no other declarations of uninhabited property from the first century except for SB XII 10788B (62). Such declarations 'presumably have the function of assuring the government that there are no persons to be registered outside of those listed in the sum total of household declarations' (Bagnall–Frier, *Demography* 14).

The text bears no date, but the reference to the royal scribe Nicander establishes that the census is that of 75/6. Three other declarations for this census are known: II **361** descr. and the Arsinoite BGU XI 2088 and P. Minnesota inv. 1381982 (described in Bagnall–Frier, *Demography* 186). Only **361** preserves a date, and this points to 76/7, though the reading of the year-number is uncertain (Bagnall, *GRBS* 32 (1991) 258 n. 12). It has been observed that census declarations from the Oxyrhynchite, the Arsinoite, and other nomes were usually filed in the year following the decree of the prefect (see M. Hombert, C. Préaux, *Recherches sur le recensement dans l'Égypte romaine* (1952) 76–84; Bagnall–Frier, *Demography* 16–18), but this pattern does not apply to the first century: 'filing during the census year itself seems prevalent at least through 61/2 and perhaps through 75/6' (Bagnall–Frier, *Demography* 6); see also **4980–82**, filed during the year of the census. These early declarations date from between Phamenoth (February–March) of the census year (P. Oxy. Hels. 10, **4980**) and Phaophi (September–October) of the year after (II **255** = W. *Chr.* 201). We may thus assume that **4983** was filed some time in 76 or even in 77.

4983 displays some well-known features of first-century declarations, especially from the Oxyrhynchite nome. These are mostly omissions of certain elements common in later documents of this type: the term ἀπογραφή does not occur; there is no mention of the year of the census; and there is no reference to the edict of the prefect ordering the census.

The text runs parallel to the fibres. The back is blank.

(m.2)   >
(m.1)   Τιβερίωι Κλαυδίωι Ἡρακλείδηι
        cτρα(τηγῷ) καὶ Νικάνδ(ρῳ) βα(cιλικῷ) γρ(αμματεῖ) καὶ Διονυcίῳ
        τοπ(ο)γρ(αμματεῖ) ἄνω{ι} τοπαρχ(ίας) καὶ Cαραπίω(νι)
5   κωμογρα(μματεῖ) Κερκεμούν(εως) καὶ (vac.)
        (vac.)   λαογρά(φοιc) τῆ(c) α(ὐτῆc) Κερκεμού(νεως)
        παρὰ Cιεάπιος τῆc Cαραπίωνος
        τοῦ Ἀπολλωνίου μητρὸc Ἀριστοῦτ(ος)
        τῆc Ἀρίcτωνος τῶν ἀπ' Ὀξυρύγχ(ων)
10   πόλεως μετὰ κυρίου τοῦ
        υἱοῦ Ἀρίcτωνος τοῦ Διογέν[ο]υ[c.

ἀπογράφομαι τὴν ὑπάρχουcάν
μοι καὶ τῆι ἀδελφῆι Θαΐδι
οἰκίαν θηcαυρὸν λεγομένη[ν
15 ἐν τῆι αὐτῆι κώμηι, ἐν ἧι οὐ-
δεὶc ἀπογράφεται οὐδὲ
καταγίνεται.] καὶ ὀμνύω [

. . .

3 cτρ^α   νικαν^δ β^α ϙ̄   διονυcι^ω   4 τοϙ̄ϙ̄   τοπαρ^χ   και: κ corr. from c   cαραπι^ω
5 κωμογρ^α κερκεμου^ν   6 λαογρ^α τη͞α κερκεμο^υ   8 αριcτου^τ   9 οξυρυγ^χ   15 αυτη:
υ corr. from τ

'To Tiberius Claudius Heraclides, strategus, and Nicander, royal scribe, and Dionysius, district-scribe of the Upper toparchy, and Sarapion, village-scribe of Cercemunis, and (blank) registrars of the same Cercemunis, from Sieapis daughter of Sarapion son of Apollonius, mother Aristous daughter of Ariston, from the city of the Oxyrhynchi, with her son Ariston son of Diogenes as guardian. I register the house that belongs to me and to my sister, Thais, the so-called 'granary', in the same village, in which no one is registered nor lives; and I swear . . .'

1 Just above and to the left of the beginning of the text there is the sign >. Its purpose is unknown, but it may have been a kind of official mark; cf. the cross at the top of the census return XII **1547** (119) and the *epikrisis* applications VII **1028** (86) and XII **1452** (127/8).

2–6 All but one of the first-century census returns from Oxyrhynchus that have their top preserved are addressed to more than one official; the only exception is P. Oxy. Hels. 10 (34), addressed to the strategus. II **254** (19/20 or 33/4) is addressed to two *topogrammateis-komogrammateis*, II **255** (48) adds the strategus and the royal scribe, and SB XII 10788B (62) and **4983** further add the *laographoi*. Declarations addressed to a plurality of officials have been attested only from the Oxyrhynchite and the Arsinoite nomes. See Hombert–Préaux, *Recherches* 84–97, 101–2; Bagnall–Frier, *Demography* 21; Th. Kruse, *Der Königliche Schreiber und die Gauverwaltung* i (2002) 113–18 (for the Oxyrhynchite nome).

2–3 Τιβερίωι Κλαυδίωι Ἡρακλείδηι cτρα(τηγῷ). This strategus is new. He should be placed between Coυτώριοc Cωcίβιοc, attested in 72/3, and Κλαύδιοc Ἡράκλειοc, who first occurs on 5.ix.77 (II **276**); see J. Whitehorne, *Strategi and Royal Scribes of Roman Egypt*² (2006) 92. However, one may question whether Tiberius Claudius Heraclides and Claudius Heraclius are one and the same person, the difference in the names being due to the scribe of the present document. We find Ἡρακλείωι in XLV **3264** 7 (80/81); in **276** 15 the name is restored, Ἡρακλε[ίο]υ, and seems fairly certain (the on-line image indicates that it suits the space better than Ἡρακλε[ίδο]υ).

3 Νικάνδ(ρῳ) βα(cιλικῷ) γρ(αμματεῖ). Nicander is attested in office in several documents of 72/3; see Kruse, *Königliche Schreiber* ii 1016. X **1266** refers to two royal scribes in office during this same year (72/3): Pamphilus (line 2) and Nicander (l. 27); it has been thought that Pamphilus succeeded Nicander in the course of the year (see Kruse, *Königliche Schreiber* ii 1016 n. 267; the same order is adopted by Whitehorne, *Strategi and Royal Scribes*² 160), but **4985** suggests that the opposite was the case (it would be uneconomical to reckon with a second stint of Nicander as royal scribe).

4 τοπ(ο)γρ(αμματεῖ). On this office, see F. Oertel, *Die Liturgie* (1917) 164–5; S. L. Wallace, *Taxation in Egypt from Augustus to Diocletian* (1938) 100, 397 n. 19.

5 Κερκεμούν(εωc). Cf. 6. This is a well-attested village, located in the Upper toparchy of the Oxyrhynchite nome.

6 λαογρά(φοιc). Cf. **4991** 1. On these officials, see L. Capponi, *ZPE* 140 (2002) 179, with

references. In villages their number varied from two to six, so that it is probably correct to resolve the abbreviation in the plural; cf. Hombert–Préaux, *Recherches* 95–7. The space left blank at the end of line 5 and the beginning of 6 indicates that the names of *laographoi* were to be added later, which never happened.

7–13 The text includes many names in the self-identification of the declarant despite its early date and the presence of a guardian; see Hombert–Préaux, *Recherches* 102, and Bagnall–Frier, *Demography* 22. (Cf. also below, 9–10 n.). None of these persons can be identified with people already attested in the papyri. The family tree may be presented as follows:

```
       Ἀπολλώνιος      Ἀρίcτων
           |              |
        Cαραπίων    =   Ἀριcτοῦc
     ┌──────────────────────┐
   Θαΐc      Διογένηc  =  Cιέαπιc
                           |
                         Ἀρίcτων
```

7 *Cιέαπιοc*. The name *Cιέαπιc is not attested, though cf. *Cιαιέπιοc* (gen.) in P. Mich. V 238.60 (Tebt., 46), which must be a version of the same name. For the frequent interchange of αι and ε, see Gignac, *Grammar* i 192–3, 278–86, and in particular 279 n. 1, and 285–6 for the interchange of α and ε. *Cιε* (*Cια*, *Cιοc*), meaning 'cedar' in Coptic, is used as a personal name for both men and women; see G. Heuser, *Die Personennamen die Kopten* (1929) 54, 72. *Cιέαπιc* could be a compound theophoric name, meaning 'the cedar of Apis'.

9–10 *τῶν ἀπ' Ὀξυρύγχ(ων) πόλεωc*. Hombert–Préaux, *Recherches* 106–7 (sim. 103 n. 7) observed that in first-century declarations from Oxyrhynchus the origin of the declarant was not indicated. This found further support from P. Oxy. Hels. 10 (34) and SB XII 10788B (62), published subsequently, but is now disproved by **4983**, which attests a formulation common in such texts in the second and third centuries.

10–11 For guardians of women in census-returns, see Hombert–Préaux, *Recherches* 59–61; Bagnall–Frier, *Demography* 13. Since the guardian of Sieapis is her son and not her husband, she may be widowed or divorced; cf. Hombert–Préaux, *Recherches* 167–8.

12 *ἀπογράφομαι τὴν ὑπάρχουcαν*. This seems to be the earliest instance of this formula, which is standard in Oxyrhynchite declarations after 146; see G. M. Parássoglou, *BASP* 7 (1970) 96 n. 31. But cf. SB XXIV 16011.3–5 (Oxy., reign of Augustus?), which attests a slightly different formula: *ἀπογράφομαι ἐν τῆι μητροπόλει ἐν [τ]ῆι ὑπαρχούcῃ μοι οἰκίᾳ*.

12–14 *τὴν ὑπάρχουcάν μοι καὶ τῆι ἀδελφῆι Θαΐδι οἰκίαν*. This is an example of fragmentation of property between siblings, which primarily results from partible inheritance. The shares of the declared property are unspecified, reflecting a *communio pro indiviso*, that is, the legal designation of a portion of a physically undivided house; see E. Weiss, *APF* 4 (1908) 330–65, and R. Taubenschlag, *Law*² 239–43. As in other first-century census returns, with the exception of P. Oxy. Hels. 10.5 (*πατρικῆι οἰκίᾳ*), there is no mention of the way in which the property devolved to its present owners, which is a common element of later returns. Despite the joint ownership, the two sisters do not file a joint declaration, which is not unusual; see Hombert–Préaux, *Recherches* 58. Contrast **4990**.

14 *θηcαυρὸν λεγομένη[ν*. Cf. SB XX 14166.15 (189) *ἐπαυλ( ) κωμογρα(μματ-) λεγομ( )*. This house may have formerly been a public or private granary at Cercemunis (a public granary in this village is mentioned or implied in XLI **2959** 12, XLIV **3170** 35, 105, 149, P. Theon. 22.2–3, SB XIV 12079.8, XVIII 13131.12). Granaries are attested as parts of private houses, cf. G. Husson, *OIKIA* (1983) 91–3, and in one case a family seems to have taken over as living quarters part of the granary of Karanis (E. M. Husselman, *TAPA* 83 (1952) 68–9).

16–17 *οὐδὲ [καταγίνεται]*. For the restoration, compare III **480** 5–6 (132) *εἰc ὃ [ο]ὐδεὶc ἀπο-*

γρ(άφεται) οὐδὲ καταγί(νεται), and P. Harr. I 71.22 (188/9), as re-read in Korr. Tyche 590, forthcoming in *Tyche* 23 (2008). Declarations of uninhabited property usually have the formulas οὐδεὶϲ ἀπογράφεται or, less often, οὐδεὶϲ καταγίνεται (only XII **1547** 30 (119) and PSI VII 874.i.14 (132/3), both from Oxyrhynchus). (In P. Wisc. I 18.8, which appears to have the singular οὐδεὶϲ κατοι(κεῖ), the plate (VII) allows reading οὐδεὶϲ καταγ(ίνεται).)

R. HATZILAMBROU

4984. REGISTRATION OF A LOAN

89A/50   6.7 × 4.8 cm   *c*.98–100

This and the following item are letters from unqualified officials to *agoranomi*, authorizing them to register certain transactions. Such documents are unique to Oxyrhynchus and are attested only within the last third of the first century AD. The function of the senders and the precise nature of the requested 'registration' are the subject of some debate. For a discussion of the issue, publication of further texts of this type that were only described in P. Oxy. II and III, and a complete list of the relevant papyri, see *ZPE* 170 (2009) 157–85.

4984 is the top of a letter from Caecilius Clemens to the *agoranomus* authorizing the registration of a loan contract. Orders to register a loan (δανείου ϲυγγραφή) rather than a sale are relatively rare among letters to *agoranomi*, paralleled only by II **241** (*c*.98/9) and **329** descr. (late first century). The loan in **241** is on the security of a share of a house (**329**, like **4984**, preserves only the top of the document); cf. also the orders to register a contract of mortgage (ϲυγγραφὴ ὑποθήκηϲ) in II **243** (79) and VIII **1105** (81–96). All of these documents distinguish themselves from orders to register sales (such as **4985**) by the use of ἀναγράφειν instead of καταγράφειν as their main verb; for the significance of this distinction, see H. J. Wolff, *Das Recht der griechischen Papyri Ägyptens in der Zeit der Ptolemaeer und des Prinzipats* ii (1978) 200–201.

Upper and left margins are preserved. The papyrus is complete on the right but with no free margin. The writing runs along the fibres and the back is blank.

    Καικίλλιϲ Κλήμηϲ τῷ
    ἀγορανόμ(ῳ) χ(αίρειν). ἀνάγρα(ψον) δα(νείου)
    ϲυνγρα(φὴν) Διον(υϲίου) Θέω(νοϲ) τοῦ
    Διον(υϲίου) μητ(ρὸϲ) Πτολέμ(αϲ) Θέω(νοϲ)
5   τοῦ [. . .]⁻ [. .]υ[.]α[. .] . [

    .   .   .   .

1 l. Καικίλιοϲ   2 αγορανοᵘχᒪαναγρᒪδᵃ   3 ϲυνγρᒪδιοῡθεᵚ, l. ϲυγγραφήν
4 διοῡμηᵀπτολεᴴθεᵚ

'Caecilius Clemens to the *agoranomus*, greetings. Register a contract of loan from Dionysius son of Theon son of Dionysius, mother Ptolema daughter of Theon son of . . .'

1 Caecilius Clemens is known as the sender of other letters to *agoranomi*: II **241** (date not preserved), **340** descr. (98/9), III **581** descr. (29 August 99), and II **338** descr. (99/100). **4984** must therefore date from around the years 98–100.

3–4 A Dionysius son of Theon grandson of Dionysius is attested in I **94** 4 (83). He may be identical to the person here, but both 'Dionysius' and 'Theon' were exceedingly common names in first-century Oxyrhynchus, and the mother's name is not given in **94**.

A. BENAISSA

4985. Registration of a Sale

9 1B.172/A 11.7 × 8 cm Late first century

A letter from Heracleides and Ammonius to the *agoranomus* authorizing the registration of a sale of house property.

The document is complete on all sides but the bottom. The writing, in a rapid cursive hand, runs along the fibres and the back is blank. A small loose fragment is not transcribed.

    Ἡρακλείδης καὶ Ἀμμώνιος τῶι
    ἀγορανόμωι χ(αίρειν). κατάγραψον
    ὠνὴν Διοκλεῖ Πτολεμαίου τοῦ
    ἐπιβάλλοντος τῶι διατιθεμένωι
5   μέρους οἰκίας καὶ αὐλῆς καὶ τῆς εἰς ταύτ(ας)
    εἰσόδου καὶ ἐξ[ό]δου καὶ τῶν συνκυρόντων
    κοινῶν [καὶ ἀ]διαιρέτων πρὸς τοὺς ἑ-
    αυτοῦ ̣ ̣[̣ ̣ ̣ ̣] ̣ ̣ ̣ερα καὶ το ̣[̣ ̣ ̣ ̣] ̣ε
    [c.14   ]εντω ̣ ̣ ̣[̣ ̣ ̣ ̣ ̣] ̣

2 χ̅ς̅ 3 υ of -μαιου corrected 5 ταυ^τ 6 l. συγκυρόντων

'Heraclides and Ammonius to the *agoranomus*, greetings. Register a sale for Diocles son of Ptolemaeus of the share that falls to the one disposing of it, of a house and courtyard and the entrance and exit to these and the appurtenances, (being) common and indivisible with his . . . and . . .'

1 Ἡρακλείδης καὶ Ἀμμώνιος. This pair of officials does not recur in other letters to *agoranomi*.
3 Διοκλεῖ Πτολεμαίου. Not identifiable elsewhere.
7–8 πρὸς τοὺς ἑαυτοῦ ̣ ̣[̣ ̣ ̣ ̣] ̣ ̣ ̣ερα. Presumably restore ἀδ[ελ(φούς) after ἑαυτοῦ. What follows, however, is unclear. The letter before ερα is obscured by a large blot of ink. The trace preceding this blot can hardly be η, so that καὶ τὴν μητέρα does not seem a commendable restoration (assuming the available space allows it). πατέρα may be just possible. One would not expect property to be

4985. *REGISTRATION OF A SALE* 99

owned jointly by a father and his children, unless we suppose that the seller's mother was deceased and either had divided her house property between her husband and children in a will or had jointly owned the house with her husband before bequeathing her share to her children.

A. BENAISSA

4986–4988. Census Declarations

48 5B.29/D(a)a   29 × 2.5 cm

A strip from a *tomos synkollesimos*, blank on the back except for the odd ink spot (no writing), with remains of four census declarations. Though found in Oxyrhynchus, the documents come from Antinoopolis, as suggested by the reference to a (former?) gymnasiarch of the city in one of them (**4986** 2) and the use of a particular formula in another (**4988** 4 n). That the roll was among the papers of an Oxyrhynchite who served as the nomarch of Antinoopolis (cf. XLIX **3477** introd.) is one possibility.

None of the declarations appears to have an addressee. **4986** preserves part of an official annotation added in the top margin (see **4986** 1 n.); at least one line is lost from the upper part of **4987**, and two from **4988**. Of the more fragmentary fourth item in the roll (not printed below), we have the annotation in the upper margin and a few letter-tops from the first line. All this implies that the constituents of the composite roll were not aligned at the top, which is not uncommon; see **4993–4995** introd.

Besides adding to the meagre number of census declarations from Antinoopolis, these are the earliest such documents from this city to be published, and refer to what was probably the first census held there (see Jördens, *Statthalterliche Verwaltung* 80). Their fragmentary state is thus all the more to be regretted. The Antinoite declarations published previously are VIII **1110**, PSI XII 1227 (both of 188), SB XXIV 16223 (201/2), W. *Chr.* 207 (216), and P. Col. X 269 (II/III). When verifiable, all these declarations were submitted in the course of the census year, and this is the case with **4988** too; see the discussion in Jördens, op. cit. 80–81. The 'current 9th year' in **4988** corresponds to 145/6; since no such document dates from earlier than February in the census year, it is probable that **4988** dates from the spring or summer of 146. I have assumed that the 9th year mentioned in **4987** is the 'current year', and I have posited the same date for **4986**, though it lacks a chronological indication.

For other declarations for the census of 145/6, see LXXIII **4956–7** introd.

4986

48 5B.29/D(a)a col. i   146?

(m. 2)   ] . . /
(m. 1)   ].[.] γυμν(αςιαρχ-) Ἀν[τ]ινόου πόλ(εως)
                               ]..[.]του Παςέμςεως μη-
          τρὸς   ]μη.[c.8]ομαι
5   ]...δ( ) [

2 γυμν𝄙   πο^λ   5]...δ

'... (former?) gymnasiarch of Antinoopolis ... (son of) ... (grandson of) Pasemsis, mother ...'

1 In the upper margin one sees the feet of two uprights followed by a blank space and a thick dash. The same kind of annotation occurs in the fourth item in the *tomos*: a large π, followed by blank space and dash. The traces in **4986** would admit π, but its meaning escapes me. At this point one would expect to find the number of this item number in the *tomos*, but if π = 80, the number in **4986** would have been οζ (= 77), which cannot be read. I would rule out that one has to read π(αρετέθη).

2 γυμν(αςιάρχου) or γυμν(αςιαρχήςαντος) Ἀντινόου πόλ(εως). I cannot explain what is written between Ἀντινόου and πόλ(εως) (not an attempt to write Ἀντινοέων).

The gymnasiarchs were not among the addressees of census returns, so that it seems more likely that this is the declarer, in which case restore παρά at the beginning of the line. It is probably not relevant that the (ex-)gymnasiarch of Antinoopolis attested in XLIV **3198** 6–7 (146/7?) seems to have had Oxyrhynchite connections.

3 Παςέμςεως. If correctly read, the name is new. Alternatively, read Πανεμγέως (suggested by N. Litinas), but nu is not easy.

4]μη.[c.8]ομαι. The sequence κώ]μης [ἀπογράφ]ομαι suits space and trace but is difficult to defend, also because of the reading in the next line.

5 One could think of Μ]ατιδ(ίου), but alpha is not easy to read.

4987

48 5B.29/D(a)a col. ii   146

                         traces of one line
         μητ(ρὸς) Χενανούπ(ιος) τῶν ἀπὸ κώμ(ης) Μενδ( ).
         ἀπογράφο(μαι) κατὰ τὰ κελευςθ(έντα) ὑπὸ τοῦ
         κρατίστου ἡγεμόνο[ς Οὐα]λερίου
5   Πρόκλου εἰ[ς] τὴν τοῦ θ ἔτου[ς Ἀν]τ[ω]νίνου

4987. *CENSUS DECLARATION* 101

2 μη˙χενανου` κωμ⸖μεν^δ   3 απογραφ^ο   κελευc^θ

'. . . mother Chenanupis, one of those from the village of Mend—. In accordance with the orders of the prefect Valerius Proculus, *vir egregius*, I register for the (house-by-house registration) of the 9th year of Antoninus . . .'

2 Χεναν̣ού̣π(ιος). A rare name, otherwise attested only in three documents: P. Hamb. I 60.4, 12 (Herm.; 90) Χενανούπιος; P. Yale I 78.1, 12 (Ars.; ii) Χενανούβι (l. -ει); P. Princ. III 189.2, 16, 21 (?; I/II) Χενανουβ( ).

κώμης Μένδ(ητος)? The Arsinoite village of Mendes in the division of Heraclides comes to mind. It would be no surprise if one of the early citizens of Antinoopolis were a settler from an Arsinoite village, but it is remarkable that there is no reference to a nome.

4–5 Οὐα]λερίου Πρό̣κ̣λου. See LXXIII **4956** 9–10 n.; Jördens, *Statthalterliche Verwaltung* 532.

4988

48 5B.29/D(a)a col. iii   146

. . . . .
       traces of one line
   ἀπογράφο(μαι) κατὰ τὰ κελ(ευσθέντα) ὑπὸ τοῦ κρατίστου
   ἡγεμόνος Οὐαλερίου Πρόκλου
4 εἰς τὴν πρὸς τὸ ἐνεςτ(ὸς) θ (ἔτος)
       . . . .

2 απογραφο̄ κε^λ   4 ενεϲ˙θ∫

'In accordance with the orders of the prefect Valerius Proculus, *vir egregius*, I register for the (house-by-house registration) for the current 9th year . . .'

4 εἰς τὴν πρὸς τὸ ἐνεςτ(ὸς) θ (ἔτος). Cf. VIII **1110** 7, PSI XII 1227.8–9, W. *Chr.* 207.7, and SB XXIV 16223.5 (mostly restored).

N. GONIS

4989. Census Declaration

36 4B.92/H(12–13)b   7 × 19.5+ cm   25 February – 26 March 175

Two disjointed fragments comprising the upper and lower parts of a census declaration submitted by a woman, who registers a part of a house in Oxyrhynchus that belongs to her and in which her children, and presumably she too, live. The children are *apatores*. Down to the end of fr. 1, the list contains only men's names, which conforms to the standard pattern of Oxyrhynchite declarations (men are listed first, and then women). Fr. 2 preserves the end of an entry for a person whose gender, age, or status cannot be ascertained, and then the oath and date clause. The amount of text lost between the two fragments is unknown; its possible contents are discussed below, 23–4 n. There is no reference to an addressee and no docket on the back (blank), which may suggest that this is a copy, though this is not necessary; see Kruse, *Königliche Schreiber* i 113–14.

This is the first Oxyrhynchite declaration for the census of 173/4 to be published. The evidence from other regions is much more plentiful; see Bagnall–Frier *Demography* 248–64, 318–19.

    παρὰ Διδύμης Πλουτάρχου
    τοῦ Ζωςίμου μητ(ρὸς) Ἀςκλαταρίο(υ)
    μετὰ κ(υρίου) τοῦ υἱο(ῦ) Πλουτίωνο(ς)
    ἐξ αὐτ(ῆς) χρημ(ατίζοντος) ἀμφοτ(έρων) ἀπ' Ὀξυ(ρύγχων) πόλ(εως).
5   κατὰ τὰ κελ(ευςθέντα) ὑπὸ Καλουιςίου
    Cτατιανοῦ τοῦ λαμπροτ(άτου) ἡγεμόν(ος)
    ἀπογρ(άφομαι) πρὸς τ(ὴν) τοῦ διελ(θόντος) ιδ (ἔτους) Αὐρ(ηλίου)
    Ἀντωνίνου Καίςαρος τοῦ κυρίου
    κατ' οἰκ(ίαν) ἀπογρ(αφὴν) τὸ ὑπ(άρχον) μοι ἐπ' ἀμ-
10 φόδου Ἑρμαίο(υ) μέρο(ς) οἰκ(ίας) εἰς ὃ
    ἀπογρ(αφόμεθα)· Πλουτίων χρημα(τίζων)
    μητρὸ(ς) Διδύμη(ς) ἄτ(εχνος) ἄςημ(ος) (ἐτῶν) λςʹ
    Ἀνδρόμαχος ἀδελ(φὸς) μητ(ρὸς) τῆς α(ὐτῆς)
    ἄτ(εχνος) ἄςημ(ος)   (ἐτῶν) λδʹ
15 Ἁρμίυςις ἕτ(ερος) μη[τ](ρὸς) τῆς α(ὐτῆς) ἄτ(εχνος) ἄςη[(μος) (ἐτῶν) η
    πρ(ος)γί(νεται) Ἐπι.[.].ος [Πλ]ουτίωνος
    χρη[μα(τίζοντος) μητ(ρὸς) Δι]δύμης, μητ(ρὸς)
         c.8] ἀδελ(φῆς) τοῦ πα(τρὸς) (ἐτῶν) α
            ]...προ.( ) β..λ( )
20   ]....

        .   .   .   .   .   .

        .   .   .   .   .

    ..[
    ..[
    ..[
    α[   ]..ἀμφοτ(ερ)
                      ] ὡς (ἐτῶν) ιʹ
25 κ[αὶ ὀμν]ύ(ω) τὴν Αὐρηλίου
    Ἀ[ν]τωνί[νου] Καίςαρος τοῦ

κυρίο[υ] τύχην μὴ ἐψεῦcθ(αι).
(ἔτους) ιε′ Αὐτ[οκ]ράτορος Καίсαρος
Μάρκου Αὐρηλίου Ἀντωνίνου
30 Cεβ[αcτοῦ] Ἀ[ρ]μενιακοῦ Μηδικοῦ Παρθικοῦ
Γε[ρμανικοῦ Μεγίcτου], Φαμενωθ.

. . . . . .

2 μη ͭ αcκλαταρι ͦ   3 κ⁻ υι ͦ πλουτιων ͦ   4 αυ ͭ χρημ ϛ αμφο ͭ   οξ ͮ πο ^λ   5 κε ^λ
6 λαμπρο ͭ ηγεμο ͮ   7 απογρ ϛ προc ͭ   διε ^λ ιδ ϛ αυρ—   9 οι ͨ απογρ ϛ   υ ͫ   10 ερμαι ͦ μερ ͦ οι ͨ
11 απογρ ϛ   χρημ⁻   12 μητρ ͦ διδυμ ͫ α ͭ αcη ͪ Lλϛ′   13 αδε ^λ μη ͭ   ᾱ   14 αταcη ͪ Lλδ
15 ε ͭ μη ͭ   ᾱα ͭ αc[16 ͳγι   17 μη ͭ   18 αδε ^λ   π ʾ α L   23 αμφο ͭ   24 Lι
25 ομν ͮ ?   27 εψευcθ   28 Lιε

'From Didyme, daughter of Plutarchus son of Zosimus, her mother being Asclatarion, with her guardian, her son Ploution, officially described as her son, both from the city of the Oxyrhynchi. In accordance with the orders of the prefect Caluisius Statianus, *vir clarissimus*, I register for the house-by-house registration of the past fourteenth year of Aurelius Antoninus Caesar the lord, the part of a house that I own in the district of the Hermaion, in which we are registered:

'Ploution, officially described as son of Didyme, of no trade, with no distinguishing marks, aged 36.

'Andromachus, his brother, of the same mother, of no trade, with no distinguishing marks, aged 34.

'Harmiysis, another (brother), of the same mother, of no trade, with no distinguishing marks, aged *n*.

'An addition (to the declaration) is Epi—us son of Ploution, officially described as son of Didyme, his mother being [name], sister of his father, aged 1(?).

'. . .

'. . . both . . . aged about 10.

'And I swear by the fortune of Aurelius Antoninus Caesar the lord not to have lied.

'Year 15 of Imperator Caesar Marcus Aurelius Antoninus Augustus Armeniacus Medicus Parthicus Germanicus Maximus, Phamenoth.'

4 ἐξ αὐτ(ῆc) χρημα(τίζοντοc). On this expression, typical of Oxyrhynchite documents (the term ἀπάτωρ is used elsewhere), see M. Malouta in *Pap. Congr. XXIV* (2007) 615 ff.

5–6 ὑπὸ Καλουιcίου Cτατιανοῦ. See G. Bastianini, *ZPE* 17 (1975) 298, *ZPE* 38 (1980) 83, and *ANRW* 10.1 (1988) 510; add LV **3782** (172/3) and the undated SB XX 14683 (= SPP XXII 97) and P. Bodl. 61(f), and remove P. Berl. Leihg. II 28 (see Kruse, *Königliche Schreiber* ii 756 n. 5) and P. Thmouis I 1 80.16, redated to 180–92 [HGV].

C. Caluisius Statianus is first attested in office on 24 February 170 (SB V 7528), and was still a prefect in the earlier part of 175. Besides XII **1451**, which attests him in office in the month of Phamenoth, and perhaps also later, we have P. Amst. 27, in which Statianus announces the accession of C. Auidius Cassius, and which no doubt dates from April. The first securely dated document to mention Caluisius' successor, C. Caecilius Saluianus, is BGU I 327 of 1 April 176. BGU III 847 = W. Chr. 460.13–14 (182/3), ὑπὸ Καλου[ιcίου Cτατιανοῦ τοῦ ἡγεμο]νεύcαντοc, is the last document that refers to Caluisius Statianus.

λαμπροτ(άτου) ἡγεμό(νοc). Caluisius Statianus was still in office at the time when this document was written (see previous note), hence the expansion of the abbreviations adopted (see Bastianini, *ANRW* 10.1 (1988) 584 n. 7).

9–10 ἀμφόδου Ἑρμαίο(υ). This quarter took its name from the nearby temple of Hermes. They were both in the vicinity of the Serapeum, and the quarter's western border coincided with the city walls. See J. Krüger, *Oxyrhynchos in der Kaiserzeit* (1990) 83; S. Daris, *ZPE* 132 (2000) 215–16.

10 μέρο(c) οἰκ(ίας). The part owned by the declarant of the rest of the house is not revealed, and no description is made thereof; in general this is unusual, and in Oxyrhynchus in particular it is so far unprecedented.

12 ἄτ(εχνος). With the dubious exception of P. Oslo III 97 and P. Strasb. VI 530 = C. Pap. Gr. II.1 42.13 and 57.9 (the readings are doubtful), the term is characteristic of Oxyrhynchite documents. Hombert–Préaux, *Recherches* 120, have argued that the term refers to an occupation rather than a fiscal status, though this indication certainly had a fiscal purpose. Bagnall–Frier associate the Oxyrhynchite ἄτεχνοι with the Arsinoite ἰδιῶται and the ἀργοί of Memphis, people who did not do any manual labour but lived from their landed revenues or other accumulated wealth (*Demography* 24, 46). However, it is not easy to apply this explanation to the slaves described as such (see **4998** 12 n.; cf. C. Pap. Gr. II.1 15.9 n.), nor to the five- and three-year-old girls in PSI I 53.i.16 and iv.54 (132), whose lack of profession would not need special mention.

15 ἕτ(ερος), sc. ἀδελφός. Cf. P. Oxy. Hels. 10.10 (34), P. Col. II 1a.v.2 (after 134/5 [*HGV*]), etc.

16 πρ(οc)γί(νεται). For a description of this abbreviation, π arching over ρ, see XL **2915** 20 n. Besides **4989**, the verb occurs in one other census declaration, LXXIII **4957** 16, 18 (147). Its meaning in this context may be deduced from PSI XII 1240 a.9 and b.8 (Oxy.; 222), a petition for change of status: the petitioner says that he no longer has the status under which he was declared in previous census declarations, and quotes parts of the original documents. At the time of the first of them, he was five years old, and was declared by his father as a πρωταπόγραφος, i.e., one being registered for the first time. The verb used in the declaration is προ⟨c⟩γείνεται. Therefore, it would appear that the verb in question is used to introduce πρωταπόγραφοι to a declaration that in other respects remains the same in consecutive cycles.

Ἐπι. [.] . ος. Ἐπίμ[α]χος, a name common in Oxyrhynchus, is likely.

17 μητ(ρός). This cannot refer to Didyme, because in the formula χρηματίζων μητρός, μητρός comes before the name. This suggests that the damaged name in 16 is that of a son of Ploution, followed by the formula μητρός + *name*.

18] ἀδελ(φῆς) τοῦ πα(τρός). The collocation μητρὸς *name* ἀδελφῆς (τοῦ) πατρός is fairly common; cf. PSI VIII 875.6 (1/II), BGU II 562 = W. *Chr.* 220.21 (after 117), P. Ryl. II 103.8 (134), SB XVIII 13369.9–10 (188/9), BGU II 406.iii.1 (II/III), XLIII 3096 12, 16 (223/4), etc. Here this would mean that the mother of the child is the sister of the father, i.e., of Didyme's own child. However, the type of the abbreviation poses a problem: the scribe wrote πα and added a curved stroke over π. This way of abbreviating a form of the word πατήρ seems to be unattested.

(ἐτῶν) α. One may also wish to read β.

19] . . . προ . ( ) β . . λ( ). The letter after προ, raised above the line, is τ or τ, suggesting προγ(εγραμμέν-) or πρότ(ερον); the former is more likely (the latter refers to previous ownership of property). In this case, we expect a name to follow, but the remains do not obviously suggest one. Another possibility is *name + relation*] τῆς προγ(εγραμμένης); cf. PSI I 53.i.9. At the end of the line, perhaps read βεβλ(αμμέν-), a participle used for persons with visual impairment; cf. e.g. P. Flor. I 1 = M. *Chr.* 243.2 (153) βεβλ(αμμένου) τὸ(ν) ἀριc(τερὸν) ὀφθ(αλμόν), XLI **2993** 12 (323) βεβ⟨λ⟩αμμένου τὰς ὄψεις (most other examples are Ptolemaic).

23–4] . ἀμφοτ(ερ) | [ ] . ὡς (ἐτῶν) ι. The number of lines and entries lost between these lines and line 20 is a matter for speculation. One would expect Didyme to be the first of the women to be declared, being the most senior as well as the declarant. If 16–18 have been read and interpreted correctly, then Ploution's son, being one year old, is probably the last male member of the family to be declared. If so, the entry for Didyme must have followed directly underneath, followed by Ploution's wife at some point. If this is correct, the persons mentioned in 23 would be female members of the family or slaves (of either sex), if any were present in this household. Alternatively the word ἀμφοτ(ερ) might refer back to the parents, Ploution and his wife, rather than the person concerned in this entry, or possibly one of the other brothers, about whose marital status there is no information.

The likeliest interpretation is that the combination of ἀμφοτ(ερ) and ὡc (ἐτῶν) ι´ in the next line is a reference to 'twins': Bagnall and Frier observe that instances of siblings recorded as having the same age occur too often to be credible (and more notably, in PSI I 53.i there is a case of 'twin' half-siblings; cf. BL X 235). Such references to siblings of the same age are the result of a rough rounding of ages, rather than an unusually high number of real twins (*Demography* 43–4; W. Scheidel, *BASP* 33 (1996) 48–9).

24 ὡc (ἐτῶν) ι´. Contrast 12, 14, 18, where the ages are not rounded off. On the reporting of ages in census returns, see Scheidel, *BASP* 33 (1996) 25–59.

25–7 κ[αὶ ὀμν]ύ(ω) . . . μὴ ἐψεῦcθ(αι). This short oath formula with μὴ ἐψεῦcθαι is characteristic of Oxyrhynchus.

28–31 The readings and restorations of the imperial titles assume that they were written in *Verschleifung* rather than that they were abbreviated.

M. MALOUTA

4990. Census Declaration

69/54(a)   11.5 × 12.8 cm   188/9

This is the seventh Oxyrhynchite declaration for the census of 187/8 to be published, after XXXVI **2762**, **2800**, LVIII **3918**, P. Harr. I 71, (P. Princ. III 129 =) SB XX 14310 i–ii. All were filed during the year after the year of the census. For a full list of declarations for this census, see Bagnall–Frier *Demography* 264–82, 319.

What is preserved follows the standard pattern of such documents from Oxyrhynchus. The declaration, addressed to the strategus and royal scribe (cf. I **171** descr. = SB XXII 15353), is submitted by two men who jointly own a share of a small house in the city. The papyrus breaks off at the beginning of the listing of persons. Above the main text a second hand wrote the verb ἐνε(τάγη), a novelty in texts of this type; see below, 1 n.

The back is blank.

(m.2)   ἐνε(τάγη)[
(m.1)   Ἡράμμωνι τῷ κα[ὶ Κάcτορι cτρατηγῷ καὶ Cαραπανού-
     βιδι βαcιλι[κῷ γραμματεῖ
     παρὰ Πετεαρ.[
5   Διοδώρου μητρ[ὸc
     θέcει Διογένουc ἐπικαλουμ[ένου c.4 καὶ c.4
     γένουc τοῦ κ(αὶ) Διον(υcίου?) Ἑρμογένο[υc τοῦ c.4 μητρὸc

Ἀρτέμειτος ἀμφοτ(έρων) [ἀπ' Ὀξυρύγ(χων) πόλ(εωϲ). κατὰ
τὰ κελευϲθέντα ὑπ[ὸ Τινηΐου Δημητρίου τοῦ λαμ(προτάτου)
10 ἡγε(μόνοϲ) καὶ Αὐρηλίου Οὐηριαν[οῦ] τοῦ [ἡγεμονεύϲ(αντοϲ)
ἀπογρ(αφόμεθα) πρὸϲ τὴν τοῦ διελ(θόντοϲ) κη (ἔτουϲ) Αὐρηλίο̣[υ Κομμόδου
Ἀντωνίνου Καίϲαροϲ τοῦ κυρίου κατ' [οἰκ(ίαν) ἀπο(γραφὴν)
τὸ ὑπάρχον ἡμεῖν ἐξ ἴϲου ἐπ' ἀμφόδ(ου) Δρ[όμου
Θοήριδοϲ πρότ(ερον) Ἐπιτέλουϲ Ἐπιτέλουϲ [τοῦ Ἐπι-
15 τέλουϲ μητ(ρὸϲ) Θαΐδοϲ ἀπὸ τῆϲ (αὐτῆϲ) πόλ(εωϲ) κληρο[νομι-
κῷ δικαίῳ ἀκολούθ(ωϲ) ᾗ ἔθετο διαθ(ήκῃ) τῇ καὶ λυθ[εί-
ϲῃ οἰκείδιον [ ]..... μέροϲ ἐφ' οὗ ἀπογρ[αφόμεθα
αὐτὸϲ [ἐ]γὼ [Πετεαρ.].. ( ) [.].[

1 εν^ε   7 του^κ Διο̄   8 l. Ἀρτέμιτοϲ   αμφο^τ   10 ηγε^−   11 απογρ∫   διε^λ κη∫
13 ὕπαρχον   αμφο^δ   l. ἡμῖν   14 προ^τ   15 μη^τ θαϊδοϲ   ᾱπο^λ   16 ακολου^θ
δια^θ   17 l. οἰκίδιον   18 .. ⁻

(2nd hand) 'It has been enrolled (or: attached).'
(1st hand) 'To Herammon alias Castor, strategus, and Sarapanubis, royal scribe, from Petear—son of . . . , grandson of Diodorus, mother . . . , adopted son of Diogenes surnamed . . . , and from —genes alias Dionysius(?) son of Hermogenes, grandson of . . . , mother Artemis, both from the city of the Oxyrhynchi. According to the orders of the prefect Tineius Demetrius, *vir clarissimus*, and Aurelius Verianus, the ex-prefect, we register for the house by house registration of the past 28th year of Aurelius Commodus Antoninus Caesar the lord, a . . . part of a small house, formerly belonging to Epiteles son of Epiteles, grandson of Epiteles, mother Thais, from the same city, in the quarter of the Avenue of Thoeris, belonging to us in equal shares by right of inheritance in accordance with the testament that was opened, in which we register ourselves:
'I, myself, Petear— . . .'

1 ἐνε(τάγη). The verb is part of archival annotations in XL **2892** i 31 = ii 31 (269) ἐνετάγη β (ἔτουϲ) Φαῶφι; the same verb form but in a different context occurs XL **2906** ii 23 (270/71?) and **2936** ii 9, 12, 15, 18, 21 (271/2). There are similar annotations in a very few census declarations, but other terms are used: ἐλ(ήφθη) ι (ἔτουϲ), μη(νὸϲ) Καιϲαρείου α in SB XII 10788c.45; παρε(τέθη) in XII **1547** 4 (119); ἐγδ(όϲιμον) in XII **1548** 1 (202/3). For other verbs used at the end of such documents, see L. Capponi, *ZPE* 140 (2002) 179 (notes to ll. 18 and 19).

If something was written in the lost part of the line, this could have been the date in which the census was filed.

2 Ἡράμμωνι τῷ κα[ὶ Κάϲτορι ϲτρατηγῷ. See Whitehorne, *Strategi and Royal Scribes*² 100.

2–3 Ϲαραπανού]βιδι βαϲιλι[κῷ γραμματεῖ. See Whitehorne, *Strategi and Royal Scribes*² 164.

4 Πετεαρ.[. Names beginning Πετεαρ- are not common in the Oxyrhynchite nome, and so it is a pity that too little remains of the letter on the edge to allow a reading.

4–6 There are two possible reconstructions of this sequence of names: Πετεαρ.[— *name of father τοῦ*] Διοδώρου μητρ[ὸϲ *name* (υἱοῦ)] θέϲει Διογένουϲ κτλ. (adopted in the translation above); or Πετεαρ.[— ὁ καὶ *name*] Διοδώρου μητρ[ὸϲ κτλ.

6 θέϲει. On adoption, see Taubenschlag, *Law*² 133–4 with n. 12; Berger, *EDRL* 350 s.v. Adoptio. θέϲει occurs in papyri from the first to the third century, mostly in documents from Oxyrhynchus. It is

added to the name of a person either before or after the name of the mother; the following constructions are attested: ὁ δεῖνα + *name of father* + *name of grandfather* (with τοῦ) + μητρὸς δεῖνος + θέcει δεῖνος (VII **1123** 2, SB XIV 11337.1–2, SB XX 14395.8–11, P. Mich. XVIII 789.5–6); ὁ δεῖνα + *name of father* (with τοῦ) + θέcει δεῖνος + μητρός δεῖνος (P. Wash. Univ. I 2.2–3); ὁ δεῖνα + *name of father* (+ *name of grandfather* with τοῦ) + θέcει δεῖνος (P. Mert. I 18.17–18; PSI VII 732.1–3, I **46** 5–7; III **502** 6–7; XIV **1719** 4–5; LXVI **4531** 3–4); ὁ δεῖνα θέcει δεῖνος (XXXI **2583** 2).

ἐπικαλουμ[ένου refers to Petear—, not to Diogenes, since the usual formula is ὁ δεῖνα + *name of father* + ἐπικαλούμενος δεῖνα; see R. Calderini, *Aegyptus* 21 (1941) 254–5; P. Petaus pp. 54–63; D. Hobson, *BASP* 26 (1989) 168–71.

7 —γένους τοῦ κ(αὶ) Διον(υcίου?) Ἑρμογένο[υς τοῦ *c*.4 μητρὸς]. At the beginning, read Διο]|γένους, Ἑρμο]|γένους, etc. The name of the grandfather would have been *c*.4 letters long; it is of course possible that this was not written, but without it the line would be short.

8 Ἀρτέμειτος. The name Ἄρτεμις is attested between the second and the early fourth centuries; see O. Masson, *ZPE* 66 (1986) 126–30.

8–9 κατὰ τὰ κελευσθέντα. After this phrase the name of the prefect almost always follows except for some documents from the Arsinoite nome. The edicts of the prefects contained the order for the census return, and described the procedures involved; when they were issued is uncertain. See most recently Jördens, *Statthalterliche Verwaltung* 68–9, 81–6.

9–10 For references to the prefects Tineius Demetrius and his predecessor Aurelius Verianus in census declarations, see Jördens, *Statthalterliche Verwaltung* 532–3.

11 πρὸς τὴν τοῦ διελ(θόντος) κη (ἔτους). The time limit for the implementation of the census edict was the last day of the year following the census year (no declaration dates from the year after that); cf. Kruse, *Königliche Schreiber* 67.

13 ἐξ ἴcου. For declarations of property held jointly, see Hombert–Préaux, *Recherches* 57–9; also above, **4983** 12–14 n. A declaration is very rarely submitted by all the owners, who in most cases are relatives; for examples of more than one owner, see Hombert–Préaux, *Recherches* 58 n. 1.

13–14 ἐπ' ἀμφόδ(ου) Δρ[όμου] Θοήριδος. For this *amphodon*, see S. Daris, *Dizionario* Suppl. iv 98.

14–15 πρότ(ερον) Ἐπιτέλους Ἐπιτέλους [τοῦ Ἐπι]τέλους. The name Ἐπιτέλης is rare in the papyri; it is attested in other parts of the Greek world, mostly in the Classical and Hellenistic periods; see the various volumes of *LGPN*, under the name. It is remarkable that three generations had the same name, though this practice was not unusual (see Hobson, loc. cit. 167).

15–16 κλη[ο[νομι]κῷ δικαίῳ. For this phrase, attested only in Oxyrhynchite documents, see S. Daris, *ZPE* 85 (1991) 272.

16 ἀκολούθ(ως) ᾗ ἔθετο διαθ(ήκῃ). This collocation with minor variations also occurs in BGU VII 1662.7 (182), P. Heid. IV 301.2 (192), P. Oslo II 24.13 (131?), CPR I 102.10–11 (I/II); cf. also P. Freib. II 8.10 (143), and XIV **1648** 53 (II). The phrase τίθεμαι διαθήκην was used in the second century. From then onwards other phrases were in use such as ἀκολούθ(ως) ᾗ παρέθετο διαθήκῃ (SB XVI 12950.18; XIV **1725** 21), ἀκολούθ(ως) ᾗ ἀπολέλοιπεν διαθήκῃ (IX **1208** 11), or ἀκολούθ(ως) τῇ διαθήκῃ (PSI VIII 940.24; X 1101.10; LIV **3756** 11; SPP XX 5.12).

16–17 διαθ(ήκῃ) τῇ καὶ λυθ[εί]cῃ. See N. Litinas, *ZPE* 117 (1997) 210 no. 5.

17 οἰκείδιον [ ] . . . . . μέρος. For the term οἰκίδιον, see G. Husson, *OIKIA* 207–9. The itacistic spelling is common; cf. XII **1538** 2, 8, XIX **2236** 12, 24, L **3560** 26.

We have not been able to read what comes between οἰκείδιον and μέρος. Only some letter-tops survive, while something may have been added above the line. One expects to find an adjective qualifying οἰκείδιον or a numeral modifying μέρος, but the construction is in any case unusual: when a part of a property is declared, we have μέρος + genitive(s). The late P. J. Sijpesteijn tentatively suggested [κα]τὰ δ' μέρος, which would give good sense but is unparalleled. It is also unclear whether τὸ ὑπάρχον in line 13 refers to οἰκείδιον or to μέρος.

18 αὐτὸς [ἐ]γὼ [. The standard formula for introducing the first name in Oxyrhynchite second- and third-century census declarations is (ὁ) αὐτὸς ἐγώ; see Hombert-Préaux, *Recherches* 113. But contrast **4989** 11.

N. LITINAS

4991. Census Declaration

20 3B.36/H(1–5)b   3.9 × 9.5 cm   216/17

The upper part of a declaration for the census of 215/16, submitted some time after the year of the census. It is addressed to the *laographoi* of the district of Metroon in Oxyrhynchus; the docket on the back may suggest that the document was filed in their archives. Aurelius Polycarpus, the declarant, is a dependant (ἴδιος) of Marcus Aurelius Achilleus alias Isidorus, an eminent Oxyrhynchite (see 4–6 n.). The text breaks off at the point where the property registered was described. This probably belonged to Achilleus, as the docket implies (see 22 n.). Compare BGU VII 1580 (147), where a slave registers vacant property belonging to his mistresses, or BGU I 57.ii (160/61?) (re-ed. *ZPE* 163 (2007) 150–52), XIII 2223 (175), and P. Mich. VI 370 (189), in which *phrontistai* of various women likewise declare vacant properties.

Besides **4991**, the other Oxyrhynchite declarations for this census are XLVII **3347** and SB XXVI 16671–74; for declarations from other regions, see Bagnall–Frier, *Demography* 291–9, 320–21 (note that P. Bakchias 137 = SB XXVI 16538).

     λαογρ(άφοις) Μητρῴου
     παρὰ Αὐρηλίου
     Πολυκάρπ[ο]υ ἰδίου
     Μάρκου Αὐρηλ[ίο]υ
5   Ἀχιλλέως τοῦ καὶ Ἰσιδώ(ρου)
     καὶ ὡς χρη(ματίζει). κατὰ τὰ κελ(ευσθέντα)
     ὑπὸ Οὐαλερίου Δάτου
     τοῦ λαμ(προτάτου) ἡγε(μόνος) καὶ Αὐ-
     ρηλίου Ἀντινόου
10   τοῦ κρ(ατίστου) διαδεξα(μένου) τὴν
     ἡγε(μονίαν) ἀπογρ(άφομαι) πρὸς τὴν
     τοῦ δι[ελ]θ(όντος) [κ]δ [(ἔτους)] Μάρκου
     Αὐρηλίου Σεουήρου
     Ἀντ[ωνίνου Ε]ὐσε[βο]ῦς
15   [Εὐτυχοῦς Σεβαστοῦ κατ' οἰκίαν
     ἀπ[ογραφὴν τὴν ὑπάρχου-

ca[ν
αυ̣[
κε̣.[
20   κυρι̣.[
α̣.τ.[
. .

Back, downwards along the fibres:
(m.2)   //Μητρῴου (vac.) Αὐρηλ(ίου) Ἀχιλλ(έως) . . . . . [

1 λαογρϚ   5 ιϲιδ̅ω̅   6 χρη̅   κε̅λ   8 λαμϚηγε̅   10 κρϚδιαδεξα̅
11 ηγε̅απογρϽ   22 αυρη̅λαχιλλ'

'To the registrars of Metroon from Aurelius Polycarpus, dependant of Marcus Aurelius Achilleus alias Isidorus and however he is styled. In accordance with the orders given by the prefect Valerius Datus, *vir clarissimus*, and by Aurelius Antinous, *vir egregius*, the former acting prefect, I register for the house-by-house registration of the past 24th year of Marcus Aurelius Severus Antoninus Pius Felix Augustus, the (house?) belonging to . . .'
Back: (2nd hand) '(District) of Metroon; of Aurelius Achilleus . . .'

1 λαογρ(άφοιϲ). For the resolution in the plural, see A. Papathomas, *APF* 42 (1996) 203–4, but contrast L. Capponi, *ZPE* 140 (2002) 179. The addressing of Oxyrhynchite declarations solely to *laographoi* is a third-century feature; this is the earliest among them.

Μητρῴου. For this Oxyrhynchite quarter, named after the temple of Cybele located there, see J. Krüger, *Oxyrhynchos in der Kaiserzeit* (1990) 84; S. Daris, *ZPE* 132 (2000) 218.

2–3 Αὐρηλίου Πολυκάρπ[ο]υ ἰδίου. On the use of the term ἴδιοϲ in the sense of 'dependant, agent, employee', see H. Cuvigny, *BIFAO* 102 (2002) 148–9. The absence of Polycarpus' patronymic and *origo* may point to his dependent status, but the presence of the *gentilicium* Aurelius implies that he was not a slave, as ἴδιοι often were; see H. Koskenniemi, *Studien zur Idee und Phraseologie des Griechischen Briefes bis 400 n. Chr.* (1956) 104, and L **3597** 15 n. Perhaps Polycarpus was Achilleus' freedman. Cf. XIV **1711** 4–5 (late III), which attests another ἴδιοϲ of a prominent person.

4–6 Μάρκου Αὐρηλ[ίο]υ Ἀχιλλέωϲ τοῦ καὶ Ἰϲιδώ(ρου) καὶ ὡϲ χρη(ματίζει). Assuming that the alias is correctly resolved (Ἰϲιδω(ρίωνοϲ) or Ἰϲιδω(ριανοῦ) are much less likely alternatives), he may be identified with Achilleus alias Isidorus in VI **908** = W. *Chr.* 426.15–16 (199), described as ex-*exegetes*, gymnasiarch and eutheniarch, perhaps the same person as Aurelius Achilleus alias Isidorus in VII **1046** 10 (218/19); see P. Hamb. IV p. 228 with n. 46 (no. 74). The phrase καὶ ὡϲ χρη(ματίζει) is an implicit reference to his titles, those mentioned in **908** and perhaps others too.

7–11 On Valerius Datus and Aurelius Antinous in census declarations, see Jördens, *Statthalterliche Verwaltung* 84–6, 533.

16–18 τὴν ὑπάρχου]ϲά[ν μοι οἰκίαν is what we would expect if this were Polycarpus' own house, with αὐ[λήν following in 18. But if the house belonged to his employer (see introd.), the text may have run τὴν ὑπάρχου]|ϲα[ν τῷ προγεγρ(αμμένῳ) Μάρκῳ] Αὐ[ρηλίῳ Ἀχιλλεῖ κτλ.

19 κε̣.[. The damaged letter may be tau; it is not iota.

20 κυρι̣.[. It is difficult to account for a form of κύριοϲ or κυριεύειν in this part of the declaration.

21 α̣.τ.[. Perhaps αὐτό[ϲ, which recalls phrases such as ἀπογράφομαι αὐτὸϲ ἐγώ.

22 Μητρῴου (vac.) Αὐρηλ(ίου) Ἀχιλλ(έως) . . . . . [. The unread part of the line does not seem to refer to Polycarpus. The prominence given to Achilleus suggests that the property declared was his. Compare the docket of P. Col. X 262 (Oxy., 160), the only parallel among documents of this type: ἀπογρ(αφὴ) Ὀξυρύγχων πόλεως· Ἀμόι(τος) καὶ τ(ῶν) τέκ(νων).

R. HATZILAMBROU

4992. NOTIFICATION OF DEATH

26 3B.49/H(1–4)a   6 × 20.8 cm   223/4

A father gives notice of the death of his son, which took place in the very year when the son turned fourteen years old and thus became of fiscal age (and in this case, one may think, eligible for admission to the metropolitan or gymnasial classes). A curious feature is that the date clause contains no reference to month and day. There is no addressee, but the declarant's subscription, in the gawky capitals of the 'slow writer', indicates that this is not a copy. On this type of document, see **4996–8** introd.

The back is blank.

```
     παρὰ Αὐρηλίου Cαρᾶτος Βηcᾶ-
     τος μη(τρὸς) Ζωϊλοῦτ̣[ος] ἀπ' Ὀξυ(ρύγχων)
     πόλεως. ὁ υἱός μου
     Β[η]c̣ᾶς μη(τρὸς) Cιντοτοῆ[το]c ἐπ(ικαλουμένης) Εὐ-
5    δα̣[ι]μονίδος προcβὰc εἰc (τεccαρεcκαιδεκαετεῖc)
     τῷ ἐνε(cτῶτι) γ (ἔτει) ἐτελεύτηcεν
     τῷ α(ὐτῷ) γ (ἔτει). διὸ ἐπιδίδωμι
     τὸ ὑπόμνημα ἀξιῶν ἀναγρ(αφῆναι)
     α[ὐ]τὸν ἐν τῇ τῶν τετελ(ευτηκότων)
10   τ[άξ]ει ὡc καθήκει καὶ ὀμνύω
     τὴν Μάρκου Αὐρηλίου
     Cεουήρου Ἀλεξάνδρου Καίcαροc
     τοῦ κυρίου τύχην μὴ ἐψεῦcθαι.
     (ἔτουc) γ̄ Αὐτοκράτοροc Καίcαροc Μάρκου
15   Αὐρηλίου Cεουήρου Ἀλεξάνδρου
     Εὐ[cεβοῦc Εὐ]τυχοῦc Cεβαcτοῦ.
(m.2) Αὐ[ρ]ήλιοc Cαρᾶc Βηcᾶτοc
     ἐπιδέδωκα̣ καὶ ὀμώμεκα
     τὸ[ν] ὅρχον.
```

2, 4 μη   2 οξυ   4 ἐπ   5 ιδϛ   6 ἐνεϛγϛ   7 αγϛ   8 αναγρϛ   9 τετελ   14 L   18 l. ὀμώμοκα   19 l. ὅρκον

4992. NOTIFICATION OF DEATH

'From Aurelius Saras son of Besas, mother Zoilous, from the city of the Oxyrhynchi. My son Besas, mother Sintotoes called Eudaemonis, having advanced into (the category of) the fourteen-year-olds in the current 3rd year, died in the same 3rd year. For this reason I submit this application, requesting that he be registered in the list of the dead as is fitting, and I swear by the fortune of Marcus Aurelius Severus Alexander Caesar the lord not to have lied. Year 3 of Imperator Caesar Marcus Aurelius Severus Alexander Pius Felix Augustus.'

(2nd hand) 'I, Aurelius Saras son of Besas, have submitted (the application) and sworn the oath.'

1 For the absence of the addressee, not common in texts of this type, see LXV **4479** 1 n.

2 Ζωϊλοῦτ[ος]. This name has occurred in two other papyri from Oxyrhynchus, viz. I **91** 4 (187) and PSI III 164.6 (287).

4 ἐπ(ικαλουμένης). See **4990** 6 and n.

5 προϲβὰϲ εἰϲ (τεϲϲαρεϲκαιδεκαετεῖϲ). This expression has not occurred in any other such text; it is mostly found in the context of the *epikrisis* procedure (e.g. VII **1028** 11–12 or IX **1202** 18–19). The age of the deceased is specified only in a very few texts, and then it mostly refers to children under the age of fourteen; cf. C. Pap. Gr. II.1 p. 14.

7–8 διὸ ἐπιδίδωμι . . . ἀξιῶν. See **4479** 8 ff. n.

18–19 On this phrase, see **4479** 25–6 n.

N. GONIS

4993–4995. Registrations of Children

14 1B.203/K(1)a 24 × 15 cm

A part of a *tomos synkollesimos* with portions of four *kollemata*. Its inventory number is adjacent to **4996–4998**, from a *tomos* of notices of death, which date from the same period. **4994** and **4998** are addressed to the phylarch of Oxyrhynchus, and there is no reason to doubt that the other items were addressed to the same official. It seems likely that there were two distinct rolls originally kept in the same office and discarded at the same time rather than that they all belonged to the same composite roll. On the issue of such rolls in general, see W. Clarysse, 'Tomoi Syncollesimoi', in M. Brosius (ed.), *Ancient Archives and Archival Traditions* (2003) 344–59; for a list, see http://www.trismegistos.org/arch/tomos.xls.

The two items that are better preserved (**4994–5**) request the registration of two boys aged two and thirteen years respectively. Both boys belong to the privileged class of *dodekadrachmoi*, and one of them was born into a family who are members of the gymnasium (cf. also **4993**). The aim of these documents seems to have been to register children in their parents' status, which was usually a privileged one. The discussion offered by P. Mertens, *Les Services de l'état civil et le contrôle de la population à Oxyrhynchus* (1958) 49–65, remains fundamental. There are some forty published documents this type, most of which come from Oxyrhynchus. A list is given by N. Cohen in R. Katzoff et al. (edd.), *Classical Studies in Honor of David Sohlberg* (1996) 391–2 (reproduced in P. Berl. Cohen 12 introd.), supplemented by

A. Jördens, P. Bingen 105 introd., who also offers an overview of earlier views with further reflections on the issue. Cf. also Kruse, *Königliche Schreiber* i 143 n. 256. Other such texts published more recently are P. Gen. inv. 341 (ed. *ZPE* 141 (2002) 155–7), and SB XXVI 16803. See also **4999**.

Of the first *kollema*, only the ends of lines are preserved, and only a few preserve more than three or four letters, while of the last *kollema* (not transcribed below) no more than ten not consecutive lines survive, which mostly contain one or two letters. Parts are missing from the top and foot of the first, third, and fourth *kollemata*. Since the second *kollema* is the only one preserved at full height, no conclusions can be drawn about the technical aspects of this *tomos*. The second and third *kollemata* seem to have been aligned at the lower end, which was normal practice (Clarysse, 'Tomoi Syncollesimoi' 354). If indeed, as the preserved part of the first *kollema* would indicate, the first two *kollemata* were also aligned at the top, this might point to a roll where the sheets all have the same height; but it may only be a coincidence. The reason why such rolls were aligned at the foot may have been that it was easier to align the part closer to the person who was sticking the *kollemata* onto the roll, or it may have to do with the way the *tomoi* were stored; if they were stored upright (in *capsae*?), they would need to have one level surface when rolled up, or else they would be subject to damage. But even if they were stored horizontally, it would be practical to have a level surface propped up against the wall.

Under the signed declaration, the two *kollemata* whose lower part is preserved (**4994–5**), contain official dockets that summarize the contents of the declaration, giving the district of provenance, the name of the person declared, his age and status. After the documents were glued into the *tomos*, numbers were added at the top (intact only in **4994**), repeated after the docket (**4994** 36, **4995** 33), in both documents by the same scribe; this is the number of the *kollema* within the *tomos*, as was common practice. This part of the roll will have contained *kollemata* numbered 33–36. Another official annotation (again, by the same scribe in both cases) was added below, and this refers to another *kollema*; its purpose is unclear (see **4994** 37 n.).

The back is blank.

4993

14 1B.203/K(1)a col. i   253/4?

        Top?

            πό]λεως
            ]
            ]ου
            ].ε..
5   ]. ος
            ]ευς
            ].cτου
            ]αρ..
            ].
10   ].ορ.α[.]
           ]τρ...[.]
       Αὐ]⟦ρήλιον⟧
           ]οντα πρὸς
   ἀπὸ γυμ]ναςίου
15   ].ξ......
           ]...ος
           ]
     Οὐαλερι]ανοῦ
           ]
20   ]
  . . .

4994

14 1B.203/K(1)a col. ii   26 May or 24 June 254

(m.5)   ⦻ λδ′
(m.1) Αὐρηλίῳ Ἡρᾷ, φυλάρχῃ τῆc Ὀξυρυγχ-
      ειτῶν πόλεωc τοῦ ἐνεcτῶτοc α (ἔτουc),
      παρὰ Αὐρηλίου Διοcκόρου Ἀντωνᾶ-
5   τοc μητ(ρὸc) Ἰcαρίου καὶ τῆc τούτου γυ-
      ναικὸc Ϛαραποῦτοc Ἁρμιύcιοc τοῦ
      Ἡρακλείδου μητρὸc Διογενεί-

δος ἀπ' Ὀξυρύγχων πόλεως.
βουλόμεθα πρώτως ἀναγρα-
10 φῆναι ἐπὶ τῆς ὑπαρχούςης ἐ-
μοὶ τῷ Διοςκόρῳ ἐπ' ἀμφόδου
Πλατείας οἰκίας τὸν γεγονότα ἡ-
μεῖν ἐξ ἀλλήλων υἱὸν Αὐρή-
λιον Ἀρτεμίδωρον (δωδεκάδραχμον) ἀπὸ
15 γυμναςίου ὄντα πρὸς τὸ ἐνε-
ϲτ{ωτ}ὸϲ α (ἔτος) (ἐτῶν) β ὡς καθήκει
καὶ ὀμνύομεν τὴν τῶν κυρίω(ν)
ἡμῶν Οὐαλεριανοῦ καὶ Γαλλιηνοῦ
Ϲεβαςτῶν τύχην μὴ ἐψεῦ-
20 ϲθαι. (ἔτους) α' Αὐτοκρατόρων
Καιϲάρων Πουπλίου Λικιννίου
Οὐαλεριανοῦ καὶ Πουπλίου
Λικιννίου Οὐαλεριανοῦ
Γαλλιηνοῦ Εὐςεβῶν
25 Εὐτυχῶν Ϲεβαςτῶν, Παῦνι ..
(m.2) Αὐρήλιος Διόςκορο⟨ς⟩ ἐπιδέδωκα καὶ ὤμοςα
τὸν ὅρκον. (m.3) Αὐρηλία Cαραποῦς
Ἁρ]μιύϲιος ςυνεπιδέδωκα καὶ ὤμοςα τ[ὸν
30 ὅρκο]ν. Αὐρήλ(ιος) Βηςαρίων ἔγραψα ὑπὲρ αὐτῆς
φαμ]ένης μὴ εἰδέναι γράμματα.
(vac.)
(m.4) Πλατείας
Ἀρτεμίδωρος Διοςκόρου τοῦ
Ἀντωνᾶτος μητ(ρὸς) Cαραποῦτος
35 ⟦Ἡρακλ⟧ Ἁρμιύϲιος τοῦ Ἡρακλ[εί]δου
(ἐτῶν) β (δωδεκάδραχμος) ἀπὸ γυμ(ναςίου). (m. 5) λδ
(vac.)
(m.6) κατεκ( ) κολ(λημα-) ρμη

3 l. -ιτῶν   αϛ   5 μη²·ι·ϲαριου   7 l. Διογενί-   13 l. -μῖν   14 ιβϛ
16 αϛLβ   17 κυριω̄   20 L   27 ὤμοϲα: ο corr. from α   30 αυρηλ   34 μητ
36 Lβ ιβϛ   γυμϛ   37 κατεκκολ

(5th hand) '34'
(1st hand) 'To Aurelius Heras, phylarch of the city of the Oxyrhynchites for the current 1st year,

4994. REGISTRATION OF A CHILD 115

from Aurelius Dioscorus son of Antonas, his mother being Isarion, and his wife Sarapous daughter of Harmiysis son of Heraclides, her mother being Diogenis, from the city of the Oxyrhynchi.

'We wish to register for the first time, in the house that belongs to me, Dioscorus, in the quarter of Plateia, our son Aurelius Artemidorus, who was born to us from one another, a payer of twelve drachmae and a member of the gymnasium, and who in the current 1st year is 2 years old, as is fitting, and we swear by the fortune of our lords Valerianus and Gallienus Augusti not to have lied.

'Year 1 of Imperatores Caesares Publius Licinius Valerianus and Publius Licinius Valerianus Gallienus Pii Felices Augusti, Payni 1 (or 30).'

(2nd hand) 'I, Aurelius Dioscorus, have presented (the notification) and have sworn the oath.'

(3rd hand) 'I, Aurelia Sarapous daughter of Harmiysis, have joined in presenting (this notification) and sworn the oath. I, Aurelius Besarion, wrote on her behalf since she claims not to know letters.'

(4th hand) 'The quarter of Plateia. Artemidorus son of Dioscorus son of Antonas, his mother being Sarapous daughter of Harmiysis son of Heraclides, two years old, a payer of twelve drachmae (and) a member of the gymnasium.' (5th hand) '34'

(6th hand) '. . . *kollema* 148.'

1 At the top left of the *kollema*, there are two long slanting strokes. These strokes appear in a characteristic pattern in both this roll as well as **4996–8** (lost in certain points). They were added after the separate sheets were glued together (see **4997** 33; cf. a comparative selection illustrating the position of the sheet before the writing in G. Messeri Savorelli, R. Pintaudi, *ZPE* 100 (1994) 196–8). They occur at the top of the document, to mark the point where the main body of the text starts, and then again before the official docket that contains the name of the person being declared. They were probably a kind of demarcation, intended to facilitate reference. Something similar may be seen at the top of C. Pap. Gr. II.1 40, an Oxyrhynchite death declaration of *c*.150.

2 Αὐρηλίῳ Ἡρᾷ. The phylarch Aurelius Heras is also the addressee of **4998** and probably of **4995**. The dated documents that attest him are VIII **1119** = W. *Chr.* 397 (16 August 253; see BL I 332, II.2 98), which refers to him as phylarch-to-be in 'year 4' (of the Galli); XXXVI **2763**, a surety for Heras during his term of office, dated year 1 = 253/4; **4994** of May/June 254; and **4998** of 253/4. The 'incoming' year 4 of **1119** came to be year 1 of Valerian and Gallienus, and so all references to Heras relate to year 253/4. Assuming that the phylarch served only for one year (Mertens, *Services* 22; Lewis, *Compulsory Public Services*[2] 50), Heras is not the addressee of **4996**, which dates from year 2; but his name should be restored in **4995** 1, dated 6 January 254. We do not know the name of the phylarch of 254/5.

φυλάρχῃ. The office of a phylarch was a liturgy (cf. IX **1187** of 254). Candidates were nominated by the *demos*, not the *boule*, and were chosen by the strategus; see Mertens, *Services* 25–8. His office was held within the city, and he acted on his own, but contrast SB IV 7375, possibly from Hermopolis (see Mertens, *Services* 23), of 222–35, which refers to four phylarchs. This latter document offers the only attestation of the office before 245–8 (XXXIII **2664** 15), by which time the phylarch had replaced the *amphodogrammateus*; see P. J. Parsons, *JRS* 57 (1967) 136). The expressions used to determine his term of office, administrative duties and geographical limits are the same as those used for the *amphodogrammateus*. The declarations of birth are part of the relevant evidence: we find them addressed to the *amphodogrammateus* (X **1267**, XII **1552**), the phylarch (PSI XII 1257; cf. XLVI **3295**, P. Köln II 87), and later to the *systates* (P. Corn. 18, P. Fuad 13, PSI III 164, XLIII **3137**, XLIV **3183**), who took over the phylarch's responsibilities. The same succession of officials may be observed in the declarations of death. The phylarch continued to function even in years when his tribe was not serving, and was still responsible for keeping records (but as an 'ex-phylarch'), at least records of the corn dole (XL **2892–2940** introd., pp. 7–8). For further bibliography and documentation, see Mertens, *Services* 16–29, and R. Alston, *The City in Roman and Byzantine Egypt* (2002) 145–6.

2–3 Ὀξυρυγχ|ειτῶν. The reason for this wrong syllabification is unclear; the scribe does not make such a mistake anywhere else, and in most other lines he does not seem as pressed to make the most of the whole width of the line.

8 Ὀξυρύγχων. At this time, Ὀξυρύγχων denotes provenance, and refers to the name of the city as a geographical term, while Ὀξυρυγχιτῶν (here in 2–3) is used 'als ein politisches Gebilde', and complements descriptions of municipal officials (D. Hagedorn, ZPE 12 (1973) 279).

Two minor corrections may be recorded here. In P. Fouad 52.2 (after 272), where the edition reads ἐνάρχῳ πρυτά[νει τῆς λαμπρ]ᾶς καὶ λαμπροτάτης Ὀξυρύγχ(ων) π[όλεως, read Ὀξυρυγχ(ιτῶν); sim. in the restored P. Col. VIII 222.2 (160/61) [τοῖς ἀγορανόμοις | Ὀξ(υρύγχων)].

9 πρώτως. The child is being declared here for the first time. The boy is two years old; there are, however, documents where a πρωταπόγραφος can be up to thirteen years old, and such a case is found in **4995**; cf. also **4999**, where the child is twelve years old. The declaration could be made any time up to the child's fourteenth birthday.

11–12 ἀμφόδου Πλατείας. The location of this quarter is uncertain. In his schematic representation of the twelve names preserved in XL **2928**, Krüger, Oxyrhynchos 371, places it in the south/south-east, in the vicinity of ἄμφοδον Κρητικοῦ and ἄμφοδον Ἑρμαίου. Alston suggests it is the Πλατεία τοῦ θεάτρου, and since the area where the theatre was situated is known, he places this quarter in that vicinity, i.e., very centrally in the city, towards the south-west. The district had gymnasial residents, and a magistrate owned property here (Alston, The City 154). See further S. Daris, ZPE 132 (2000) 219–20, who is sceptical about the identification with the ἄμφοδον Πλατείας θεάτρου.

12–13 ἡμεῖν ἐξ ἀλλήλων. This is a standard phrase, though it may seem rather pleonastic, and indeed ἐξ ἀλλήλων is often omitted.

14 (δωδεκάδραχμον). Cf. **4995** 12, **4996** 9. This is the term used in the Oxyrhynchite nome for privileged citizens who had to pay a lower rate of poll-tax. In order to acquire this status, eligible boys had to undergo the process known as ἐπίκρισις.

14–15 ἀπὸ γυμνασίου. Cf. **4993** 14, **4996** 9–10. The class of οἱ ἀπὸ γυμνασίου, instituted in Oxyrhynchus in 4/5, designates an elite class within that of the metropolites. It was a hereditary privilege and was under strict control, whereby one's Greek ancestry had to be confirmed, and the person who wanted to be recognized as belonging to this class had to go through the ἐπίκρισις. See the recent summary by S. Bussi, Le élites locali nella provincia d'Egitto di prima età imperiale (2008) 17–20.

16 ὡς καθήκει. We expect something on the lines of διὸ ἐπιδίδομεν τὸ ὑπόμνημα to come before this (cf. **4995** 14–15), or one of the longer variants of the formula. The scribe seems to have omitted this by accident.

25 Παυνι . The figure is ⳼ or λ. Under this line there is a long paragraphus, showing the end of the main body of the document. Cf. **4997** 24.

26–31 It is not surprising that the mother of a member of the gymnasial class was illiterate, but it is remarkable that his father is a βραδέως γράφων, signing the declaration with evident difficulty in a shaky capital.

32–6 We find a similar docket in **4995** 29–32; see also XLVI **3295** 28 (285), P. Corn. 18.25–31, XXXVIII **2855** 17–18 (both 291), XLIII **3137** 18–21, XLIV **3183** 21–5 (both 292).

37 κατεκ( ). The abbreviation is marked by a long oblique stroke crossing through κ, and is followed by a short blank space. The same annotation occurs at the foot of **4995**, and seems to be the same as the note added at the end of **4996** and **4997**, where, however, it is followed by a different text. Its meaning is unclear. One could think of κατεκ(ολλήθη), though the verb is not attested in any other papyrus, but this is not the word written in **4996** 45 and **4997** 37.

κολ(λημα-) ρμη. The purpose of this reference is unknown. For another obscure mention of kollemata in an official subscription, see L **3565** 40, a census return of 245, discussed by Kruse, Königliche Schreiber i 117 n. 174.

4995

14 1B.203/K(1)a col. iii   6 January 254

      Ἀ[ὐρηλίῳ Ἡρᾷ
      .[
      τ.[
      δ[
5   θ[
      .[
      [
      [
      . . . .
10 Αὐρ]ήλ(ιον) Τούρβωνα
      μητρὸς Φιλοῦτος
      .].τα γενο( ) (δωδεκαδραχμ-)..
      πρὸς τὸ ἐν(εστὸς) α (ἔτος) (ἐτῶν) ιγ.
      δι[ὸ] ἐπιδίδωμι τὸ
15 ὑπ[ό]μνη(μα) ὡς καθήκ(ει).
      (ἔτους) α″ Αὐτοκρατόρων
      Καισάρων Πουπλίου
      Λικιννίου Οὐαλεριανοῦ
      καὶ Πουπλίου Λικιννίου
20 Οὐαλεριανοῦ Γαλλιηνοῦ
      Εὐσεβῶν Εὐτυχῶν
      Σεβαστῶν, Τυβι ια.
(m.2) Αὐρήλ(ιος) Ἀχιλλεὺς ἐπι-
      δέδωκα. Αὐρή(λιος) Θέων
25 ὁ] καὶ Ἀσκληπιάδης ἐπικα-
      λούμενος Ζωίλος ἔγρα-
      ψα ὑπὲρ αὐτοῦ μὴ εἰδ[ό-
      τος γράμματα.
            (vac.)
(m.3) Κρητικ[οῦ
30 ⟋Τούρβ[ων Ἀχιλ-
      λέως [μητ(ρὸς) Φιλοῦ-
      τος [
(m.4)   λε [

(m.5)   κατεκ( ) [

(vac.)

10, 23 αυρη^λ   12 γενο̄ ιβ∫   13 ε̄ῡ α∫Lιγ   15 καθη^κ   16 L   24 αυρ^η
34 κατεκ

'... (10ff.) Aurelius Tourbon, his mother being Philous ..., payer of twelve drachmae, and in the present 1st year 13 years old. Therefore I present the notification as is fitting.

'Year 1 of Imperatores Caesares Publius Licinius Valerianus and Publius Licinius Valerianus Gallienus Pii Felices Augusti, Tybi 11.'

(2nd hand) 'I, Aurelius Achilleus, have presented (the notification). I, Aurelius Theon, also known as Asclepiades and also called Zoilus, wrote on his behalf, since he doesn't know letters.'

(3nd hand) 'The Cretan quarter. Tourbon son of Achilleus, his mother being Philous.'

(4th hand) '35.'

(5th hand) '...'

12 [.].τα γενο( ). A patronymic for Philous may be appropriate (cf. X **1267** 17–18), but the traces do not obviously suggest any known male name: only [C]ωτᾶ could be considered, but omega is hard to reconcile with the remains (apparently not [M]έλα: tau is a better reading than lambda). γενο( ) is surely a form of γενόμενος, a participle often used for deceased persons; could it refer to the father of Philous, γενο(μένου) (δωδεκαδράχμου)?

What is written at the end of the line is also puzzling. One possibility is υἱό(ν), but the position of the word would be awkward; another is καί, but is even more difficult. What follows is usually preceded by ὄντα, but this is not written.

22 Τῦβι. The document that comes before this in the tomos (**4994**) is dated to the month of Payni. Usually the *kollemata* run chronologically from left to right; but see **4996–7**.

24–6 Αὐρή(λιος) Θέων [ὁ] καὶ Ἀσκληπιάδης ἐπικαλούμενος Ζωίλος. This person recurs in L **3595** (243) and XIV **1636** (249) performing the same function as here; see H. Cockle, *JRS* 71 (1981) 89. His wife is attested in IX **1199** 4–5 (275/6 or 281/2; see BL XI 147).

The way Theon styles himself, with two aliases, is not common; this combination recurs in P. Iand. VII 139.13–14 (148), XLVII **3345** ii 60 (209), and VI **964** 1–2 (263), all from Oxyrhynchus. On the issue, see the references collected in **4990** 6 n., especially Hobson's article. It seems that ὁ καί is the expression denoting the formal alternative of a name, while ἐπικαλούμενος introduces sobriquets and nicknames.

29 Κρητικ[οῦ. Krüger, *Oxyrhynchos* 84 (cf. 371) places this *amphodon* in the southern part of the city. Alston, *The City* 154, further suggests that it is identical with the *amphodon Ioudaikes*. This must have been of a similar social makeup to the *amphodon Plateias*, also being residence for members of the gymnasial class and a magistrate. See further Daris, *ZPE* 132 (2000) 217.

32 Probably nothing was written in the lost part of the line; contrast **4994** 35.

34 In the break there perhaps stood κο'λ(λημα?) ρμθ, 'sheet no. 149', if the numbers were consecutive; see **4994** 37 with n.

M. MALOUTA

4996–4998. Notifications of Death

14 1B.203/K(2)   19 × 33 cm

Four *kollemata* from a *tomos synkollesimos*, apparently found with **4993–4995**. The *kollemata* have different heights; the bottom parts are aligned, but the tops vary visibly (the fourth *kolléma* is approximately 4 cm shorter than the second).

Of the first *kolléma* only scant line-ends from the middle and lower parts of the document survive. These remains (not transcribed below) are too exiguous to identify it as a death notice, but it was surely one. The second *kolléma* (**4996**) is a notification submitted by a father, informing an official of his son's death. It is dated to Year 2 of Valerian and Gallienus (254/5), which shows that the *kollemata* were not arranged chronologically, since the next *kolléma* is from year 1 (cf. **4994–5**, in which the documents come from year 1, but the order of months is not chronological). Most of the lower half is missing, apart from the last eight lines. In the third *kolléma* (**4997**), dated to May/June 254 (Year 1), another father reports the death of his son. The text is largely complete, apart from a few lines missing at the top and a hole at the middle.

In the fourth *kolléma* (**4998**), also dated to Year 1 (253/4), Aurelius Amoitas declares the death of Vibius Publius, of whom he was the guardian or manager, and of two of Publius' slaves. As was common practice, the reason for the deaths is not given. Accident or foul play readily comes to mind, but the date of the document may suggest a further possibility: Egypt in the middle of the third century suffered from a plague epidemic, which lasted for about fifteen years (H. Braunert, *Die Binnenwanderung* (1964) 270; list of literary sources in G. Casanova, *Aegyptus* 54 (1984) 174 n. 53; P. Salmon, *Population et dépopulation dans l'Empire romain* (1974) 134–6). Indeed the whole of the Roman Empire was attacked by an epidemic of plague, which lasted from 251 to 268; it came from Ethiopia, was very contagious, and had devastating repercussions (H. Zinsser, *Rats, Lice and History* (1935) 138–41). According to Eusebius, *HE* 7.21, by 260 the population of Alexandria had been halved (Salmon, *Population et dépopulation* 140–41). In the papyri there are references to possibly contagious diseases even shortly after 260, for example P. Mert. I 26, where the fate of an orphan boy is at stake, both of whose parents had died, presumably suddenly, ἀπό τινος φρεικώδους νόσου. The possible connection between such epidemics and death declarations is discussed by Casanova, *Aegyptus* 54 (1984) 172–3, and *Pap. Congr. XVII* iii 951. On diseases and their effect on the demography of Roman Egypt, see W. Scheidel, *Death on the Nile: Disease and the Demography of Roman Egypt* (2001).

All preserved *kollemata* carry official annotations, in the form also found in **4993–5**: **4996** and **4998** preserve the top left of the documents, and the same slanting strokes marking the beginning of the text can be seen. **4998** also preserves the middle part of the upper margin, where, as in **4993–5**, there is a numeral. **4996** and **4997** preserve the slanting strokes to the left of the summarizing subscription, but these are in a different place in **4998**; all three preserve the final docket. **4996** and **4997** seem to have the same puzzling wording as in **4994** and **4995** (see **4994** 37 n.); in **4998** the subscription is different.

The notifications published down to the early 1980s were re-edited with introduction and commentary by L. Casarico, *Il controllo della popolazione nell'Egitto romano: 1. Le denunce di morte* = C. Pap. Gr. II.1 (1985). For further references, see LXV **4478–80** introd., with Kruse, *Königliche Schreiber* i 143 n. 256. There are several documents of this type that survive as parts of *tomoi synkollesimoi*; see C. Pap. Gr. II.1 30–31, 38, 47–48, 49, 62, 65, 71, 78, 79. Cf. also **4992**.

4996

14 1B.203/K(2) col. ii   254/5

```
        ⫽[
        Αὐ[ρηλίῳ - - - -
          τ[οῦ ἐνεcτῶτοc β (ἔτουc)
        παρὰ [Τι]βερίου Κλαυ[δίου
        Δημητρίου υἱοῦ Τιβερίου
   5    Κλαυδίου Κοπρέωc.
        ὁ υἱὸc μου Δημέαc ἐκ μη-
        τρὸc Τανεχώτιδοc Πετ-
        τειρᾶτοc ἀπ' Ὀξυρύγχων
        πόλεωc (δωδεκάδραχμοc) ἀπὸ γυμνα-
  10    cίου ἀναγραφόμενοc ἐπ' ἀμ-
        φόδου Πλατείαc ἐτελεύ-
        τηcεν τῷ ἐνεcτῶτι ἔτει.
        διὸ ἐπιδίδωμι τὸ ὑπόμνη-
        μα πρὸc τὸ ἀναγραφῆ-
  15    ναι αὐτὸν ἐν τῇ τῶν ὁμοί-
        ων τάξει ὡc καθήκει.
        καὶ ὀμνύω τὴν Οὐαλεριανοῦ
        καὶ Γαλλιηνοῦ Καιcάρων
        τῶν κυρίων τύχην
  20    μὴ ἐψεῦcθαι.
        (ἔτουc) β″ Αὐτοκρατόρων
        Καιcάρων Πουπλίου
```

4996. NOTIFICATION OF DEATH

    Λικιννίου Οὐαλεριανοῦ
    καὶ [Πο]υπλίου Λικιννίου
25 Οὐαλεριανοῦ Γ]αλλιηνοῦ
    Εὐcεβῶν Εὐ]τυχῶν
    Cεβαcτῶν, month, day]

(m.2)   ].ει.
          ]..
30   ].του
         ].αι
          ]...
        ].οι...οc
         ].ηc
35   ]....αc
         ]..υ
         ]..μου
         ]..

(m.3)   ].. (δωδεκαδραχμ)
40 ⤴[ ].....Τιβερίο(υ) Κλ(αυδίου) Δη-
    μητρίου υἱο(ῦ) Τιβερίο(υ) Κλ(αυδίου)
    Κοπρέωc μη(τρὸc) Τανεχώτι-
    δοc Πετcειρᾶτοc
    ἐξ (ὑπομνήματοc) τοῦ πατρόc.

(m.4) 45 κατεκελ( ) γρ( )..η ι..
    νγ.

    4 υἱου 5 κοπρεωc– 6 υἱοc 7–8 πετ'τειρατοc 9, 39 ιβ∫ 13 ὑπομνη-
21 L 39 ιβ∫ 40, 41 τιβεριºκλ' 41 υἱº 42 μ^η 44 ἐξ/ 45 κατεκε^λ γρ∫

'To Aurelius ... (phylarch of the city of the Oxyrhynchites?) of the present 2nd year, from Tiberius Claudius Demetrius son of Tiberius Claudius Copreus.

'Demeas, my son by Tanechotis daughter of Petteiras from the city of the Oxyrhynchi, payer of twelve drachmae and a member of the gymnasium, registered in the quarter of Plateia, died during the current year. Therefore I present the notification, so that he may be registered in the list of those of a similar category as is fitting. And I swear by the fortune of our lords Valerianus and Gallienus Caesares not to have lied.

'Year 2 of Imperatores Caesares Publius Licinius Valerianus and Publius Licinius Valerianus Gallienus Pii Felices Augusti, (month, day).'

  (2nd hand) '....'

  (3rd hand) '... payer of twelve drachmae ... of Tiberius Claudius Demetrius son of Tiberius Claudius Copreus, his mother being Tanechotis daughter of Petseiras, from the notification of the father.'

  (4th hand) '...'

On the checkmarks above line 1, see **4994** 1 n.

1 Probably not Αὐ[ρηλίῳ Ἡρᾷ φυλάρχῃ]; see **4994** 2 n.

2 τ[οῦ ἐνεστῶτος β (ἔτους). The year figure is guaranteed by line 21.

7–8 Πεττειρᾶτος (πετ'τειρατος pap.) is a variant of the name Πετcειρᾶc, written Πετcειρᾶτοc in 43 by a different scribe. The name occurs also in P. Oslo III 111.297 (235) and P. Giss. 101.13 (iii), both Oxyrhynchite. The assimilation of the two consonants is often attested with the name Πέτc(ε)ιριc, as well as other names starting Πετc-. From the third century onwards, the apostrophe is often written between the two taus; see P. Köln I 55.19 (238–44?), XIV **1699** 8 (240–80), PSI Congr. XXI 12 v 12 (261), LIV **3738** 18 (312), PSI X 1106.15 (336), BGU VII 1628.14 (iv), SPP III2 98.1 (vi).

9–10 (δωδεκάδραχμοc) ἀπὸ γυμναcίου. See **4994** 14 n., 14–15 n.

10–11 ἀμφόδου Πλατείαc. See **4994** 11–12 n.

18 Καιcάρων: Cεβαcτῶν in **4994** 19, **4997** 16. Καιcάρων also occurs in XLIII **3109** 25 (253–6), while in XXXVI **2763** 9 (253/4) it was cancelled and replaced by Cεβαcτῶν. All these passages come from imperial oaths, not dating formulas.

28–36 This part would have contained the signature of the person presenting the notification and the statement that he has sworn the oath, and very probably an illiteracy formula.

39 ff. These lines were written in by an official after the *kollema* had been glued onto the roll: before the text of the second of these lines starts, there are two slanting strokes that start on the left side of the *kollesis* and onto the right, i.e., the *kollema* in question. For their function, see **4994** 1 n.

40 υἱόν cannot be read at the beginning of the line.

44 ἐξ (ὑπομνήματοc). Cf. **4997** 36. The particular symbol as abbreviation for ὑπόμνημα is unattested. The phrase, however, is widely attested; see especially P. Col. II 1.iii, where it occurs throughout the text also in reference to deaths.

45 κατεκελ( ) reminds one of what was transcribed as κατεκ( ) at the beginnings of **4994** 37 and **4995** 34, but what follows is different. After γρ( ), there is a stroke of obscure import followed by what may be the *artaba* symbol; then an upright stroke, followed by the fractions η̄ ιβ̄ κδ̄ (it is hard to take the upright as the fraction for ½). Apparently not κατέβαλ(εν) γρ(αμματεῖ).

4997

14 1B.203/K(2) col. iii   26 May – 24 June 254

```
      ].ος Ἀντιόχου τοῦ Θέω[νος
      μητρὸς Ἱερακιαίνης
      ἀπ' Ὀξυρύγχων πόλεως.
      ὁ υἱὸς μου Κοπρεὺς
  5   ὁ] καὶ Μέλας μητρὸς
      Τεκλώμιος τέλειος ἄτε-
      χνος ἀναγραφόμενος
      ἐπ' ἀμφόδου Ἱπποδρό-
      μου ἐτελ(εύτηcεν) τῷ ἐνεcτῶ(τι) ἔτει.
 10   διὸ ἐπιδίδωμι τὸ ὑπόμνη-
```

4997. NOTIFICATION OF DEATH

μα πρὸς τὸ ἀναγρα(φῆναι) αὐτὸν
ἐν τῇ τῶν ὁμοίων τάξει
ὡς καθήκει. καὶ ὀμνύ-
ω τὴν τῶν κυρίων
15 ἡμῶν Οὐαλεριανοῦ
καὶ Γαλλιηνοῦ Cεβαστῶν
τύχην μὴ ἐψεῦcθαι.
(ἔτουc) α// Αὐτοκρατόρων
Καιcάρων Πουπλίου
20 Λικιννίου Οὐαλεριανοῦ
καὶ Πουπλίου Λικιννίου
Οὐαλεριανοῦ Γαλλιηνοῦ
Εὐcεβῶν Εὐ[τυχῶ]ν
Cεβαcτῶν, [Παχω]ν.
(m.2) 25 Αὐρήλ(ιοc) Πλουτ[ί]ων ἐ-
πιδέδ[ω]κα καὶ ὤμοcα
τὸν ὅρκον ὡc πρόκει-
ται. Αὐρήλιοc Διονύcιοc
ἔγραψα ὑπὲρ αὐτοῦ μὴ
30 ε]ἰδότοc γράμματα.
(m.3) Ἱπποδρόμου τέλειοc
Ἱππέων Παρεμ(βολῆc)
(m.4) ⟋Κοπρεὺc Πλουτίωνοc
τοῦ Ἀντιόχου Θέωνοc
35 μη(τρὸc) Ἱερακιαίνηc
ἐξ (ὑπομνήματοc) τοῦ πα[τρόc.
(m.5) κατεκε.[...].

2, 35 ϊερακιαινηc   4 first o very large   ϋιοc   9 ετε^λ   τῷ: ω corr from ε   ενεcτ^ω
10 ὑπομνη-   11 αναγραϛ   18 L   32 παρε̄   35 μ^η   36 εξ/

'... (son) of Antiochus, grandson of Theon, his mother being Hieraciaena, from the city of the Oxyrhynchi. My son Copreus also called Melas, his mother being Teclomis, adult, without a profession, registered in the quarter of the Hippodrome, died during the current year. Therefore I present the notification, so that he may be registered in the list of those of a similar category as is fitting. And I swear by the fortune of our lords Valerianus and Gallienus Augusti not to have lied.

'Year 1 of Imperatores Caesares Publius Licinius Valerianus and Publius Licinius Valerianus Gallienus Pii Felices Augusti, Pachon(?).'

(2nd hand) 'I, Aurelius Ploution, have presented (the notification) and sworn the oath as is written above. I, Aurelius Dionysius, wrote on his behalf, for he does not know letters.'

(3rd hand) 'The quarter of the Hippodrome, adult, the quarter of Hippeon Parembole.'

(4th hand) 'Copreus son of Ploution, grandson of Antiochus son of Theon, his [= Ploution's] mother being Hieraciaena, from the notification of the father.'
(5th hand) '...'

1 The first letter may be ν, so that one may read [παρὰ Αὐρηλίου Πλουτίω]|νος. Before this, the address would have taken up another two lines; cf. **4996** and **4998** 2–3.

6 Τεκλώμιος. A rare name, attested otherwise only in BGU VII 1641.8 (127).

τέλειος. Cf. 31, **4998** 13. On this term see LXV **4479** 5 n.

8–9 ἀμφόδου Ἱπποδρόμου. This quarter is well attested in documents dating from the early first century until 259; it is conspicuously absent from I **43** of 295 (Krüger, *Oxyrhynchos* 83). See further Daris, *ZPE* 132 (2000) 217.

24 [Παχω]ν. Only the name of the month is stated, which is unusual, but the remains of the letter only match nu.

31 ff. See **4996** 39 ff. n.

31–2 Ἱπποδρόμου, Ἱππέων Παρε(μβολῆς). It is not easy to understand why the subscription refers to two quarters; there is no parallel. Perhaps the quarter of the Hippodrome was where the deceased was registered at some point after he became of age, whereas originally he was registered in Hippeon Parembole; or perhaps the notification was entered in the quarter of Hippeon Parembole, assuming that his father, the declarant, came from there. IV **786**, a census return of 119, carries a subscription that also names two quarters. It has been suggested that the declaration may have been carried from the one quarter to the other and deposited there, or else that the dual statement of quarter may reflect an update of an individual's official address (L. Capponi, *ZPE* 140 (2002) 179–80).

32 Ἱππέων Παρεμ(βολῆς). For a list of attestations, see Daris, *ZPE* 132 (2000) 217. This ἄμφοδον was located in the north to north-west of the city (Krüger, *Oxyrhynchos* 371). The cavalry barracks were originally associated with the Ptolemaic cavalry. The name continued to be used, in spite of the fact that by 64 there was no παρεμβολή anymore (Krüger, *Oxyrhynchos* 86). For possible later uses of the barracks, see Capponi, loc. cit. 180.

35 μη(τρὸς) Ἱερακιαίνης. Dr A. Benaissa remarks that it is odd for the father's metronymic to be given at this point, where one expects the metronymic of the deceased; cf. e.g. in **4996** 34. This may be due to scribal carelessness.

37 κατεκε.[...]. See **4996** 45 with n.

4998

14 1B.203/K(2) col. iv   253/4

(m.?)   ξε[
(m.1)   Αὐρ(ηλίῳ) Ἡρᾷ φυλάρχῃ τῆ[ς Ὀξυ(ρυγχιτῶν) πόλ(εως)
         τοῦ ἐνεςτῶτος α (ἔτους) [
         παρὰ Αὐρ(ηλίου) Ἀμοϊτᾶ Ἀμοϊ[τᾶτος μητρὸς
5   Θαήςιος ἀπ᾽ Ὀξυρύγχων [πόλεως ἐπι-
         τρόπου Οὐειβίου Πουπ[λίου - - - Ἀπολ-
         λωνίας μητρὸς καὶ ὡς [χρηματίζει(?). Οὐ(ε)ίβιος
         Πούπλιος Πτολεμαίου [τοῦ name
         μητρὸς Ἀπολλωνί[ας (ἐτῶν) ..

4998. NOTIFICATION OF DEATHS 125

10 ἄτεχνος ἀναγρ(αφόμενος) ἐπ' ἀ[μφόδου name
καὶ Ἀνείκητος ἀνθ' [οὗ - - -
της δοῦλ(ος) Πουπλίου [(ἐτῶν)
ις τέλ(ειος) ἄτεχ[νος ἀναγρα(φόμενος)
ἐπ' ἀμφόδ(ου) Παμμένο[υς Παραδείσου
15 καὶ Εὐφράτης δοῦλ(ος) Πουπ[λίου (ἐτῶν) . .
ἄτεχνος ἀναγρ(αφόμενος) ἐπ' ἀμφ[όδου
⸍ Νεμεσίου, οἱ γ̄ ἐτελ(εύτησαν) [- - -
διὸ ἐπιδίδομι τὸ ὑπ[όμνημα
πρὸς τὸ ἀναγρ(αφῆναι) αὐτ[οὺς ἐν τῇ
20 τῶν ὁ[μοί]ων τ[άξει ὡς καθήκει.
καὶ ὀμνύω [τὸν ἔθιμον Ῥωμαίοις
ὅρκον μὴ ἐψεῦς[θαι. (ἔτους) α
Αὐτοκρατόρων [Καισάρων
Πουπλίου Λικ[ιννίου Οὐαλεριανοῦ
25 καὶ Πουπλίου [Λικιννίου Οὐαλεριανοῦ
Γαλληεινοῦ [Εὐσεβῶν Εὐτυχῶν
Σεβαστῶν, [(month, day). Αὐρήλιος Ἀμοϊτᾶς
Ἀμοϊτᾶτος [ἐπιδέδωκα καὶ ὤμοσα
τὸν ὅρκον ὡς π[ρόκειται.
    (vac.)
(m.2) 30 δι(ὰ) Ἀπίωνος . . . φελ( )
    (vac.)
(m.3)   λα
    κς
    ξε

2, 4 αυρ/   3 α∫   10, 16, 19 αναγρ∫   11 l. Ἀνείκητος   12, 15 δουλ   13 ι∫ʃ/
τελ   14 αμφοδ   17 ετελ   18 l. ἐπιδίδωμι   ὑπ[26 l. Γαλλιηνοῦ   30 . . . φελ

(? hand) '65.'
(1st hand) 'To Aurelius Heras, phylarch of the city of the Oxyrhynchites, for the current 1st year, from Aurelius Amoitas son of Amoitas, his mother being Thaesis from the city of the Oxyrhynchi, guardian (or: steward) of Vibius Publius, . . . Apollonia, his mother, and however he(?) is officially described.

'Vibius Publius son of Ptolemaeus, grandson of . . . , his mother being Apollonia, n years old, of no trade, registered at the quarter of . . . , and Anicetus also called . . . , a slave of Publius, sixteen years old, adult, of no trade, registered at the quarter of Pammenous Paradeisos, and Euphrates, a slave of Publius, n years old, of no trade, registered at the quarter of Nemesion, died, all 3, [during the current year(?)]. Therefore I present the notification so that they may be registered in the list of those of a similar category as is fitting. And I swear the oath customary to Romans not to have lied.

'Year 1 of Imperatores Caesares Publius Licinius Valerianus and Publius Licinius Valerianus Gallienus Pii Felices Augusti, *month*, *day*.

'I, Aurelius Amoitas son of Amoitas, have presented (this notification) and sworn the oath as is written above.'

(2nd hand) 'Through Apion . . .'

(3rd hand) '31. 26. 65(?).

4 Αὐρ(ηλίου) Ἀμοϊτᾶ Ἀμοϊ[τᾶτος. The restoration is guaranteed by line 28. Father and son have the same name but use different forms of its genitive; for a similar case, cf. LXVII **4600** 4, 13–14. Ἀμοϊτᾶς is a typical Oxyrhynchite name; see P. Bingen 105.3 n.

5–6 ἐπι]τρόπου. The term here either refers to a tutor or guardian for a minor or the overseer of an estate. We have one parallel for such a notice being submitted by guardians, P. Tebt. II 301 = C. Pap. Gr. II.1 64 (190). If this is a guardian, the implication is that the deceased Vibius Publius is under fourteen years of age, but this cannot be ascertained, since his age is lost. See further next note.

6 Οὐειβίου Πουπ[λίου. A certain Οὐίβιος Πούπλιος καὶ ὡς χρημα(τίζει) is listed among the landowners in Ἡρακλείδου ἐποίκιον in XII **1537** 7 (ii/iii); XIV **1646** 1 (268/9) attests the heirs of Vibius Publius, a veteran, late *officialis* on the prefect's staff, and late councillor of Alexandria. If we are dealing with the same person, the present document, dated to 253/4, cannot refer to a minor, in which case Aurelius Amoitas would be an 'overseer' of privately owned property. Examples of this kind of ἐπίτροπος are found in XII **1577**, **1578**, (possibly) XIV **1680**, P. Brem. 15, P. Ross.-Georg. III 7, and P. Köln III 143. III **501** might also offer such an example, though G. Hamza, in *Symposion* 7 (1988) 349–60, takes the word to mean a guardian. From **1578** and **1680** it would seem that the ἐπίτροπος had a similar function to that of φροντιστής (P. Jouguet, *La Vie municipale dans l'Egypte romaine* (1911) 419), but was higher up in the hierarchy of administration. Being a landowner, it would be justified for Vibius Publius to have had a manager for his land. What is unparalleled is the overseer's entitlement to declare the death of his master.

6–7 Ἀπολ]λωνίας μητρός. Something must have come between the name of Vibius Publius and that of his mother. The order Ἀπολλωνίας μητρός is odd, if the phrase is taken to be the standard statement of the name of the mother in filiations; it would further suggest that Publius is officially described as her son, which is impossible, since his patronymic is stated in the next line, where his name is officially registered. Thus we may assume that Publius is mentioned as an explanation of the role of Amoitas. Likewise, the name of Apollonia is mentioned not as an official filiation, but to explain her role in the practical side of the declaration. If she is a widow, and what is stated at the beginning of the declaration is that Amoitas is the guardian of her son, what is lost is either a degree of relation with Apollonia, which would require no other explanation as to how he came to be a guardian (ἀδελφός, θεῖος, etc.), or a preposition giving the meaning 'appointed through', 'on behalf of', etc. This could be διά or ὑπό, explaining his appointment, or ὑπέρ, suggesting that, since he was the guardian, he drafted the declaration on the mother's behalf. If so, μητρός would be in apposition to Ἀπολλωνίας.

7 ὡς [χρηματίζει(?). This could be taken with Vibius Publius (cf. **1537** 7), though in that case we would probably have ἐχρημάτιζεν, or refers to his mother. It is also conceivable though less likely that we have to resolve χρημα(τίζω), which would refer to Amoitas.

8 Πούπλιος Πτολεμαίου[. The name here must be the same as the one in line 6. Apart from the obvious similarity, it facilitates the transition from the prescript to the main part of the declaration by serving as the connection between the declarant and the deceased. So the line above must have ended with the word Οὐ(ε)ίβιος. The patronymic is given as Πτολεμαίου and after the break the line must have contained the name of the grandfather, in the form τοῦ + *name* in the genitive.

11–12 The first three letters of 12 must be the ending of the alternative name given for

4998. *NOTIFICATION OF DEATHS* 127

Ἀνείκητος. This name may be N(ε)ικητής: when ἀνθ' οὗ is used, the names given are often similar, or indeed variations of the same name. Cf. BGU IV 1062 = W. *Chr.* 276.1 Ἑρμίας ἀνθ' οὗ Ἑρμῆς; BGU IX 1897.5 Ἁρποκρα( ) ἀνθ' οὗ Ἁρποκ( ), 168 Χάρης ἀνθ' οὗ Χάρεις; XII **1475** 15 Νείκωνος ἀνθ' οὗ Νεικομήδους; and most curiously, P. Lond. III 1170.727 Ἑκύςεως ἀνθ' οὗ Ἑκύςεως.

12 δούλ(ος). Cf. 15. Several notifications of death relate to slaves; see LXV **4479** 5 n. Two slaves are mentioned in XLIX **3510** = C. Pap. Gr. II.1 15.

13 The crossed sinusoid after ις may be a mere numerical marker. The purpose of the oblique stroke that follows is unclear.

ἄτεχ[νος. Cf. 16. For the term, see **4989** 12 n. It is used for slaves also in **3510** 9 (78/9), XXXI **2564** 7 (153), and VII **1030** 8 (212) (= C. Pap. Gr. II.1 15, 44, 71).

14 ἀμφόδ(ου) Παμμένο[υς Παραδείςου. This quarter was situated in the south-west of the city, and was adjacent to the city walls (Krüger, *Oxyrhynchos* 371, 85). Since each of these slaves was registered in a different quarter (cf. 17), their master or his family must have owned property in both of these quarters.

16–17 ἀμφ[όδου] Νεμεςίου. This quarter of Oxyrhynchus must have been near that of Θερμῶν Βαλανείων, since parts of the Eastern Stoa of the city seem to have belonged to both (Krüger, *Oxyrhynchos* 84, 87). Not attested in papyri before the third century.

17 ἐτελ(εύτηςαν) [. This would have been followed by τῷ ἐνεςτῶτι μηνὶ *name of month* τοῦ ἐνεςτῶτος ἔτους or τῷ ἐνεςτῶτι ἔτει μηνὶ *name of month*, or even simply by τῷ ἐνεςτῶτι ἔτει, as in the other two examples preserved in this roll. The phrase was probably abbreviated.

18 On the left of this line there appear the two characteristic strokes used throughout these documents. Here, however, the use of the strokes is slightly different, unavoidably so, since the layout of this document also differs from that of the others. Since in this case there is no official docket at the end, the strokes come before the line that states the deaths. The use is therefore the same, i.e., to mark the place where it is stated whom the declaration concerns.

21 ὀμνύω [τὸν ἔθιμον Ῥωμαίοις. The collocation as restored suits the space, but does not occur in any of the other documents in this roll or in **4993–5**. On this formula, see CPR XXIII 12 introd. and pp. 232–3 (table).

30 δι(ὰ) Ἀπίωνος . . . φελ( ): τοῦ Ὀφελ(λίου)? But the article is hard to justify. For the subscription, cf. C. Pap. Gr. II.1 76.18 (229).

33 ξε. The third of the numbers scribbled at the foot of the document is the same as that written at the top of the *kollema*. It may not be a coincidence that there are three numbers in a document in which three people are declared dead. However, the exact purpose of the numbers is not clear.

M. MALOUTA

4999. Registration of a Child

28 4B.60/B(1–3)b　　　　　　　4.7 × 18.5 cm　　　　　　　12 August 292

This is an application to register a twelve-year old boy, submitted by a friend of the boy's deceased father. The beginnings of the lines are lost, but much the most of the main text can be securely restored; the reconstruction of the official docket (23 ff.), however, is problematic. The absence of the declarant's signature is noteworthy; it is also absent from XLIV **3183** but present in XLIII **3136**, both of which date from summer 292. The dockets, written in hands other than those of the main texts, indicate that these were not private copies.

On this type of document, see **4996–4998** introd. A close parallel is XXXVIII **2855**, which dates from the previous year (291). Both **2855** and **4999** concern the sons of deceased fathers, and are addressed 'to the board of *laographoi* through one of them', Aurelius Diogenes alias Hermias. This person was previously attested as the *systates*, to whom other such applications were addressed: PSI III 164 (287), P. Corn. 18 (291), and XLIV **3183** (292). Three years later, a similar registration was submitted to the board of *systatai* (XLIII **3137** of 295). 'It is a probable conclusion that the term laographus was at this period equivalent to systates' (**3137** introd.); in any case, the use of the term *laographoi*, common in earlier times (cf. above, **4983** and **4991**), for the collectivity of *systatai* was not long-lived.

The inventory numbers of these registrations of children dated to 291 and 292 imply that they were found in relatively close proximity, which may suggest an archival connection. **4999** comes from metal packing box no. 60 of the fourth excavation campaign at Oxyrhynchus; **3183** (28 4B.61/B(8)a) comes from box 61, **2855** (29 4B.56/C(7)a) from box 56; it is unclear whether the same applies to **3136** (292), which comes from box 71 (35 4B.71/H(1–3)a).

The back is blank.

  τῷ κοινῷ τῶν] λαογράφων διὰ τοῦ
   ἑνὸς αὐτῶν] Αὐρηλίου Διογένι
  τοῦ καὶ Ἑρμείου τ]ῆc λαμ(πρᾶc) καὶ λαμ(προτάτηc) Ὀξυρυγχιτῶν πόλεωc το]ῦ ἐνεcτῶτοc η (ἔτουc) καὶ ζ (ἔτουc)
5 παρὰ Αὐρηλίου] Ὡρίωνοc Θέωνοc μη(τρὸc)
   c.6 ἀπὸ τῆ]c λαμ(πρᾶc) καὶ λαμ(προτάτηc) Ὀξυρυγχιτῶν πόλεωc. βού]λομαι πρῶτοc ἀπογράψα-
  cθαι παρὰ coὶ τὸ]ν τοῦ φίλου μου καὶ μετηλ-
  λαχότοc *c.4*] ίωνοc Cαραπίωνοc υἱὸν
10   *c.12*]ην ἐκ μη(τρὸc) Ἀδωρᾶc ἐπ᾿ ἀμφόδου ὄ]ντα πρὸc τὸ ἐνεcτὸc
  η (ἔτοc) καὶ ζ (ἔτοc)] (vac.) (ἐτῶν) ιβ
   c.12] διὸ ἐπιδίδωμει τὸ ὑπόμνημα ἀξιῶν ταγῆ]ναι αὐτόν εἰc τὴν τῶν ὁ-
15 μηλίκων τά]ξιν ὡc καθήκει καὶ
  ὀμνύω τὸν ἔθι]μον Ῥωμαίοιc ὅρκον
  μὴ ἐψεῦcθαι. (ἔτουc)] η/ Αὐτοκράτοροc Καίcαροc
  Γαΐου Αὐρηλίου] Οὐαλερίου Διοκλητιανοῦ
  καὶ (ἔτουc) ζ Αὐτο]κράτοροc Καίcαροc Μάρκου
20 Αὐρηλίου Οὐαλερ]ίου Μαξιμιανοῦ Γερ-
  μανικῶν Μεγίcτ]ων Εὐcεβῶν Εὐτυχῶν

4999. REGISTRATION OF A CHILD

        Cεβαcτῶν,] Μεcορη   ιθ.
        (vac.)

(m.2)   ]υc
        ]. (ἐτῶν) ιβ′
25   ]ου υἱοῦ μεγάλω
        ]. Μερμέρθων
        (vac.)
        ]. α. ηc

. . . . .

2 l. Διογένουc   3, 6 λαμ∫ (bis)   οξυρυγ'χι   4 ∫ (bis)   5, 10 μη?   7 l. πρώτωc
9 υἱον   12, 24 L   13 l. ἐπιδίδωμι   25 υἱοῦ   l. μεγάλου?

'To the board of *laographoi* through one of them, Aurelius Diogenes alias Hermias, of the splendid and most splendid city of the Oxyrhynchites, for the current 8th year and 7th year, from Aurelius (?)Horion son of Theon, mother . . . , from the splendid and most splendid city of the Oxyrhynchites. I wish to register with you for the first time the son of my deceased friend —ion son of Sarapion, —es, of mother Adora, in the quarter of . . . , who in the current 8th year and 7th year is 12 years old (of the twelve-drachma gymnasial class?). Therefore I submit the application requesting that he be enrolled in the category of his age group as is appropriate, and I swear the oath customary to Romans not to have lied. Year 8 of Imperator Caesar Gaius Aurelius Valerius Diocletianus and year 7 of Imperator Caesar Marcus Aurelius Valerius Maximianus Germanici Maximi Pii Felices Augusti, Mesore 19.'

(2nd hand) '. . . 12 years old . . . son of the great(?) . . . Mermertha . . .'

1–4 The order of the constituents of the prescript is confused; it should have been τῷ κοινῷ τῶν λαογράφων τῆc λαμπρᾶc κτλ. τοῦ ἐνεcτῶτοc κτλ. διὰ τοῦ ἑνὸc κτλ. We find a peculiar order in **2855** 1–4 too: τῷ κοινῷ κτλ. τῆc λαμπρᾶc κτλ. διὰ κτλ. τοῦ ἐνεcτῶτοc κτλ.

2–3 Αὐρηλίου Διογένι (l. -ουc) τοῦ καὶ Ἑρμείου. For a list of attestations of this *systates*, see P. Leid. Inst. p. 277.

5 Αὐρηλίου] Ὡρίωνοc Θέωνοc. Assuming that the name was not Δ]ωρίωνοc, it is tempting to identify this person with the *systates* of this name, who was Aurelius Diogenes' successor; see the listing in P. Leid. Inst. pp. 277–8.

7 πρῶτοc, l. πρώτωc. See **4994** 9 n.

8 Restored after **2855** 8.

10 Ἀδωρᾶc. The genitive of this name is usually Ἀδωρᾶ, like the nominative. The ending in -ᾶc recurs in P. Herm. 67 = SB XIV 12133.7 (vi).

11 Παμμένουc Παραδείcου, suggested by]υc in 23 (see n.), is long unless abbreviated. This is the *amphodon* mentioned in **2855**.

13 The break most probably took away the sequence (δωδεκάδραχμον) ἀπὸ γυμναcίου.

14–15 ὁ|[μηλίκων suits the space better than ὁμοίων; on these terms, see **3136** introd.

17–22 For this regnal formula (2), see $CSBE^2$ 226.

23 ff. The annotation seems to begin according to the usual pattern, with the name of amphodon followed by the name and age of boy declared; cf. **2855** 27 ff., **3136** 18 ff., **3183** 21 ff., P. Corn. 18.25 ff. The genitives in 25 may refer to the boy's father. The village mentioned in 26 may be the father's *origo*; see note below.

23]υc. Since the name of an *amphodon* is expected, this can only be [Παμμένο]υc. It occurs

without Παραδείcου in a similar docket in **3183** 21 (copy B); cf. also XL **2928** i 12, 14, ii 14, P. Fuad I Univ. 29.6.

26] . Μερμέρθων. The letter on the edge seems to be nu: ἐ]ν? Cf. ἐν Θω[c.6] (a village name) in **2855** 29–30, and ἐν Τήει in **3183** 24; these villages were thought to be the places where the fathers belonged, while the sons were registered in the city.

27 Perhaps read cυc]τάτηc; if so, this is the first such document signed by this official. **2855** and **3183** end with a mention of the person through whom the registration was made.

N. GONIS

5000–5012. Documents Relating to Village Police

5000. Sworn Undertaking

32 4B.91/K(1–3)e   6.5 × 20 cm   166–9

Two village policemen, an *archephodos* and an *eirenophylax*, declare on oath that they will search for three persons (two from the same village and one Alexandrian) and present them to the authorities within sixty days. The text breaks off halfway through the guarantor-clause; the date formula will have followed.

This is the first document of this kind to be published, but the exercise itself is not unknown. In P. Giss. 84 (Apoll. Hept.; early II), an *eirenophylax* had to pledge that within thirty days he would present one person to the authorities and take another to prison; in SB VI 9105 (Ars.; late II), someone selected for the post of *eirenophylax* is petitioned to take an accused person (a 'repeat offender' whom the *eirenophylax* has previously punished) as well his victim to the metropolis. What occasioned this oath can only be a matter for speculation. Given the instructions in various summonses for the *archephodos* to 'come up' himself, especially in the event he failed to produce the wanted person (see e.g. **5004–5**), it is conceivable that this oath was taken at the metropolis, where the village policemen would have been summoned after they failed to respond to an earlier summons.

The text runs along the fibres. A stroke added at about the middle of the top margin does not look like a column-number. The back is blank.

    Πνεφερῶc Πνεφε-
    ρῶ[τ]οc τοῦ Ναυάρχου
    μη[τ]ρὸc Τcενθ . τοc
    ἀπὸ [Τυ]χινφάγων ἀρχέ-
5   φοδ[ο]c τῆ[c] αὐτῆc κώ-
    μηc καὶ Ὧροc Θοτ . . . . . -
    οc μητρὸc Θιν . . . . . . -
    τ[ο]c ἀπὸ τῆc αὐτῆc
    Τυχινφάγων εἰρη-

5000. SWORN UNDERTAKING

10 νοφύλαξ τῆς αὐτῆς
    κώμης ὀμνύομεν
    τὴν [τ]ῶν κυρίων
    Αὐτοκρατόρων Ἀντωνί[νου
    καὶ [ ] Οὐήρου Ἀρμενιακῶν
15 Μηδικῶν Παρθικῶν
    Με[γ]ίςτων τ[ύ]χην
    ἐν[τ]ὸς ἡμερῶν ἑξή-
    κο[ν]τα ἀπὸ τῆς ἐνες-
    τώ[c]ης ἡμέρας ἀνα-
20 ζητήςειν καὶ παρα-
    ςτήςει[ν] Θῶνιν Παυ-
    έως μητρὸς Τνε-
    φε[ρ]ῶτος καὶ Πετό-
    ςειριν Πε[τ]ςέμιος
25 τοῦ Ψενήςιος μη-
    τρὸς Θινπαυνίεως,
    το[ὺ]ς δύο ἀπ[ὸ] τῆς αὐ-
    τῆ[ς] κώμης, καὶ Νεῖ-
    λ[ον] Νείλου Ἀλεξαν-
30 δ[ρέ]α, τοὺς τρεῖς ο[
    . .]. οθέντας ὡςω.
    . . .]υο ἢ ἔνοχοι εἴ-
    ημεν] τῷ ὅρκῳ. παρές-
    χομεν δὲ ἑ]αυτ[ῶν

24 πε[τ]ςεμιος: μ written over ιρ   32 η ε- written over ειη

'We, Pnepheros son of Pnepheros, grandson of Nauarchus, mother Tsenthe(u)s, from Tychinphagon, *archephodos* of the same village, and Horos son of Thot—, mother Thin—, from the same village Tychinphagon, *eirenophylax* of the same village, swear by the fortune of the lords emperors Antoninus and Verus, Armeniaci Medici Parthici Maximi, that within sixty days from today we shall search out and present (to the authorities) Thonis son of Paues, mother Tnepheros, and Petosiris son of Petsemis, grandson of Psenesis, mother Thinpayniis, both from the same village, and Nilus son of Nilus, an Alexandrian, the three . . . , or may we be liable to (the penalties for breaking) the oath. And we provided (as guarantors) for ourselves . . .'

2 Ναυάρχου. This is the first occurrence of the name (not the office) in a papyrus, otherwise attested in Ptolemaic inscriptions. For names derived from shipping and maritime activity, see G. Neumann, *BN* 22 (1987) 1–10, esp. 6; A. B. Tataki, *Tyche* 20 (2005) 209–15, esp. 210.

3 Τϲενθ̣․τοϲ. The uncertain letter seems to be η. If this is correct, the nominative of the name would be Τϲενθῆϲ or Τϲενθεῦϲ; cf. XLIV **3169** 64 (200–212 [HGV]) Τϲενθεῦ[ϲ, or Ψενθέωϲ in O. Strasb. 319.3 (126 BC), and Ψενθηουϲ in IGChEg 687.1 (no date). Although the name is not attested in Demotic, its formation is plausible, and its meaning would be 'daughter of Thoth' (communication from Professor W. J. Tait); cf. the name Ψενθώτηϲ (*DemNb* 274–5).

4 Τυχινφάγων was a village in the Lower toparchy of the Oxyrhynchite nome. See Pruneti, *I centri* 211; Calderini–Daris, *Dizionario* v 40, Suppl. ii 233, iii 153, iv 133. An εἰρηνοφύλαξ of Tynchinphagon appears in LXV **4486** 5.

4–5 ἀρχέφοδ[ο]ϲ. On the office, see N. Lewis, *Compulsory Public Services*² (1997) 15; H.-J. Drexhage, in *Migratio et Commutatio: Festschrift Thomas Pekáry* (1989) 108 ff.; C. Drecoll, *Die Liturgien im römischen Kaiserreich des 3. und 4. Jh. n. Chr.* (1997) 158–63; C. Homoth-Kuhs, *Phylakes und Phylakon-Steuer im griechisch-römischen Ägypten* (2005) 94–8. The office is mentioned only rarely in papyri after the mid third century but survives well into the fourth; see P. Horak 11.2 n. (to the examples add SB XXVI 16496).

6–7 Θοτ̣․․․․․|οϲ. The letter after tau is epsilon or sigma, followed by what looks like upsilon. If we opt for Θοτευ-, no known variant of the common name Θοτεύϲ can be read in what follows. If we read Θοτϲυ-, Θοτϲυτάι̣|οϲ (not Θοτϲύτμιοϲ) may be possible. This is a rare name, attested only in P. Meyer 34.4 (III BC) Θοτϲυτάιν, and IV **797** (103/102 BC) Θοτϲυταῖοϲ. For the genitive in -ιοϲ, see Gignac, *Grammar* ii 78–9.

7–8 Θιν․․․․․|τ[ο]ϲ. The two letters after Θιν look most like λα, followed by three or four letters, of which the first could be β, κ, or μ, the second ω or ο, and the third ν or ϲι. No known name is suggested.

9–10 εἰρηνοφύλαξ. Most attestations for this office come from the second century (occasionally 'second/third'). The εἰρηνοφύλαξ was, like the ἀρχέφοδοϲ, one of the δημόϲιοι κώμηϲ, and his office was a liturgy, incumbent upon the εὐϲχήμονεϲ (SB VI 9105); see Lewis, *Compulsory Public Services*² 23; Homoth-Kuhs, *Phylakes und Phylakon-Steuer* 93, 108–9. Their number ranged from two (XVII **2121**, P. Achm. 7, P. Lond. II 199, P. Ryl. II 89) to four (P. Berl. Leihg. 6, SB XIV 12136); Horos may not have been the only εἰρηνοφύλαξ of Tychinphagon. A very few papyri refer to their police or other enforcement duties; besides those mentioned in the introduction, cf. P. Brem. 14, in which he is to deal with workers; P. Brem. 26, where we also hear that an εἰρηνοφύλαξ was killed; P. Vind. Sal. 2; and perhaps P. Harr. II 192.

9 At the end of the line there is a very small stroke. The scribe perhaps began to write the ν of εἰρηνοφυλαξ, but gave up because he ran out of space.

12–16 The imperial titulature is new. The victory titles point to a date between mid 166, when the two emperors assumed the titles of Medici and Parthici maximi, and early 169, when Verus died; see D. Kienast, *Römische Kaisertabelle* (1996²) 139, 144.

14 καὶ [̣] ̣. After καί there is a break that could accommodate one letter, to which the lower part of the tail visible after the break may belong. Did the scribe write καιϲα for Καίϲαροϲ, and then deleted ϲα?

17–19 ἐν[τ]ὸϲ ἡμερῶν ἑξήκο[ν]τα ἀπὸ τῆϲ ἐνεϲτώ[ϲ]ηϲ ἡμέραϲ. On such official deadlines, see R. Taubenschlag, *Opera minora* ii (1959) 171–87, and N. Litinas, *APF* 45 (1999) 69–76.

19–21 ἀναζητήϲειν καὶ παραϲτήϲει[ν]. These two verbs occur together in P. Panop. Beatty 1.214 (298) and VI **897** 10 (346); cf. also P. Panop. Beatty 1.197 ἀναζήτηϲιϲ [καὶ παράϲτα]ϲιϲ. For the procedure, see A. Łukaszewicz in *Symposion* 1985 (1989) 363–8.

21 Θῶνιν. This is a typical Oxyrhynchite name; see P. Köln IV 202.1 n., LXIX **4741** 3 n.

22–3 Τνεφερῶϲ. See *DemNb* 1068. The name is attested from the Ptolemaic period until the third century.

24 Πε[τ]ϲέμιοϲ. The name is new, but cf. Πετϲιμίου in CPR XIII 6.1.8 = P. Count 24.51 (III

BC). The scribe first wrote Πε[τ]ϲείριοϲ (there is no space for Πε[το]ϲείριοϲ), and then corrected it by writing μ over ιρ.

26 Θινπαυνίεωϲ. Female names such as Θινπαυνιίϲ, Θινπαυνιεῦϲ, or Θινπαυνιῆϲ are not attested in the papyri. However, cf. the male names Παῦνιϲ in P. Cair. Zen. IV 59727.16 (mid III BC) and Παῦνιοϲ in O. Strasb. 521.1 (II).

27 το[ὐ]ϲ δύο. This is not a common expression, with ἀμφότεροι being mostly used; cf. e.g. I **101** 3, II **275** 5, **290** 12, XXXVIII **2863** 5, **2876** 27–8.

30 τοὺϲ τρεῖϲ. This collocation too is not very common; it occurs in P. Köln II 100.6 (133), III **491** 4 (126), XLVII **3346** 13 (207–10/11), SB IV 7362.18 (188); cf. also SB XVIII 13871.6 (200–150 BC). We find similar expressions such as τοὺϲ τέϲϲαραϲ (P. Fouad 32.25, P. Sakaon 51.27) or τοὺϲ πέντε (P. Mil. Vogl. IV 236.11), but generally, the adjective πᾶϲ is preferred.

30–31 ο[ ]|[. . .] ͺοθέντας ωϲω ͺ. One letter may have been lost at the end of 30. In 31, one may wish to read]δοθέντας, but delta is not easy. In any case, if the division is correct, we have the end of a participle that probably indicates the reason for which these people were wanted. The reading and articulation of what follows is even more difficult.

32]υο. Probably δ]ύο, which should refer to the two policemen.

33–4 παρέϲ[χομεν (or παρέϲχαμεν) δὲ ἑ]αυτ[ῶν ἐγγυητὴν τὸν δεῖνα παρόντα καὶ εὐορκοῦντα, assuming that there was only one guarantor (there are numerous parallels); or, less likely . . . ἐγγυητὰϲ ὁ μὲν Πνεφερῶϲ Πνεφερῶτοϲ τὸν δεῖνα, ὁ δὲ / καὶ ὁ Ὧροϲ Θοτ ͺ ͺ ͺ ͺ τὸν δεῖνα (cf. P. Köln V 229.23–31). Other variations of the formula, e.g. those involving the collocation παρόντα καὶ εὐορκοῦντα, occur in later documents, and are less likely to have occurred here. This clause is the commonest and is found from the second half of the second century until the beginning of the fourth, mainly in Oxyrhynchite documents; the only exceptions are P. Mil. Vogl. IV 237.18–19 (Ars.; 212), and PSI VII 734.26–7 (Herm.; 218–22). Our papyrus seems to offer its earliest example.

N. LITINAS

5001–5012. Summonses ('Orders to Arrest')

The twelve texts published in this section belong to a very frequently exampled and extensively discussed type of document. The common term 'order to/for arrest' nowadays appears hardly appropriate, and 'summons' seems to be the one recommended.

A 'consolidated' list was given by A. Bülow-Jacobsen, *ZPE* 66 (1986) 95–8 (78 items); a list of addenda (16 items) was offered by T. Gagos and P. J. Sijpesteijn, *BASP* 33 (1996) 95–6.[1] A new update (30 items) is presented overleaf.[2]

N. GONIS

---

[1] Half of the items in this list of addenda now have SB numbers: no. 1 (P. Tebt. II 535) = SB XX 15130; no. 3 = SB XXIV 16005; no. 11 = SB XX 15094; nos. 12–13 (P. Cair. Preis. 6a–b) = SB XX 15095; no. 14 = SB XXIV 16006; no. 15 = SB XXIV 16008; no. 16 (P. Lond. III 1074) = SB XX 14967. PSI XV 1536–1538 have been given new editions, and SB XVI 12967 = P. NYU II 49.

[2] Not included in the list is BGU XIX 2773. SB XXII 15628 (as P. Yale inv. 1347) and P. Strasb. V 309 were mentioned in P. Oxy. LXI **4114–4116** introd. (p. 90) but not in the *BASP* article (I owe the observation to Margaret Mountford, who is editing a number of summonses in her PhD dissertation at UCL).

134   DOCUMENTARY TEXTS

publication	date	sender	recipient	village	w × h	fibres[a]
LXXIV **5001**	I/II		*archephodos*	Nemera, Oxy.?	8.9 × 6.9	→
LXXIV **5002**	I/II	*strategos*	*nomophylax* + [*archephodos*]	Naouis, Oxy.?	9 × 7	→
SB XXXVI 16429	I/II		[*archephodos*]	Tholthis Kato, Oxy.	5.8 × 5.3	→
LXXIV **5003**	II		*archephodos*	Pakerke, Oxy.	9.3 × 7.5	→
LXV 4485	II		*archephodos*	Iseion Tryphonos, Oxy.	10.1 × 7.1	→
LXV 4486 i[b]	II/III		*archephodos*	Takona, Oxy.	(26 × 5)	*→
LXV 4486 ii	II/III		*archephodos*	Tychinphagon, Oxy.	(26 × 5)	*→
SB XXXVI 16465	II/III		*archephodos*	Soknopaiou Nesos, Ars.	18.2 × 7.5	→
SB XXXVI 16466	II/III		?	Philadelphia, Ars.	10 × 8.7	→
SB XXXVI 16467	II/III		?	?Soknopaiou Nesos, Ars.	6.6 × 3	→
PSI XV 1552	III		*proestotes, epi tes eirenes, demosioi*	Mnachis, Herm.	13 × 17	→
SB XXII 15628	III		*archephodos*	Mermertha, Oxy.	7.5 × 12	→
LXXIV **5004**	III		*archephodos*	Takona, Oxy.	15.3 × 6.5	→
LXXIV **5005**	III/IV	*decurio*	*phylakes, demosioi*	T—, Oxy.(?)	11.3 × 6.2	*→
LXXIV **5006**	III/IV	*decurio*	*comarchs, demosioi*	Syron, Oxy.	9.6 × 7.6	*→
LXXIV **5007**	III/IV	*decurio*	*comarchs, demosioi*	Paomis, Oxy.	9.5 × 7.2	→
LXXIV **5008**	III/IV	*decurio*	*comarchs, epistates eirenes*	Pakerke East, Oxy.	10 × 7.2	→
LXXIV **5009**	III/IV	*decurio*	*comarchs, epistates eirenes*	?, Oxy.(?)	8.9 × 6.1	→
BGU XVII 2700	III/IV	*eirenarch*	*comarch, epistates eirenes*	Enteeis, Oxy.	11 × 9	→
BGU XVII 2701	III/IV	*vir egregius*	*comarch, lestopiastai*	Senoabis, Herm.	25.5 × 6.5	→
LXXIV **5010**	III/IV	*vir egregius*	*comarchs, demosioi*	Berky, Oxy.	20.8 × 5.7	→
LXXIV **5011**	III/IV	*beneficiarius*	*comarchs, epistates eirenes*	Arabon, Ars.?	19 × 7.4	→
LXXIV **5012**	IV	?	?	?	21 × 3.1	→

5001–5012. SUMMONSES ('ORDERS TO ARREST')

P. Horak 11	IV	?	*archephodos, nomianos*(?)	?	15.8 × 11.5	→
P. Kell. inv. D/1/75.13.1[c]	IV	*archiereus*	comarchs	Kellis, Moth.	25 × 5.3	→
P. Kell. inv. D/1/75.13.2[c]	IV	*archiereus*	comarchs	Kellis, Moth.	4.2 × 6	→
P. Kell. inv. D/1/75.25[c]	IV	*archiereus*	priest	Kellis, Moth.	13 × 7	*→
P. Strasb. V 309	IV	*exactor*	eirenarch	Philadelphia, Ars.	26 × 8	→
BGU XIX 2772	IV	*riparius*?	eirenarchs	Psobthonyris, Herm.	27.3 × 4.8	→
BGU XIX 2774	V/VI	*comes*	eirenarchs	Pois, Herm.	31.2 × 7	→

[a] * = along the fibres but on reused papyrus.
[b] **4686** i–ii are written on the same strip of papyrus, on the back of a piece cut from a larger document.
[c] These three Kellis papyri were published by K. A. Worp in C. A. Hope, G. E. Bowen (eds.), *Dakhleh Oasis Project: Preliminary Reports on the 1994–1995 to 1998–1999 Field Seasons* (2002) 334–6. The third item is addressed to the person summoned without the intervention of village officials.

5001

36 4B.93/M(1–3)b   8.9 × 6.9 cm   First/second century

A relatively early example of an Oxyrhynchite text of this type, not distinguishable in content or wording from others of slightly earlier date. However, its almost square format and the direction of the writing, along the fibres, place it in the minority. The back is blank.

    ἀρχεφόδωι Νεμέρων.
    πέμψον Πλουτίωνα
    Πλουτίωνος γεωργὸν
    ἐντυχόντος Ζωίλου.
5   μη(νὸς) Καισαρείο(υ) ι.

5 μη καισαρειο

'To the *archephodos* of Nemera. Send Ploution son of Ploution, farmer, at the petition of Zoilus. In the month of Caesarius, (day) 10.'

1 ἀρχεφόδωι. See **5000** 4–5 n.
Νεμέρων. A village in the Middle toparchy. Another such text addressed to an *archephodos* of this village is LXI **4115** (III).
2 πέμψον. See U. Hagedorn, *BASP* 16 (1979) 62.
5 Caesarius 10 = August 3. For dates in summonses, see D. Hagedorn, *ZPE* 159 (2007) 266. Cf. **5002** 4.

N. GONIS

5002

45 5B.57/D(5–7)a   9 × 7 cm   First/second century

This text displays the same structure as P. Mich. X 590 (?; I/II) and SB XVIII 13172 (Ars.?; 88–96), re-ed. D. Hagedorn, *ZPE* 159 (2007) 264–6. The order is addressed by a strategus to the *nomophylax* and another official, probably the *archephodos*, of a village not known otherwise. That the papyrus was found in the rubbish dump of the city that served as the strategus' seat suggests that the village was Oxyrhynchite.

The writing is across the fibres. The back is blank.

    ὁ ϲτρατηγὸϲ νομοφύλακι κ[αὶ ἀρχεφόδῳ
    κώμηϲ Νάουεοϲ. ἐκπέμψ[ατε c.7

5002. SUMMONS

Νααρω[ο]ῦτος ἐ.[.].[c.15
Φαρμοῦθι ιδ̄. οφ.η..[

2 l. Νάουεως   ἐκπεμψ[ατε: π corr. from μ

'The strategus to the *nomophylax* and *archephodos* of the village of Naouis. Send out . . . (son/daughter) of Naaroous . . . Pharmouthi 14. . . .'

1 ὁ στρατηγός is the issuing authority also in P. Mich. X 590 and SB XVIII 13172; the same holds for P. Tebt. II 290, where the phrase ὁ στρατηγός σε καλεῖ is written on the seal. Though it is highly likely that down to the mid third century such summonses stem from the strategus' office, there is no reference to this official again until the fourth century.

νομοφύλακι κ[αὶ ἀρχεφόδῳ. Restored after P. Mich. 590.1. SB 13172 is addressed πρεσβ(υτέροις) καὶ ἀρχεφ(όδῳ).

On the office of *nomophylax*, see XLIV **3190** 3–4 n., XLVII **3344** 5–6 n.; P. Freib. IV 62 introd. Cf. also **5007** 7 and n.

2 ἐκπέμψ[ατε. This compound is used in Arsinoite, Hermopolite, and Oxyrhynchite orders; see U. Hagedorn, *BASP* 16 (1979) 65–6, 69, 71.

3 ἐν[κ]αλ[ούμενον ὑπὸ + *name*? If so, the name would have been short. This participle is used in P. Mich. 590.4 and SB 13172.3. But ἐντυ[χόντος is possible too.

4 Pharmouthi 14 = April 9.
I cannot tell what was written at the end of the line.

N. GONIS

5003

29 4B.56/B(4–7)a   9.3 × 7.5 cm   Second century

An order to a village *archephodos* to 'send up' two *presbyteroi*. No reason is stated, but it is conceivable that this concerned their dealings during their term of office. An unusual feature is that the persons summoned are presented in the form of a list.

The writing is along the fibres and the back is blank.

ἀρχεφόδῳι Πακερκη. ἀνάπεμψον
   τοὺς πρεσβ(υτέρους)·
Πατέρμουθιν Διογᾶτος, μη(τρὸς) Ἀμμωναρίου῾,
Κοπρέαν ['Ο]φελλίου, μη(τρὸς) Ταύριος.

2 πρεσβ—   3, 4 μ^η

'To the *archephodos* of Pakerke. Send up the *presbyteroi*:
'Patermouthis son of Diogas, mother Ammonarion.
'Copreas son of Ofellius, mother Tayris.'

1 Πακερκη. There were two villages of this name, one in the Eastern (cf. **5008**) and the other in the Middle toparchy.

2 πρεϲβ(υτέρουϲ). These were the πρεϲβύτεροι τῆϲ κώμηϲ; see A. Tomsin, 'Étude sur les πρεϲβύτεροι des villages de la χώρα égyptienne II', *BAB* 38 (1952) 477–8 (nos. 514–15). They often assisted the *archephodos*; see H. J. Drexhage in *Migratio et commutatio: Festschrift Th. Pekáry* (1989) 115–16. Things could occasionally go wrong: see BGU III 891 v (144), a surety for *presbyteroi* who were under accusation.

H. MAENO

5004

36 4B.98/F(1–2)a   15.3 × 6.5 cm   Third century

A son and his father are involved in the summons, but there is no mention of an accusation. The address to the *archephodos* suggests that the text is not later than c.250.

The writing is across the fibres. The back is blank.

ἀρχεφόδῳ Τακονα. ἐξαυτῆϲ ἀνάπεμψον
Ἀκύλαν Ἀπoληγίου ἢ τὸν πατέραν ἐγ[γ]υητ[ὴν
αὐτοῦ ὄντα ἢ ϲὺ αὐτὸϲ ἄνελθε.

2 l. πατέρα

'To the *archephodos* of Takona. Send Aquila son of Apoleius, or his father who is his guarantor, or else come up yourself.'

1 Τακονα was a village in the Lower toparchy. Two other such orders are addressed to *archephodoi* of this village, namely LXV **4486** i and SB XVI 12313.

ἐξαυτῆϲ ἀνάπεμψον. Four other Oxyrhynchite orders attest this opening: XII **1507** (III) and XLII **3035** (256), both addressed to comarchs and *epistatai eirenes*, lacking the accusation formula, and closing with the order that the officials should come up themselves if they fail to send up those summoned; **5010** (III/IV), addressed to comarchs and *demosioi*; and the Hermopolite PSI XV 1552.3–4 (III). One may thus assume that the formula is not attested earlier than the mid third century. However, the concept is already present in earlier texts; cf. SB XVIII 13854.3–4 (I) ἐξαυτῆϲ ἐ[κπέμ]ψατε, XVI 12649.3 (II) ἐξαυτῆ[ϲ] πέμψον.

2 Ἀπoληγίου. This name is usually found in the spelling Ἀπολήιοϲ. For the insertion of γ before a front vowel, see Mayser, *Grammatik*[2] i 142–3, Gignac, *Grammar* i 71–2.

πατέραν, l. -α. For the form, see Gignac, *Grammar* ii 45. Relatives are often mentioned in documents of this type; a father and his son also occur in PSI XV 1536.

ἐγ[γ]υητ[ήν. This word is not attested in any other such text. Surety was required for a wide range of purposes: for instance, a person could act as surety for someone in the case of a trial, in the case of payment of money or in the appointment of liturgists. See in general R. Taubenschlag, *The Law of Greco-Roman Egypt*[2] (1955) 411–17; J. Hermann, *Kleine Schriften zur Rechtsgeschichte* (1990) 94–121. If we suppose that Aquila was nominated for a liturgy and his father acted as a guarantor, the summons

5004. *SUMMONS* 139

could relate to something that happened when taking up the liturgy or during its performance; see N. Lewis, in *Pap. Congr. XI* (1966) 537 and n. 1, and *Compulsory Public Services*² 69.

3 ἢ cὺ αὐτὸc ἄνελθε. Cf. SB XVI 12313.3, (I **172** =) SB XVI 12706.3–4; sim. SB XII 11106.5. See also **5011** 3 n., and PSI XV 1536 introd.

P. M. PINTO

5005

71/11(a)   11.3 × 6.2 cm   Third/fourth century

In such documents the police functionaries of a village are ordered to send up persons to the *metropolis* or to come up themselves; here and in **5006** it is the local police that are summoned to appear; cf. also **5007**. Somewhat comparable is PSI XV 1536, which orders the *archephodos* to come up with two other persons—acting as a guard or because he was accused, is unclear. The addressees of the order are the φύλακεc and δημόcιοι, a combination not attested elsewhere. The issuing authority is a *decurio*, previously found only in two such documents, I **64** = W. *Chr.* 275 and the ostracon SB XVI 12469; see also **5006–9**. The reference to comarchs suggests a date after *c.*245.

The text is written along the fibres but on the back of a document, of which there are only scant remains (this is written along the fibres).

      π(αρὰ) τοῦ (δεκαδάρχου).
      ἐξαυτῆc ἥκετε ἅμα τῷ πεμ-
      φθέντι ὑπ' ἐμοῦ cτρατιώτῃ.
         (*vac.*)
      φ[ύ]λαξι καὶ δημοcίοιc
5   T[

1 π/   ✗

'From the *decurio*. Immediately come with the soldier sent by me.
'To the guards and *demosioi* of T—.'

1 (δεκαδάρχου). This military officer has been studied in detail by H. Melaerts in *Studia Varia Bruxellensia* 3 (1994) 99–121.

2 ἥκετε. This imperative occurs in a similar position in P. Cair. Isid. 131.3, and P. Kell. inv. D/1/75.13_2.3 (see above, p. 135 n. c); at the close of an order in P. Wisc. I 24.5, P. Kell. inv. D/1/75.25.4 and **5011** 3. The collocation ἐξαυτῆc ἥκετε is found in VII **1025** 10 and SB XIV 11452.3, but the context is different.

2–3 ἅμα τῷ πεμφθέντι. Cf. **5006** 4, **5007** 6–7.

3 cτρατιώτῃ. A soldier is mentioned in I **64** 3 and **5006** 5, issued by *decuriones* (cf. also BGU VII 1612, but the context is different), and in P. Wisc. 24.3, which stems from a procurator.

4 φ[ύ]λαξι. Guards are mentioned only in two other such texts (SB XII 11107, XXIV 16005), in

which they are said to accompany persons who are to be sent up (cf. also XXXI **2577**). The φύλακες were subordinate to *archephodoi*, and there were two or more per village; see Homoth-Kuhs, *Phylakes* 94–8 (relevant Oxyrhynchite texts: IX **1193**, **1212**, XVII **2122**).

5 *T*[. This is no doubt the beginning of a village name.

N. GONIS

5006

11 1B.147/B(a)　　　　　　9.6 × 7.6 cm　　　　　　Third/fourth century
　　　　　　　　　　　　　　　　　　　　　　　Plate VIII

This document conveys the same kind of order as **5005**. The signature, in a different hand from the main text, causes difficulty; see 6 n.

The text is written along the fibres but on reused papyrus; the other side, written along the fibres, carries parts of a text in prose. Offsets under the subscription in 6 suggest that the piece was rolled up from foot to top before the ink was dry.

　　π(αρὰ) τοῦ (δεκαδάρχου)
　　κωμάρχαιc καὶ δημοcίοιc κώ-
　　μηc Cύρων. ἐξαυτῆc ἀνέρ-
　　χεcθε ἅμα τῷ πεμφθέντι
5　cτρατιώτῃ.
　　(*vac.*)　　(*m.2*) . . . .

1 π/　　⳨

'From the *decurio* to the comarchs and *demosioi* of the village of Syron. Immediately come up with the sent soldier. (2nd hand) . . .'

2 κωμάρχαιc καὶ δημοcίοιc. See **5010** 6 n. P. Giss. Univ. I 15 is a similar order addressed to the comarchs of this village by a *centurio*.

3 Cύρων. This was a village in the Western toparchy.

6 I am not sure whether the writing is Greek or Latin. If the latter, it is not *signavi* (cf. **5007** 6), though the first letter could well be Latin *s*. If the former, it might be ἐcημ for ἐcημ(ειωcάμην).

N. GONIS

5007

27 3B.39/K(5–8)a　　　　　　9.5 × 7.2 cm　　　　　　Third/fourth century
　　　　　　　　　　　　　　　　　　　　　　　Plate VIII

The content of this document is unusual: the comarchs and *demosioi* of a village are ordered to go and meet a *decurio* at(?) the border of their village. The *decurio* seems to have been in the countryside and for some reason did not wish these officials to abandon the territory of their village, unless the border was simply a suitable place for a meeting. Another point of interest is the signature in Latin, unique in texts of this kind, and ultimately to be connected with the military function of the *decurio*.

Written across the fibres. Back blank.

    παρὰ τοῦ (δεκαδάρχου) κω (*vac.*) μάρχαις
    καὶ δημοςίοις κώμης Πα-
    ώμεως. ἐξαυτῆς λαβόντες
    γράμματα φροντίςατε
5   ςυναντῆςαί μοι μέχρι τῆς
    ςυνορίας ὑμῶν ἅμα τῷ
    πεμφθέντι νομοφύλακι.
(*m.2*)   seg(navi).

  1 ✗   8 *SEG*; l. *sig(navi)*

'From the *decurio* to the comarchs and *demosioi* of the village of Paomis. Immediately after you receive (my) letter, see to it that you meet me with the dispatched *nomophylax* as far as your border.' (2nd hand) 'I signed'.

2–3 Παώμεως. A village in the Thmoisepho toparchy.

3–4 ἐξαυτῆς λαβόντες γράμματα. Cf. I **62** = W. *Chr.* 278.4–5 (III), in a related order from a *centurio*: [ἐξα]υτῆς λαβών μου τὰ [γρ]άμματα πέμψον; for similar formulas, see IX **1193** 2–3, XII **1506** 2–3, P. Cair. Isid. 131.3, P. Horak 11.4–5, SB XXVI 16008.2, P. Kell. inv. (see above, p. 135 n. c) D/1/75.13_1.1, D/1/75.13_2.2–3, and D/1/75.25.2–3, all of the fourth century.

5 ςυναντῆςαι. This verb is fairly common in papyri of the Ptolemaic period but almost disappears thereafter; its latest attestations are in SB XX 15077.11–12 (45) and here.

7 νομοφύλακι. A *nomophylax* occurs in one other text of the same period, **3190**, in which he is said to be sent by a *prytanis*. For other instances, see **5002** 1 n.

8 *seg(navi)*, l. *sig(navi)*. Abbreviated as *sig* in P. Mich. VII 439 = ChLA V 301.18a. This is the Latin equivalent to Greek ςεςημείωμαι (see **5010** 5 n.).

N. GONIS

5008

18 2B.70/C(1–3)a   10 × 7.2 cm   Third/fourth century

A *decurio* orders the comarchs and *epistates eirenes* of a village to hand over—it is unclear to whom—two persons at the petition of a woman.

The writing is along the fibres and the back is blank.

    π(αρὰ) τοῦ (δεκαδάρχου)
    κωμάρχαις καὶ ἐπιςτάτηι εἰρή-

νης Πακερκη ἀπηλιώτου.
ἐξαυτῆς παράδοτε Κολλοῦθον υἱὸν Τνεφερϲόιτοϲ καὶ γυναῖκα
Λέοντοϲ Θρακίδου ἐντυχούϲηϲ
Αὐρηλίαϲ Ἰϲιδώραϲ.

1 π/ ✗

'From the *decurio* to the comarchs and *epistates eirenes* of Pakerke East. Immediately hand over Colluthus son of Tnephersois and the wife of Leon son of Thracidas at the petition of Aurelia Isidora.'

2–3 ἐπιϲτάτηι εἰρήνηϲ. Cf. **5009** 2; **5011** 4 and n. On this official, see G. Geraci in *Hestíasis: Studi di tarda antichità offerti a Salvatore Calderone* iii (1991) = *Studi tardoantichi* 3 (1987) 235–45.

3 Πακερκη ἀπηλιώτου. See above, **5003** 1 n.

4 ἐξαυτῆϲ παράδοτε. For the formula, see LXI **4116** 2–3 n.; add P. Wisc. I 24.2–3, BGU XVII 2701.2, and **5009** 3. It is unusual that there is no reference to the person to whom the accused are to be handed over.

5 υἱὸν Τνεφερϲόιτοϲ. An *apator*. The name Tnephersois is chiefly attested in Oxyrhynchite documents.

N. GONIS

5009

15 2B.40/C(c)a   8.9 × 6.1 cm   Third/fourth century

This is yet another order from a *decurio* to comarchs and an *epistates eirenes*, who would have to hand over three (or more) persons to someone he had sent. The break at the right has taken away the name of the village and some details concerning the accuser and accused.

The writing is across the fibres. Back blank.

π(αρὰ) τοῦ (δεκαδάρχου)
κωμάρχαιϲ καὶ ἐπιϲτάτῃ εἰρήνηϲ κ[- - -
ἐξαυτῆϲ παράδοτε τῷ διαπεμφθέν[τι - - -
τᾶν καὶ Ϲαραπίωνα καὶ Πετέμουν[ιν - - - ἐντυ-
χόντοϲ Ἀμμωνιανοῦ [- - -
.[..]..ατίων[ο]ϲ ἐξηγητ[εύϲαντοϲ.

1 π/ ✗

'From the *decurio* to the comarchs and *epistates eirenes* of . . . Immediately hand over to the dispatched . . . —tas and Sarapion and Petemunis . . . at the petition of Ammonianus . . . —ation, ex-*exegetes*.'

2 κ[: κ[ώμης or K[- (beginning of village name).

3 τῷ διαπεμφθέν[τι may have been followed by ϲτρατιώτῃ, but this is not the only possibility; cf. **5007** 7. The use of this compound is new in this context, but has occurred with a soldier in XIX **2230** 10–11 (119–24).

5 The lacuna took away Ammonianus' patronymic, in which case the name in 6 would be his father's alias; or Ammonianus' alias, his patronymic following in 6; or some other term or occupation.

6 .[.]. .ατίων[ο]ϲ. The letter before alpha looks like pi. Πατίων[ο]ϲ is one possibility; the name is attested in a couple of Arsinoite documents, but we should not expect to find it for a member of the Oxyrhynchite elite. Not Ὑπατίων[ο]ϲ?

ἐξηγητ[εύϲαντοϲ rather than ἐξηγητ[οῦ. It is unclear whether this refers to Ammonianus or to —ation. Whatever the case, he cannot be identified with any of the known *exegetai*. For officials mentioned in such documents, see **5012** 3 n.

N. GONIS

5010

31 4B.11/E(1–3)b   20.8 × 5.7 cm   Third/fourth century

A long strip written across the fibres, blank on the back. The hand suggests a date towards the end of the third century or the beginning of the fourth; cf. BGU XVII 2703 (283), P. Col. X 281 (287), P. Hamb. IV 268 (289), P. Mich. XV 720 (308), P. Gen. I² 10 (316). Apart from slight variations described in the notes, **5010** uses a formula attested for such texts in the Oxyrhynchite nome between the mid third and the fourth centuries: see U. Hagedorn, *BASP* 16 (1979) 69–70, 73–4; LXI **4114–4116** introd. (pp. 90–91). A date in the late third or early fourth century may further be suggested by prosopography; see below 1 n. (on Achilles), and 4 n. (on Aurelius Plutarchus).

The text is an order from Achilles, whose rank (κράτιϲτοϲ) is indicated but not his official function, to the comarchs and *demosioi* of Bercy, a village on the Hermopolite border, to 'send up' two persons escorted by a soldier, following an accusation made against them.

    π(αρὰ) τοῦ κρατίϲτου Ἀχιλλέωϲ.
    ἐξαυτῆϲ ἀναπέμψατε διὰ τοῦ ἀπεϲταλμένου ϲτρατιώτου
    Παφιβ Πρειτέλουϲ ϲὺν τῷ υἱῷ Ἀμάει καταμένονταϲ ἐν τῷ
    Μεικρῷ Ταρουθίνου προϲελθόντοϲ Αὐρηλίου Πλουτάρχου.
5   (vac.)   (m.2) ϲεϲημ(είωμαι).
(m.1) κωμάρχ(αιϲ) καὶ δημοϲ(ίοιϲ) Βερκυ.

1 π/   3 παφιβ'   4 l. Μικρῷ   5 ϲεϲη^μ   6 κωμαρ^χ δημοϲ'

'From Achilles, *vir egregius*.
'At once send up, through the soldier despatched, Paphib son of Preiteles with his son Amaeis, both dwelling in the Small Tarouthinou; Aurelius Plutarchus is the plaintiff.'

(2nd hand) 'I have signed (it).'
(1st hand) 'To the comarchs and the *demosioi* of Bercy.'

1 τοῦ κρατίϲτου. The appellation *vir egregius* or κράτιϲτοϲ, its Greek equivalent, was used for lower equestrian officials and military officers; see O. Hornickel, *Ehren- und Rangprädikate* (1930) 19–22; F. Millar, *JRS* 73 (1983) 90–91; P. Köln XI 458.7 n. (with references). Achilles could have been an equestrian procurator, like the one in P. Wisc. I 24 (late III [HGV]), an order to the *archephodoi* and *demosioi* of Philadelphia ἐξ ἐνκελεύϲεων Ϲαραπίωνοϲ ἐπιτρόπου; or a military officer who does not specify his exact function. The despatch of a soldier may seem to favour the latter alternative, but a soldier too is sent by the procurator in P. Wisc. 24.

τοῦ κρατίϲτου Ἀχιλλέωϲ. An Aurelius Achilles alias Ammonius, *vir egregius*, whose official capacity is not known, occurs in XXXI **2568** of 264. According to J. R. Rea, P. Oxy. XL pp. 31–2, this person has a fair chance of being the *hypomnematographus* Marcus Aurelius Achilles, *vir egregius*, mentioned as one of the addressees of **2915**, **2918**, **2920**, which date from the period 270–75; add the undated SB XIV 12158 (see P. Hamb. IV p. 229 n. 47). It is unclear whether he is to be identified with the *archidicastes* Aurelius Achilles in XXXVI **2768** 10–11 (undated but before 269; see P. Hamb. IV p. 224 with n. 29).

Another well-known Achilles active in this period was *corrector* and the right-hand man of the usurper L. Domitius Domitianus in the Egyptian rebellion of 297–8; for an overview of this revolt and references, see W. Kuhoff, *Diokletian und die Epoche der Tetrarchie* (2001) 185–96, and A. K. Bowman in *CAH*² xii 81–2. We know so little about him that an identification with Marcus Aurelius Achilles alias Ammonius cannot be totally ruled out. (A. H. S. el-Mosallamy, *ÉtPap* 9 (1971) 153–64, suggested identifying the *corrector* with the *archidicastes* of **2768**, but on flimsy grounds; see J. Schwartz, *L. Domitius Domitianus* (1975) 92, 120. The revised dating of **2768**, from the later third century to some time before 269 (see above), renders Mosallamy's suggestion even more difficult.)

3 Παφιβ'. This name is new, though cf. Παφαβ in O. Strasb. 657.4 (Thebaid; IV/V) and Παφῖβιϲ in P. Rain. Cent. 65.3 (Lycop.; 234). The apostrophe at the end indicates that the name is indeclinable; cf. P. Kell. IV p. 21.

Πρειτέλουϲ. The name Πρειτέληϲ is also an *hapax*.

3–4 ἐν τῷ Μεικρῷ (l. Μι–) Ταρουθίνου. This locality is new. The ἐποίκιον, later κτῆμα, Ταρουθίνου is well attested (see Pruneti, *I centri abitati* 198; Calderini–Daris, *Dizionario* iv 363, Suppl. ii 206, iii 145); it may have been located in the Eastern toparchy (see XXXI **2575** 1 n.). In the sixth and seventh centuries, there are references to a κτῆμα Μεγάληϲ Ταρουθίνου, apparently a different settlement (see Pruneti, *I centri abitati* 199; Calderini–Daris, *Dizionario* iii 249, Suppl. i 193, ii 118). What underlies the use of the feminine form of the adjective there and of the neuter here, is unclear, though τῷ Μικρῷ may modify an implicit ἐποικίῳ.

4 προϲελθόντοϲ. See P. Mich. X 589–91 introd. (p. 49 and n. 12); another example in BGU XVII 2700.4–5, as read in Korr. Tyche 590, forthcoming in *Tyche* 23 (2008).

Αὐρηλίου Πλουτάρχου. An Aurelius Plutarchus, former gymnasiarch and member of the board of *protostatai* of Oxyrhynchus in 296, is one of the senders of XXXVIII **2849**; I do not share the reluctance of the editor of **2849** to equate him with the *vir egregius* Aurelius Plutarchus alias Atactius of IX **1204**, who in 299 petitioned the strategus of the Oxyrhynchite nome to have his nomination as *dekaprotos* rescinded. Involvement of the person mentioned in both papyri with municipal matters in Oxyrhynchus in the 290s seems to be a good argument for such an identification. The chronological proximity between these two papyri and **5010** suggests that, although we may still be dealing with a namesake, the person mentioned in these three texts may well be the same individual.

6 κωμάρχ(αιϲ) καὶ δημοϲ(ίοιϲ). Cf. **5006** 2, **5007** 1–2. On these officials and their police duties, see N. Lewis, *CE* 45 (1970) 161–3; H. E. L. Mißler, *Der Komarch* 120–21; J. D. Thomas, *ZPE* 19 (1975)

113–9; R. S. Bagnall, *JARCE* 14 (1977) 68; Drexhage in *Festschrift Pekáry* 108–12; LXI **4116** 2 n.; CPR XXIII 7.13 n.

5005, **5010**, and **5011** are the only such documents in which the addressees are mentioned at the end of the text instead of directly after the mention of the sender.

Βερκυ. A village on the border between the Hermopolite and the Oxyrhynchite nomes, on which see most recently F. Mitthof, *APF* 49 (2003) 208–9. It belonged to the Hermopolite nome from the middle of the fourth century, but may have earlier been included in the Oxyrhynchite; **5010** now seems to offer support to this view.

M. COTTIER

5011

36 4B.100/E(1–3)b   19 × 7.4 cm   Third/fourth century

This text generally corresponds to the standard structure and wording of such documents that date from between the mid third to the late fourth century. The script points to a date in the late third or early fourth century. A remarkable feature is that the addressees are officials of an Arsinoite village, yet the chit was found at Oxyrhynchus.

The papyrus seems to have been folded horizontally three times. The writing is across the fibres and the back is blank.

> π(αρὰ) τοῦ β(ενε)φ(ικιαρίου).
> παράδοτε τῷ ἀποσταλέντι Ψάιν Οὐίβιος ἱερέα Ἀθηνᾶ[c
> ἢ ὑμεῖς ἥκετε.
> κωμάρχαις καὶ ἐπιστάτῃ εἰρήνης Ἀράβων.

1 π/   β̅   2 ψαϊν   3 ϋμεις

'From the *beneficiarius*. Hand over Psais son of Vibius, priest of Athena, to the person despatched, or come yourselves.'

'To the comarchs and the *epistates eirenes* of Arabon.'

1 β(ενε)φ(ικιαρίου). A *beneficiarius* issues a similar order in I **65** (III/IV). For the role of *beneficiarii* in the keeping of the public order, see N. B. Rankov, in E. Schallmayer (ed.), *Der römische Weihebezirk von Osterburken* ii (1994) 221–2, 230–31; R. L. Dise, *AHB* 9.2 (1995) 80; J. Nelis-Clément, *Les Beneficiarii: Militaires et administrateurs au service de l'Empire (Ier s. a.C. - Ve s. p.C.)* (2000) 228–9.

2 ἱερέα Ἀθηνᾶ[c. There seems to have been a temple of Athena in the Arsinoite 'village of the Arabs', which is probably mentioned in 4 (see n.); Athena was either an Egyptian goddess (Nēith or Thoēris) or an Arab deity (Allat). See P. Bottigelli, *Aegyptus* 22 (1942) 187; J. Quaegebeur, W. Clarysse, B. Van Maele, *ZPE* 60 (1985) 219–20; S. Honigman, *AncSoc* 32 (2002) 64–5. However, W. J. R. Rübsam, *Götter und Kulte im Faijum während der griechisch-römisch-byzantinischen Zeit* (1974) 153, considers Magdola as an alternative for the location of the temple.

Priests feature in several summonses; see XXXI **2573**, LXI **4116**, SPP XXII 1, BGU XI 2084.

Cf. also SPP XXII 55 (167), a petition addressed to a *beneficiarius* by a priest accusing one of his colleagues.

3 ἢ ὑμεῖς ἥκετε. Cf. P. Wisc. I 24.5 ἢ ὑμεῖς αὐτοὶ ἥκετε; among texts of this period, similar 'alternative' commands, but using the verb ἀνέρχεςθαι, occur in I **64** 5, XII **1507** 6, XLII **3035** 5, BGU XVII 2701.4, P. Cair. Isid. 129.3–4; for earlier parallels, see **5004** 3 n.

4 κωμάρχαις καὶ ἐπιςτάτῃ εἰρήνης. Other such orders addressed to these officials are I **64**, XII **1507**, XLII **3035** (ἐπιςτάταις), LXXIV **5008**, **5009**, and BGU XVII 2700.

Ἀράβων. This is probably the Arsinoite κώμη Ἀράβων rather than the Hermopolite or Panopolite villages of this name. For this village, also called Πτολεμαῒς (ἡ τῶν) Ἀράβων, located in the division of Heraclides, see the entry in the Fayum project at http://www.trismegistos.org/fayum/fayum2/285.php?geo_id=285/. The reference to the priest of Athena makes the identification likely; see above, 2 n.

D. COLOMO

5012

85/5(a)   21 × 3.1 cm   Fourth century

The papyrus is broken off at the top and left. There is one horizontal fold almost coinciding with line 3, and one vertical *c*.6.5 cm from the right edge. The piece is unusually thick, which may suggest that it was cut from a roll at the point of a *kollesis*. The document in its original state would have conformed to the usual pattern, that of a long rectangle, though in this case the text runs along the fibres. The back is blank.

The hand is a large official cursive of the fourth century; cf. *PGB* 38b of 348. Though much is lost, the arrangement would have been of the same type as e.g. **5010**, characteristic of Oxyrhynchite documents of this kind from after the middle of the third century.

```
        .      .      .      .      .      .
  ]..[ c.5 ]..[.].......[..].[....].[ c.3 ]..[.].
       ] οὐετρανῶν καὶ Ἀνουβᾶν ποιμένα αἰτιαθέντω(ν)
ὑπὸ   ]ωρίωνος βουλευτοῦ. (m.2) ϲεϲημ(είωμαι).
```

2 αιτιαθεντω̄; l. αἰτιαθέντας   3 ϲεϲη̄

'. . . of (the) veterans and Anoubas, shepherd, accused by . . . —orion, *bouleutes*.' (2nd hand) 'I have signed.'

1 At the end of the line, [ἀδε]λφ[ό]ν is a possibility.

2] οὐετρανῶν. What is lost in the break is unclear, but we may form an idea about it from P. Wisc. I 33.2–3 (147) Πτ]ολεμαίου Διοδώρου τοῦ καὶ Διοςκόρου τῶν ἀπὸ τοῦ Ἀρς[ιν]οείτου οὐετ[ρανῶν; CPR I 244.2 (II/III)]απιδος τοῦ καὶ Τίτου ἀπὸ οὐητρανῶν; BGU VII 1634.11 (229/30) υἱοὶ οὐετρ[αν]ῶν. There could be one or more army veterans. This is probably not an example of the collocation ἀπό + *officer* in the sense of 'former officer' (cf. *Lex. Lat. Lehn.* i 90–92).

5012. *SUMMONS* 147

ποιμένα. A ἱεροβουκόλοc (see BL VII 48) is accused in P. Fay. 37.2 (III), and an ἀρχιποιμήν in P. Prag. II 126.3 (Ars.; III).

αἰτιαθέντων (l. -αc). The mistake was presumably an influence from οὐετρανῶν. The aorist passive participle of αἰτιάομαι has occurred in BGU XI 2084.2 (Oxy.; III), P. Köln IV 189.2 (Oxy.; IV/V), and SB XX 14967.3 (Herm.; VI/VII). Cf. also P. Amh. II 146.4 (Herm.; V), P. Mil. II 42.2 (?; VI), and perhaps P. Mich. X 591.1 (Heracl.; VI), which use a different form of the verb.

3]ωρίωνοc: Ὠρίωνοc, Δ]ωρίωνοc, etc. This is either the name of the accuser (or of the last of them, if there were more than one) or a patronymic.

βουλευτοῦ. 'When the accuser is given a description he is very often the bearer of a public office'; see LXV **4486** 4 n., and for further discussion Drexhage in *Festschrift Pekáry* 112–13. BGU XVII 2700.5 and 2701.4 offer additional instances of officials in this context. A βουλευτήc is the accuser in P. Fay. 37.2.

cεcημ(είωμαι). There is no mention of the name of the official who issued the order, an established convention after the middle of the third century; see P. Cair. Isid. 131.8 n., and LXI **4116** 4 n.

R. HATZILAMBROU

5013–5016. DOCUMENTS RELATING TO PERFORMERS

Published in this section are a list and three contracts of performers. Such contracts are well attested: with the three published here, they now number twenty-five; all but one date from the Roman period. These contracts are collected in M. Vandoni, *Feste pubbliche e private* (1964) 14–27; to these add CPR XVIII 1 (Ars.; 231 BC), P. Stras. V 341 (Ars.; 85), P. Ross. Georg. II 18 (Ars.; 140), SPP XXII 47 (Ars.; II), P. Alex. Giss. 3 (Ars.; 201/2), P. Heid. IV 328 (?; III), XXXIV **2721** (III), **5014** (III), **5015** (III) and **5016** (III/IV). References to performers in the papyri are given by H. Harrauer in CPR XIII, Einleitung: D.1., s.vv. αὐλητήc, αὐλητρίc, and ὀρχήcτρια. See further W. L. Westermann, *JEA* 18 (1932) 16–27, F. Perpillou-Thomas, *ZPE* 108 (1995) 225–51 (a prosopography of artists and athletes), and M. Vesterinen, *Dancing and Professional Dancers in Roman Egypt* (diss. Helsinki 2007), forthcoming as M. Satama, *Dance, Dancers and other Performers in Graeco-Roman Egypt*, in Papers and Monographs of the Finnish Institute at Athens (2010).

The contracts indicate the employers, the employees, the place and duration of the performance, the wage, and some other conditions such as the transportation of the performers. The employer is mostly a village association (cύνοδοc κώμηc), as in the three contracts published here, represented by one or several presidents (προcτάτηc) of the association. Sometimes the employer acts as a private person, as e.g. in P. Corn. 9 (Ars.; 206) and in P. Aberd. 58 (probably Ars.; III). The employee is typically a group of performers (cυμφωνία, cύνταξιc) consisting of musicians and dancers and represented by one person, the head or 'manager' of the group (προεcτώc, πρωταύληc, προνοούμενοc, πραγματευτήc, προνοητήc). As for the form of the contracts, the majority are either *homologiai* or *cheirographa*. Oxyrhynchite contracts mostly fall into the group of objective *homologiai*. For the legal and formal aspects of the contracts, see e.g. J. Hengstl, *Private Arbeitsverhältnisse freier Personen in den hellenistischen Papyri bis Diokletian* (1972).

The contracts provide valuable information, especially about the economic circumstances of performers, albeit the wage level of individual performers is ambiguous. This is due to the physical condition of the documents or to the contents and wording of the contracts (e.g. the exact number of performers is not stated). It seems, however, that the performers were paid considerably better than an average wage-labourer. For the wages of performers, see Westermann, *JEA* 10 (1924) 140–43, and H.-J. Drexhage, *Preise, Mieten/Pachten, Kosten und Löhne im römischen Ägypten bis zum Regierungsantritt Diokletians* (1991) 410–11. Updated tables of wages and detailed discussion on economic aspects of the performers are found in Vesterinen, *Dancing and Professional Dancers*.

Besides informing us about the economic status of the performers, the contracts offer an insight into the festivities in the villages of Greco-Roman Egypt. The duration of the celebrations is given by stating the month and number of days for which the performers are hired. The exact reason for the celebrations is not, as a rule, mentioned. There are, however, good reasons for arguing that the performances belong to contexts of religious festivities, for example, because of the old Egyptian calendar used in some of the contracts. Agonistic festivals of the Greek style seem not to be concerned. Festivities in villages and towns of Greco-Roman Egypt are discussed in F. Perpillou-Thomas, *Fêtes d'Égypte ptolémaïque et romaine d'après la documentation papyrologique grecque* (1993).

M. SATAMA

5013. LIST OF PERFORMERS

A 246   9.8 × 8.1 cm   Second century

A list of names, not alphabetically arranged, with occupations of performers, including one citharode (κιθαρῳδός), two comedy actors (κωμῳδοί), one (pantomime) dancer (ὀρχηϲτής), and perhaps one mime performer (μῖμος). These performers seem to point to a theatrical context rather than to performers hired to perform in villages, as is the case in the three contracts for entertainment published in this volume (**5014–16**). All the occupational titles listed here occur in various accounts of theatrical contests (e.g. III **519** of the second century), and as members of the association of theatre performers, the Artists of Dionysus (e.g. SB V 8855, an honorary inscription from Ptolemais; III BC). For the Artists, see A. Pickard-Cambridge, *The Dramatic Festivals of Athens* (1968) 279–305; C. Roueché, *Aphrodisias in Late Antiquity* (1989) 50–57; B. Le Guen, *Les Associations de Technites dionysiaques à l'époque hellénistique* (2001). There is a short introduction with references to ancient written sources in E. Csapo, W. J. Slater, *The Context of Ancient Drama* (1994) 239–55.

The exact nature of the list is unclear. The upper margin measures 1.5 cm, indicating that the list begins from the first line. There may have been preceding sections above the surviving text. There is some blank space to the left as well (1 cm). The purpose of the list may have been stated somewhere, be it either before or after the preserved lines. The names and occupations are in the nominative, which would at first thought exclude the possibility of this being part of an account of wages paid to the performers; in accounts the case is usually the dative (see e.g. **519**). There are, however, lists of payments where the receiver is in the nominative, e.g. SB XX 14677 (Herm.?; v), ed. pr. U. Horak, *Tyche* 4 (1989) 101–7, who notes (p. 102) that the names should be in the dative. In that case, our document should begin with a phrase stating that the following persons have received a sum, which in turn would have been mentioned in the right part of the papyrus, now lost. It is also possible that these persons have paid something, in which case the nominative would cause no problem. Another possibility is that our fragment is part of a tax list. This interpretation is supported by the crossed-out name 6, which would suit better a tax list than an account of payments. Again, in the case of a tax list, the paid taxes could have been mentioned in the right part of the document. A third possibility is that it is a part of the records of some club or association of performers. The nature of the association might have been given before a list of the members, and this fragment would be only part of that list. Later, perhaps, there could have been some other information, such as (membership) fees paid by individual members and accounts of expenditures. For this kind of document, see C. Ptol. Sklav. I pp. 333–51.

Only the first two names and occupations can be deciphered properly. The right part has worn off badly, and after seven lines only some traces can be seen. After line 4 the rest of the papyrus is only loosely attached to the upper part of the papyrus. The writing is along the fibres, and the back is blank.

```
     Κάνωπος   κιθαρῳδός
     Θ]εαγένης κωμῳδ[ός
         ]ίων μ . . ος
         ]ος ὀρχηςτής
5        ]ς κω[μῳδός
         ]⟦χος⟧
         ]ανδρ . . [
         ] traces
           .   .   .
```

1 *Κάνωπος*. The name is common. In a theatrical context, one should mention the Oxyrhynchus papyrus published by W. E. H. Cockle in *Pap. Congr. XIV* (1975) 59–65: ii 3 ᾠδαὶ Κανώπου. There was also a tragedy actor named Kanopos; see I. E. Stefanis, *ΔΙΟΝΥΣΙΑΚΟΙ ΤΕΧΝΙΤΑΙ* (1988) no. 1375, p. 251.

κιθαρῳδόc. A citharode, a performer who accompanied himself with the cithara, is mentioned in only a few papyri. In P. Cair. Zen. I 59087.17 and 23 (258/257 BC) two linen chitons are given to a female citharode named Satyra employed in Apollonios' household in Alexandria (see also P. Cair. Zen. I 59028; probably 258 BC). XXVII **2476** 20, 26 (= Pap. Agon. 3; 288/289; listed in Stefanis, *ΔΙΟΝΥΣΙΑΚΟΙ ΤΕΧΝΙΤΑΙ* no. 24) mentions a citharode Agathocles also called Asterius, a citizen of Alexandria, Antinoopolis, and Lycopolis. XXXIII **2682** 21–2 (III/IV) is a private letter in which greetings are sent to a citharode called Ammonis. A considerably later instance of a citharode is in SB XIV 12124.2 = XXII 15753.2 (Ars.; VI), where the slaves of the citharode Theodosius receive oil. To the list can be added the inscription mentioned in the introduction, SB V 8855.41, concerning the Artists of Dionysus.

2 κωμῳδόc. A comedy actor is mentioned in three other papyri. In P. Cair. Zen. III 59417.11 (III BC), a private letter containing an account of payments to various persons, a comedy actor called Mikion receives 8 drachmas for some unknown reason. In an account of religious festivals, something is paid to a comedy actor (SB IV 7336.10, 22, Oxy. or Ars.; late III). A comedy actor called Syrus is mentioned in a private letter from Oxyrhynchus (PSI III 236.30–31; III/IV).

3 μ . . οc. Perhaps μῖμοc, though the second mu is difficult (μάγοc cannot be read). Mime actors occur in various lists and accounts, often in connection with other theatre- or circus-performers; see BGU XIV 2428 (Hera.; I BC), III **519**, X **1050**, SB IV 7336, P. Wash. Univ. II 95 (IV/V), XXVII **2480** (565/6?), XXXIV **2707** (VI), P. Harrauer 56 (?; VI).

4 ὀρχηcτήc. While ὀρχηcτήc is a general term for a male dancer, from the first century onwards it refers especially to a pantomime dancer. Pantomime dancers performed either in private festivities or in theatres. In many documents where tragedy and comedy actors and, e.g., citharodes occur, these male dancers are also mentioned (e.g. SB V 8855.45 and OGIS 51, an honorary inscription from Egypt of *c*.240 BC). For further references to pantomimes in ancient sources, see Csapo–Slater, *The Context of Ancient Drama* 369–89. The word ὀρχηcτήc occurs in three papyri related to a context of festivities: P. Stras. V 341.4, 9–10 (Ars., 85), a contract of performers; III **519** 6 (II), an account of a theatrical contest; SB IV 7336.14 (III), an account (also l. 27, where something is paid τῷ τοῦ ὀρχηcτοῦ δραματοθ[έτηι]. See further F. Wormald, *JEA* 15 (1929) 239 ff. The word occurs also in two private letters, III **526** 9–10 (II) and XIV **1676** 7–8 (III), and cf. the term παντόμιμοc in P. Flor. I 74.3–4 (Herm.; 181), a contract of performers.

M. SATAMA

5014. Contract of Performers

101/211(a)   7.9 × 17 cm   Third century

A contract drawn between Dioscorus and Petronis, the two presidents (προcτάται) of the village Ibion Ammoniou, situated in the lower toparchy, and Copreus, the head of a company (πρωταύληc καὶ προεcτώc) of *aulos*-players and musicians. In X **1275** 8–9 (undated, but of the third century) occurs Κοπρεὺc Cαραπάμμωνοc titled as προεcτὼc cυμφωνίαc αὐλητῶν καὶ μουcικῶν. It would be tempting to identify these persons as one and the same. Note also that in **1275** the performance takes place in Souis, which was situated in the lower toparchy too.

The closest parallels are **1275**, XXXIV **2721**, and **5015**. The end of the document is missing; to judge from the contents, only the date and signatures are lost.

5014. CONTRACT OF PERFORMERS

ὁμολογοῦσιν ἀ[λ]λήλοις Αὐρήλιοι Διόσκορος Ἡρακλᾶτος καὶ Πετρῶνις Πεσόιτος
ἀμφότεροι προστάται Ἰβιῶνος Ἀμμωνίου
καὶ Κοπρεὺς πρωταύλης καὶ προεστὼς
5   συμφωνίας αὐλητῶν τε καὶ μουσικῶν,
οἱ μὲν περὶ τὸν Διόσκορον παρειληφέναι
τὸν Κοπρέαν cὺν τῇ αὐτῇ cυμφωνίᾳ
λειτουργήcοντα τοῖc ἀπὸ τῆc κώμηc
πανηγυριζούcηc ἐπὶ ἡμέραc ἑπτὰ
10 ἀπὸ ιζ τοῦ ὄντοc μηνὸc Παυνι μιcθοῦ
ἑκάcτηc ἡμέραc δραχμῶν ἑκατὸν
εἴκοcι καὶ ἄρτων ζευγῶν μ̄, ἐλαίου
ῥαφανίνου κοτυλῶν η̄, καὶ ὅλων
τῶν ἡμερῶν οἴνου κεραμίου ἑνόc,
15 ὄξουc κεραμίου ἑνόc, πάντων ὄντων
καθαρῶν. αὐτόθι δὲ ἔcχεν εἰc λόγον
ἀραβῶνοc δραχμὰc τεccαράκοντα καὶ τοῦτον cὺν τῇ cυμφωνίᾳ
παραλήμψονται ἀπὸ τοῦ Ὀξυρυγχίτου
20 καὶ ἀποκαταcτήcαντεc ἐκεῖ παρέ-
ξονται αὐτοῖc ξενίαν ἀcφαλῆν
καὶ ἀνεπηρέαcτον καὶ μετὰ τὰc
ἡμέραc ἑπτὰ πληρώcαντεc
αὐτοὺc τοῖc μιcθοῖc καὶ ἐκτάκτοιc
25 ἀποκαταcτήcουcι εἰc τὸν
αὐτὸν Ὀξυρυγχίτην. ἐὰν μὴ
.[......]....[.]........
. . . .

Back, downwards, along the fibres.
(m.2) Ἰβιῶνος Ἀμμωνίου

17 l. ἀρραβῶνοc   21 l. ἀcφαλῆ   22 ἀνεπηρέαcτον: last α corr. from c   καί: κ corr. from μ

'Aurelius Dioscorus son of Heraclas and Aurelius Petronis son of Pesois, both presidents of the village of Ibion Ammoniou, and Copreus, the first *aulos*-player and head of a company of *aulos*-players and musicians, mutually agree, that Dioscorus' party has invited Copreus and the said company to perform for those who reside at the village as it holds a festival for seven days beginning from the 17th of the present month Payni, at a wage each day of 120 drachmas and 40 pairs of loaves,

8(?) *koṭylai* of radish-oil, and for all the days one *keramion* of wine and one *keramion* of vinegar, all free from encumbrances. And he [= Copreus] has got on the spot as earnest money forty drachmas; and they will receive him with the company from the Oxyrhynchite nome and when they have returned them there, they will provide for them safe and undisturbed lodging. And after the seven days, when they have paid them the wages and separate deliveries, they will return them (i.e. Copreus with his company) to the same Oxyrhynchite nome. If . . . not . . .'

Back: 'Ibion Ammoniou.'

2 Πεcόιτοc. The name in this spelling is not found elsewhere; Παcόιc is better known.

4 πρωταύλης καὶ προεcτώc. The same title occurs in XXXIV **2721** 5; see the note there for some remarks on the term πρωταύλης.

7 Κοπρέαν. We find Κοπρέα in X **1275** 11. The form points to a nominative Κοπρέας, but here it is a heteroclitic accusative of Κοπρεύς.

8 λειτουργήcοντα. This participle occurs in several contracts of performers, either in the singular (as here and **2721** 9) or in the plural (P. Corn. 9.5, P. Fam. Tebt. 54.10, **1275** 12, **5015** 8). The use of singular or plural may be understood as referring to either the head of the company with his company or to the whole company.

8–9 τοῖc ἀπὸ τῆc κώμης πανηγυριζούcης. Cf. **2721** 9–10 τοῖc θαλε̣ι[αζ]ομένοις ἀνδράcι; VII **1025** 11–12 ἔθοc ὑμῖν ἐcτὶν cυνπανηγυρίζειν, cυνεορτάcοντες. The noun πανήγυρις refers to a big festival, sometimes to religious or political celebrations. In papyri it occurs less frequently than ἑορτή. For πανήγυρις and ἑορτή, see L. Casarico, *Aegyptus* 64 (1984) 135–62; Perpillou-Thomas, *Fêtes d'Égypte* pp. xiv–xv and *passim*.

10–15 The items this company receives as wage are very similar to those in **1275** 16–20, and even the amounts are at points the same. See also the wages in **5015** 12–15 with the relevant notes.

13 η̄. If η is correct, the amount of radish-oil is the same as in **1275** 18.

15–16 πάντων ὄντων καθαρῶν. The phrase occurs in connection with contracts of performers also in **2721** 19–20 and **5015** 16. For καθαρός in fiscal actions, see A. Gara, *Prosdiagraphomena e circolazione monetaria* (1976) 36–8.

17 ἀραβῶνος (l. ἀρρα-). In **1275**, **2721**, and most probably **5015**, the earnest money is 20 drachmas. The word occurs also in P. Grenf. II 67.17 (with the same spelling), but the sum is not preserved.

18–26 Basically the same formula as in **1275** 22–6 and **2721** 23–34, though there is no reference to donkeys used for transportation. On transportation see P. J. Sijpesteijn in *Miscellanea Tragica in honorem J. C. Kamerbeek* (1976) 425–9.

19 ἀπὸ τοῦ Ὀξυρυγχίτου. For the phrase, which means 'from anywhere within the nome', see **1275** 25 n., and especially **2721** 24 n. It recurs in **5015** 21.

21 ἀcφαλῆν, l. -ῆ. See Gignac, *Grammar* ii 135–6. Same form in **2721** 28.

26 ἐὰν μή. This must be the beginning of a penalty clause, after which there would have come the date and signature(s). The absence of a connective is, however, a problem. A penalty clause has not been attested in any other contract of performers, and such clauses are generally rare in work contracts; see Hengstl, *Private Arbeitsverhältnisse* 113 ff.

M. SATAMA

5015. Contract of Performers

100/180(a)   8.9 × 11.2 cm   Third century

A contract drawn between Hatres and Didymus, the two presidents (προcτάται)

5015. CONTRACT OF PERFORMERS

of the village of Thosbis, and Callinicus, the head (προεcτώc) of a company of *aulos*-players and *krotalistriai* (dancers with clappers, *krotala*). The text breaks off in the middle of the phrase stating the transportation to and from the village. A concluding phrase stating that the contract is accepted by both parties, date, and signatures are lost (see e.g. XXXIV **2721**).

In this contract, the term ἐργαcτήριον occurs for the first time with musicians and dancers. It probably refers to some kind of school where dancers and musicians were trained and then hired to perform, a 'studio' or 'workshop' for performers. The term had occurred in the context of performers only in one other papyrus, the sixth-century account XXVII **2480** 43: τοῖc μίμ(οιc) τῶν β ἐργαcτηρ(ίων).

The text is written against the fibres but on what was the original recto. There are some traces of ink on the back. The sheet was probably folded from top to bottom; the folds can be detected at five points (in the text, between lines 2 and 3, between lines 5, 6 and 7, at 10, 14, and 18).

    ὁμολογοῦcιν ἀλλήλοιc Αὐρήλιοι Ἁτρῆc Κορ-
    νηλίου καὶ Δίδυμοc Ἀντέρωτοc ἀμφότεροι
    προcτάται κώμηc Θώcβεωc καὶ Καλλίνιγ-
    κοc Ἄπειτοc ἀπ' Ὀξυρύγχων πόλεωc προεc-
5 τὼc ἐργαcτηρίου αὐλητῶν τε καὶ κροτα-
    λιcτ[ρ]ι̣[ῶ]ν, οἱ μὲν περὶ τὸν Ἁτρῆν παρει-
    ληφέναι τὸν Καλλίνιγκ[ο]ν c[ὺν] τῇ αὐ-
    τῇ cυνφωνίᾳ λειτουργήcανταc τοῖc
    ἀπὸ τῆc κώμηc ἐφ' ἡμέραc ἑορτῶν πέν-
10 τε ἀ[πὸ] ι̣[γ̅ τ]ο̣ῦ Φαωφι ἕωc ι̅ζ̅ κα[ὶ] α̣[ὐτ]ῆ̣c ι̅ζ̅
    τοῦ αὐτοῦ μηνὸc μιcθοῦ ἑκάcτηc ἡμέ-
    ραc δραχμῶν ἑκατὸν εἴκοcι καὶ ἄρτων
    ζευγῶν τεccαράκοντα καὶ ἐλέου ῥαφα-
    νίν[ου...].... [.]..[......]....[....]. [.]. [τῆc ἑο]ρ-
15 τῆc οἴνου κεραμίου ἑνὸc καὶ ὄξουc ἑν(όc),
    πάντων ὄντων καθαρῶν. αὐτόθι δὲ
    μετεβάλοντο{ι} οἱ περὶ τὸν Ἁτρῆν τῷ Κα[λ-
    λιν[ί]γκ̣[ῳ c.8 ὑ]π̣ὲ̣ρ ἀ̣[ρραβῶνοc] δρ̣[α-
    χμὰ̣c̣ εἴκοcι καὶ τοῦτον ἅμα τῇ cυν-
20 φωνίᾳ παραλήμψονται χωρὶc
    θεοῦ βίαc ἀπὸ τοῦ [Ὀξ]υ̣ρ̣[υγχ]ε̣ί̣[το]υ̣ [δ]ι̣ὰ
    ....].[

3–4, 7 καλλινιγ'κος; l. Καλλίνικος   8, 19 l. ϲυμφωνίᾳ   8 l. λειτουργήϲονταϲ
13 l. ἐλαίου   20 χωρίϲ: χ corr.

'Aurelius Hatres son of Cornelius and Aurelius Didymus son of Anteros, both presidents of the village of Thosbis, and Callinicus son of Apeis from the city of the Oxyrhynchi, the head of an *ergasterion* of *aulos*-players and *krotalistriai*, mutually agree that on the one hand Hatres' party has invited Callinicus and the said company to perform for those who reside at the village, for five festive days, beginning from the 13th of Phaophi until the 17th, including the 17th of the same month, at the wage each day of one hundred and twenty drachmas and forty pairs of loaves and eight(?) *kotylai* of radish-oil, (and for all the festive days(?)) one *keramion* of wine and one of vinegar, all free from encumbrances. On the other hand, Hatres' party has remitted on the spot to Callinicus . . . (for earnest money?) twenty drachmas, and they will receive him with the company, act of God apart, from (anywhere within) the Oxyrhynchite nome . . .'

3 Θώϲβεωϲ. A village in the Upper toparchy.

5 ἐργαϲτηρίου. On the particular significance of the terms here, see introd. Otherwise, the word ἐργαϲτήριον is well attested, generally referring to a (work)shop or storage of different types (e.g. ἐργαϲτήριον λαχανοπωλ(ικόν) in XII **1461** 5–6). For ἐργαϲτήριον in Ptolemaic corn administration, see R. Düttenhöfer, *ZPE* 98 (1993) 253 ff.

κροταλίϲτρια, often translated as a castanet-dancer, occurs in three other papyri, of which P. Ross. Georg. II 18 IV fr. O 425 is the earliest (Ars.; 140); it is a fragmentary roll of *diagraphai* with a κροταλίϲτρια in one entry. In P. Corn. 9 (Ars.; 206) Isidora and two other κροταλίϲτριαι are hired, while in XXXIV **2721** the κροταλίϲτρια performs with a group of musicians (three *aulos*-players and their leader). The form κροταλίϲτρίϲ is used in III **475** 17–18 (182), a document concerning an accident on a festive occasion. The verb κροταλίζω occurs in **5016** 10 and the instruments κρόταλα (always plural when referring to the musical instruments) in P. Hib. I 54.13 (*c*.245 BC), where a certain effeminate (μαλακόϲ) Zenobios is needed to perform at some religious festival. The *krotala* were percussion instruments, usually translated as clappers or castanets, played in a variety of contexts often by a (female) dancer to give rhythm to the dance and to enhance body movements. See also Herodotus 2.60, for *krotala* played in the festival of Bastet in Bubastis.

8 λειτουργήϲανταϲ. See **5014** 8 n.

10 ἀ[πὸ] ι̣[γ̅ τ]ο̣ῦ Φαῶφι. It is interesting that in P. Grenf. II 67 the performance is set to start also on Phaophi 13, though the date is calculated according to the old Egyptian calendar (= 6 August 237).

12–13 120 drachmas and 40 pairs of loaves as wage are exactly the same as in **5014** 11–12; see the note there.

13–15 Perhaps ῥαφα|νίν[ου κοτ]υλῶν̣ [ὀ]κτ̣[ὼ καὶ ὅλ]ω̣ν τῷ̣[ν ἡμε]ρ̣[ῶ]ν̣ [τῆϲ ἑο]ρ̣|τῆϲ. Eight *kotylai* of radish-oil would be the same amount as in **5014** 12–13 and X **1275** 18.

15 The amounts of wine and vinegar are the same as in **5014** 14–15 and **1275** 19–20.

16 πάντων ὄντων καθαρῶν. See **5014** 15–16 n.

16–19 If line 18 is correctly read and restored (cf. P. Grenf. II 67.17), the reference is to the earnest money (ἀρραβών) paid to Callinicus, beginning from αὐτόθι, occupying the whole of the badly damaged l. 18 and ending with the sum, 20 drachmas, in l. 19. It seems that the clause in our document varies slightly compared with the three other contracts from Oxyrhynchus in which it is preserved (**5014** 16–18, **1275** 21–2, **2721** 20–22). In those documents, the clause consists (with some variation) of a form of the verb ἔχω followed by εἰϲ λόγον ἀρραβῶνοϲ δραχμάϲ and the sum (40 drachmas in **5014**, 20 in the other two). In **2721** 20, it is further stated that the sum is paid from the wages (ἀπὸ δὲ τῶν μιϲθῶν).

19–22 For the phrase stating the transportation to the village and from there, see **5014** 18–26 n.
22 At the beginning of the line, perhaps restore [ὄνων] followed by the number of donkeys. Cf. **1275** 22–6.

M. SATAMA

5016. CONTRACT OF PERFORMERS

100/150(b)   9.5 × 7.2 cm   Late third/early fourth century

A contract drawn up between three presidents (προςτάται) of the village Sincepha and the head of a company of performers. The contract is of the *cheirographon*-type, beginning with the greeting formula ὁ δεῖνα τῷ δεῖνι χαίρειν. This is typical of contracts of the early Byzantine period, found also in the latest contract of performers, SPP XX 78 = CPR XVIIA 19 (321).

The document is broken in two through lines 5 and 6. Only the beginnings of the first 12 lines survive, and probably almost half of the whole width of document is missing from the right side (*c*.20 letters), as suggested by the partly restored lines 6 and 7. Parts of some typical phrases occur in this contract, but on the whole it does not resemble any of the published contracts of performers to the extent that it would be possible to restore the missing parts with any certainty.

The occurrence of the collocation τῆς λαμπρᾶς καὶ λαμπροτάτης Ὀξυρυγχιτῶν πόλις (6–7, partly restored) suggests a date after 272, when this title first appears; see D. Hagedorn, *ZPE* 12 (1973) 277 ff., especially 285 ff.

The text is written along the fibres. On the back is the end of a private letter, written along the fibres in a different hand.

    Αὐρήλιοι Κοπρεὺς Ἀμουνι[
    Cοντώουτος μη(τρὸς) Θαήϲι[ος
    ϲτρ’ᾶϲ οἱ τρῖς ἀπὸ κώμης Ϲιγκ[εφα
    προστάται {προστάται} τῆς α[ὐτῆς κώμης - - - τοῦ
5   ἐνεϲτῶτος μη(νὸς) Τυβι ιζ ἕω[ς
    Αὐρη(λίῳ) Κορ[ν]ηλι... πρ.....[- - - ἀπὸ τῆς λαμπρᾶς καὶ
    λαμπροτάτης Ὀξ(υρυγχιτῶν) πόλε[ως χαίρειν. παρειλήφα-
    μέν ϲε μετὰ τῆς ϲυμφ[ωνίας
    ... τιαριων ϲυνπανη[π-
10 αίζειν καὶ κλοταρείζ[ειν
    πληροῦν ἐπὶ τὰϲ.[
    ..[...].. τῇ ὅλῃ ϲυμ[φωνίᾳ
               ]...[
    . . . . . .

3 τρις: ρ corr. from ο?; l. τρεῖς   10 l. κροταλίζειν

'Aurelius Copreus son of Amuni(u)s (and NN, Aurelius NN son of) Sontous and Thaesis, (Aurelius NN, son of NN and NN), the three from the village Sincepha . . . presidents of the same village (celebrating?) (from the?) 17th of the present month Tybi until . . . , to Aurelius Corneli(an)us the head(?) of a group of performers from the splendid and most splendid city of the Oxyrhynchites, greetings. We have engaged you with your group . . . to take part in the festivities . . . to entertain and to play the *krotala* . . . (We agree?) to pay for the (days?) . . . for the whole group . . .'

1 Ἀμούνι[ος or Ἀμουνί[ου. The broken part of the line would have contained the abbreviation μη(τρός), mother's name in the genitive and the name of the second president in the nominative.

2 At the end of the line there would have stood the name of the third president in the nominative, his patronymic, the abbreviation μη(τρός) and her name in the genitive continuing to the next line 3.

3 -στρ`α´ς. Since the next word begins the phrase 'the three presidents of etc.', this should be the end of a female name in the genitive, i.e. the mother of the third president. A tiny alpha (or iota?) seems to have been added on top of rho.

Σιγκ[εφα. This was village in the Upper toparchy.

4 Since the next line contains a date that most probably refers to the days of the festivities (see below), one may restore προστάται τῆς α[ὐτῆς κώμης ἑορταζούσης/-ούσης ἀπὸ τοῦ]; see **5014** 8–9 κώμης πανηγυριζούσης and the note there. (The verb πανηγυρίζω would be too long; thus ἑορτάζω is suggested.) The participle could also refer to the προστάται, i.e., restore ἑορτάζοντες/-οντες ('the presidents of the same village who celebrate . . .').

5 μη(νός) is abbreviated similarly to μη(τρός) in line 2. There is an oblique stroke between the day (ιζ) and ἕω[ς. The phrase states the day when the festivities begin (17th) until which day they last; cf. e.g. **5015** 10 and P. Heid. IV 328.8–9 (III). The placement of the date, either for the time of writing or for the days the group was hired, is odd compared to other contracts of performers. The date usually comes last, and the days for the festivals are normally mentioned after the other party is introduced. Syntactically, however, it is more difficult to put the date of the writing of the document in this place.

6 Αὐρη(λίῳ) Κορ[ν]ηλιανῷ rather than Κορ[ν]ηλίῳ. His patronymic or occupation should have followed next ('head of the company'). This word seems to begin with πρ-, and if it is an occupational title, three possibilities exist: προεστώς, πρωταύλης, or πραγματευτής. To judge from the traces, the third is perhaps the most likely, and was probably abbreviated as πραγ(ματευτῇ). The occupational titles of the head of the group of performers are briefly discussed in the general introduction.

6–7 [ἀπὸ τῆς λαμπρᾶς καὶ] λαμπροτάτης Ὀξ(υρυγχιτῶν) πόλε[ως. See introd.

7–8 παρειλήφα]μεν: or παρελάβο]μεν. The verb παραλαμβάνω, in the perfect or aorist, is typical in contracts of performers in the meaning 'to hire', 'to engage', 'to invite (as employees)', and hence suggested here; see e.g. X **1275** 10–11, XXXIV **2721** 7–8, 5014 6, **5015** 6–7. Other compounds or forms of the verb λαμβάνω also occur, e.g. P. Grenf. II 67.5 [ἐ]κλαβεῖν, P. Aberd. 58.2 ἔλαβον.

8 The line continues after συμφωνίας probably with a characterization of the group ('group of musicians, dancers, etc.').

9 The occupational titles in the genitive beginning in line 8 would continue to line 9, hence the genitive that ends with -τιαριων or -τιςαριων. The first three letters in 9 seem to be μαν-, although the letters are not very typical for the hand. While the resulting word, μαντιαρίων, is a possibility (the diminutive of μάντις), its occurrence in connection with performers is unexpected.

συνπανη[: some form of συνπανηγυρίζω, perhaps συνπανηγυρίζειν. In one contract of performers, this verb is used for the performers who are invited (i.e. hired) 'to take part in the festivities':

ἐξαυτῆς ἥκετε, καθὼ[ς | ἔθος ὑμῖν ἐςτιν ςυνπα|νηγυρίζειν, ςυνεορτάςον|τες (VII **1025** 10–13). In our document there would still be room for one infinitive, perhaps ςυνεορτάζειν. The infinitives continue to the next line defining the role of the hired performers at the festivities. See also **5014** 9 n. A possible restoration of lines 9–10: ςυνπανη[γυρίζειν, ςυνεορτάζειν, ςυμπ]αίζειν.

9–10 π]|αίζειν. The word division is odd, but this restoration is hardly in doubt. παίζειν is probably part of a compound, since otherwise pi would have been written at the beginning of the line, e.g. ςυμπαίζειν, ἐμπαίζειν, or προςπαίζειν. In at least one contract of performers παιςτής refers to a performer, either a musician or a dancer (P. Gen. I 73.5). The verb here can refer to playing an instrument or dancing in a playful tone. It could also refer to jesting, following the other occurrences of the verb in papyri, e.g. LV **3812** 10 and n. (late III), a private letter concerning the celebration of Saturnalia. The sender finds fault with the receiver who did not send honey to the celebration and did not arrive there, and says 'I write this . . . by way of a joke' (ταῦτα δέ ςοι γράφω . . . προςπαίζων). Perhaps the verb here refers to the performers as jesters.

κλοταρείζ[ειν, l. κροταλίζειν. For the interchange and transposition of liquids, see Gignac, *Grammar* i 102, 104. For the *krotala*-instruments, see **5015** 5–6 n.

The end of the line probably contains a phrase such as 'in the above-mentioned village' (ἐν τῇ προκειμένῃ κώμῃ).

11 πληροῦν. The infinitive is part of the stipulation of the wage paid by the employers beginning from the previous line, i.e. 'we agree/have agreed to pay'. Thus in the previous line a verb such as ὁμολογέω could be restored (e.g. ὡμολογήςαμεν).

ἐπὶ τὰς . [. The damaged letter seems to be alpha. ἡμέρας perhaps followed in the break, referring to the days the group was hired to perform.

M. SATAMA

5017–5019. Oracle Questions

The following three papyri are examples of 'ticket' oracle questions from the Roman period. The most complete list of published oracle questions of this type is found at http://www.trismegistos.org/magic/index.php. N. Litinas, *ZPE* 117 (1997) 210–12, G. Husson, 'Les Questions oraculaires d'Egypte', in W. Clarysse et al. (edd.), *Egyptian Religion: The Last Thousand Years* ii (1998) 1071), and M. G. Assante, *AnPap* 16–17 (2004–2005) 81–102, offer corrections and new interpretations to previously published questions. Husson, loc. cit. 1063–71, and W. M. Brashear, *ANRW* II.18.5 (1995) 3448–56, discuss the form of oracle questions and together provide bibliography that covers the long history of the practice from the New Kingdom to late antiquity in Hieratic, Demotic, Greek, and Coptic. Notice of unpublished Greek and Demotic oracle questions is given by Brashear, loc. cit. 3455; N. Grimal, *BIFAO* 96 (1996) 534, and 98 (1998) 534; and C. Gallazzi, *Acme* 48.3 (1995) 24, 50.3 (1997) 30, 55.1 (2002) 30. For private letters that mention the intention to solicit oracular advice or give notice of a solicitation, see P. Tebt. II 284 and R. S. Bagnall, R. Cribiore, *Women's Letters from Ancient Egypt, 300 BC – AD 800* (2006) 382–4. SB XIV 12144 is a prefectural order of 199 that aimed to outlaw the type of oracular activity the questions exemplify.

Oracle questions betray the concerns of individuals. However, observing continuity and change of the language, form, and content of the questions over their long history indicates both the resilience of the tradition and possibly also local accommodation of demands made by political authorities. See D. Frankfurter, *Religion in Roman Egypt* (1998) 145–97, and P. Ripat, *Phoenix* 60 (2006) 304–28.

A discussion of 'ticket' oracle questions in comparison with the *Sortes Astrampsychi* is found in Husson, 'Les Questions oraculaires' 1065–7. It is debated whether the *sortes* are a relation of the Egyptian tradition of oracular consultation or a product of Greek influence; see R. Stewart, *GRBS* 26 (1985) 67–73, Frankfurter, *Religion* 181–4, and Husson, loc. cit. 1065–7. The most recent edition is R. Stewart, *Sortes Astrampsychi* ii (2001); see also LXVII **4581**. Brashear, loc. cit. 3452, provides bibliography for previous editions. P. W. van der Horst's review of Stewart's edition (*BMCR* 2001.10.04) discusses the use and significance of the *sortes*. An English translation by R. Stewart and K. Morrell may be found in W. Hansen (ed.), *Anthology of Ancient Greek Popular Literature* (1998) 291–324. See also K. Brodersen, *Astrampsychos: Das Pythagoras-Orakel* (2006).

P. RIPAT

5017

29 4B.44/B(7–8)b   8.4 × 1.6 cm   First/second century

This small slip contains, like **5018**, a question to the oracle of Zeus-Helius-Serapis and associated gods. The interest of this text lies in the mention of the name of the petitioner, Euphorus, who asks the gods for a 'recovery'. From what he wishes to recover is unclear; it could have been any kind of misfortune, from diseases to financial misery, etc.

The brevity of the question (*protasis*) is also remarkable. Although the question asked is not among those included in the *Sortes Astrampsychi*, it may have figured in a list of model questions offered to petitioners, since such shortness is characteristic of the *sortes*. On the other hand, the petitioner expects the gods to know the background of his question.

The text is written along the fibres in a plain and unpractised hand assignable to the first or second century. The back is blank. There are no traces of folding.

  Διὶ Ἡλίῳ μεγάλῳ Cαράπιδι καὶ
  τοῖc cυννάοιc θεοῖc. ἀξιοῖ Εὔφοροc,
  εἰ ἀνακτήcωμαι, τοῦτό μοι δόc.

3 l. ἀνακτήcομαι

'To Zeus Helius, the great Serapis, and the associated gods. Euphorus asks: if I am going to recover, give me this.'

1 For other occurrences of this invocation, see **5018** 1 n. The combination of Helius and Serapis alone is found in VIII **1148** and XXXI **2613**. In XLII **3078** Zeus Helius Serapis has the epithet of νικαφόρος. All these oracular questions addressed to Serapis and associated gods must have been deposited at the temple of Serapis in Oxyrhynchus, on which see J. Whitehorne, *ANRW* II.18.5 (1995) 3078–9.

2 ἀξιοῖ. This verb introduces the request also in IX **1213**, SB XVI 12677, 13079, XXIV 16260, PGM XXXe. Other verbs used in this context are δεῖcθαι and ἐρωτᾶν; for examples see L. Papini, 'Osservazioni sulla terminologia delle domande oracolari in greco', in Pap. Flor. XIX (1990) 468–9.

Εὔφορος. The only other papyrus that may attest this name is P. Enteux. 26.16 Εὔφορ[. Outside Egypt, the name is found in mainland Greece and Sicily: see Pape–Benseler, *Wörterbuch der griechischen Eigennamen* 429; *RE* vi 1190; *LGPN* ii 188, iiiA 181.

3 ἀνακτήcωμαι. The verb means basically 'repossess', normally with direct object: 'regain possession' of things, 'cause to recover (from illness)' of people, 'refurbish' buildings, in the documents often 'bring back' derelict land into cultivation. For a survey of usage, see *DGE*. In our papyrus no object is stated, and the precise sense remains uncertain.

ἀνακτήcωμαι must be a phonetic spelling of ἀνακτήcομαι (future); for the confusion of ο and ω, see Gignac, *Grammar* i 277. It is less likely that we have to take it at face value, as an aorist subjunctive with future meaning (for which see B. G. Mandilaras, *The Verb in the Greek Non-Literary Papyri* (1973) §540).

The form of the apodosis is very common. For that and other possibilities see Papini, 'Osservazioni' 467–8. τοῦτο refers to the chit on which the oracular question is written. This is explicitly shown in questions to an oracle such as LV **3799** 7 τοῦτο τὸ πιττάκιν ἔνεγκ⟨ον⟩.

M. GERHARDT

5018

36 4B.95/M(1–3)a   11.5 × 5.5 cm   Second century

An oracle question addressed to Zeus-Helius-Serapis concerning the dissolution of a decision. IX **1213** provides the best parallel in form, if not subject matter. The scribe of this question may in fact be the same as the one who wrote **1213**, as there is a similarity amongst many of the letter forms, particularly the epsilon of Μένανδρος in **1213** and the Θέων of this question, and an identical way of ligaturing an alpha to a following iota. Both scripts lean to the right slightly and letter heights are of comparable size.

Written across the fibres, on the 'recto' of the original roll. The back is blank.

    Διὶ Ἡλίῳ μεγάλῳ Cαράπιδι καὶ τοῖc
    cυννάοιc θεοῖc. ἀξιοῖ Θέων ὁ καὶ
    Πτολεμαῖος· ἠ cύμφορόν μοί ἐcτι
    διαλύcαcθαι α ̣ λ ̣ τικ ̣ ν ἐπίκριcιν,
5   τοῦτό μοι δός.

3 l. εἰ

'To Zeus Helius, great Serapis and the associated gods. Theon, also called Ptolemaeus, asks: if it is beneficial for me to dissolve the . . . decision, give me this.'

1 Διὶ Ἡλίῳ μεγάλῳ Cαράπιδι. Cf. **5017** 1. Zeus-Helius-Serapis is addressed in oracle questions thus far from Oxyrhynchus only (see VIII **1149**, IX **1213**, and XLII **3078**; compare VI **923**, VIII **1148**, XXXI **2613**). On the general popularity of the designation on inscriptions of the first through the third centuries, see J. E. Stambaugh, *Sarapis under the Early Ptolemies* (1972) 79–82.

1–2 καὶ τοῖc cυννάοιc θεοῖc. Compare **1213**, P. Köln IV 201, and SB XVIII 14043. See E. G. Huzar, *ANRW* II.18.5 (1995) 3112–13, J. A. S. Evans, *YCS* 17 (1961) 150–58, and A. D. Nock, in Z. Stewart (ed.), *Essays on Religion and the Ancient World* (1972) 202–51, concerning the meaning of this phrase, which probably refers to the emperors in their divine form.

2–3 ἀξιοῖ Θέων ὁ καὶ Πτολεμαῖοc. It is not unusual for the enquirers to refer to themselves in the third person (**1149**, **1213**, P. Köln 201, P. Strasb. V 352 and 353, SB 14043). The use in an oracle question of an alias, signified by ὁ καὶ *NN*, is found also in **1149** 7–8 Cαραπίωνα τ[ὸ]ν κα[ὶ Γ]αίωνα.

3 ἤ, l. εἰ. Two unconnected strokes, bearing no resemblance to any letter, intervene between Πτολεμαῖοc and cύμφορον. εἰ cannot be read, while the strokes suggestive of н are not found elsewhere in the text. η nonetheless remains the most probable reading given the alternatives, though the second stroke suggests that another letter follows it.

4 α . λ . τικ . ν. The letter after α looks like λ; the letter between κ and ν is ligatured to κ, and resembles ι, but could also be н. One might expect either an adjective in agreement with ἐπίκριcιν, and we have considered reading ἀθλητικήν, but have little confidence in this.

ἐπίκριcιν. The terms may refer to a 'decision' in the general sense or to the process that determined a person's legal status for tax purposes; those who believed they had claim to a superior status and its accompanying lower rate of taxation would undergo ἐπίκριcιc.

P. RIPAT

5019

47 5B.43/C(2–4)a   9 × 3.5 cm   Earlier second century

An oracle question concerning the potential purchase of a female slave. This example deviates from the normal formula usually adopted by such questions (as described by Brashear, *ANRW* II.18.5 (1995) 3448–56, and A. Henrichs, *ZPE* 11 (1973) 116–17), in that it lacks the expected address to a deity or deities to whom the inquirer's question was submitted. However, XII **1567**, identified by B. Kramer, *ZPE* 61 (1985) 61–2, as an oracle question, provides a parallel, as do LXV **4470** and SB XXIV 16259 (see *ZPE* 111 (1996) 184). Another oracle question concerning the purchase of a slave is VIII **1149**. The hand may be compared to that of LXII **4335**, a rent receipt of 128.

Written across the fibres. The back is blank except for some offsets.

   εἰ οἶδαc ὅτι cυνφέρει μᾶλλον ἀγοράcαι
   παιδίcκην καὶ οὐ cυνφέρει οὕτωc
   χρήcαcθαι, τοῦτό μοι δόc.

5019. ORACLE QUESTIONS

1, 2 l. cυμφέρει

'If you know that it is more advantageous to buy a slave girl and (that) it is not advantageous to borrow(?) her like this, give me this.'

1 εἰ οἶδας. Oracle questions often initially address the god(s) in the dative, and it is unusual that the deity should be addressed with a second person verb. The expected formula would have been 'if it is advantageous for me (or N.N., in the third person) to buy the slave, etc.' rather than 'if you know that etc.'

3 χρήcαcθαι. This verb is not in the expected sense of prophetic consultation and response, but probably in the sense of 'to borrow' rather than 'to own' (LSJ B.1); in this way the two indirect statements linked by καί merely rephrase each other. Redundancy in oracle questions may be expected, as clarity was of supreme importance; compare VIII **1148**. Alternatively, it could simply mean 'make use of' (cf. XLII **3078** 2) or 'treat'.

P. RIPAT

INDEXES

Figures in raised type refer to fragments, small roman numerals to columns. Square brackets indicate that a word is wholly or substantially restored by conjecture or from other sources, round brackets that it is expanded from an abbreviation or a symbol. An asterisk denotes a word not recorded in LSJ or its Revised Supplement and previously unattested names and places. The article and (in the documentary sections) καί have not been indexed.

I. MEDICAL AND RELATED TEXTS

ἀβρύτανον **4975** [1] 20
Αἰγύπτιος **4975** [1] 9, 15–16
αἰδοῖον **4975** [1] 3, 11
αἱμορρεῖν **4975** [1] 11
ἄκοπος **4975** [1] 17
ἅλας **4978** 8
ἄλλος **4971** 16 **4972** 18 **4975** [1] 1, 17
ἅμα **4970** 6
ἄν [**4972** 16]
ἀναγκαῖος [**4971** 21]
ἀναλαμβάνειν **4977** 8
ἀναπλάccειν **4975** [1] 15
ἀνάρροπος **4972** 5
ἄνω **4973** ii 5
ἁπλοῦς **4972** 24, 26 **4974** 3
ἀπό **4970** 3 **4972** 18
ἀποβρέχειν **4975** [1] 18
ἀποδέχεcθαι **4971** 6
ἀποcτενοχωρεῖν [**4971** 13–14]
ἀπρέπεια **4972** 30
ἄπταιcτος **4970** 6
ἀραιωτικόν [**4978** 1]
(-)ἀρθρωτός **4973** iii 2
ἄρρυθμος **4973** ii 12
ἀρcενικόν **4979** 6
ἀρχή **4970** 3
ἀcθένεια **4971** 14
αὐθημερεί **4975** [1] 13
αὐτός **4972** 32
ἀφέψειν **4975** [1] 19
ἀφόδευμα **4978** 3

βαρύς **4971** 5 **4973** iii 6
βιωφελής **4970** 5
βλέφαρον **4973** ii 5–6

γάρ **4970** 5 **4972** 29, 36 **4977** 10
γίνεcθαι [**4971** 12]
γλυκύς **4975** [1] 1

γλωccόκομον **4979** 3
γνάθος **4973** ii 11
γνωρίζειν **4972** 19
γομφίος **4973** ii 12
γόμφωcις **4974** 2

δακρύδιον **4976** 2
δαῦκος **4975** [2] 4
δάφνη **4975** [1] 5–6
δέ **4972** 2, [3], 7, 11, 13, 17, 18, 25 **4973** ii 6, 10, 15, iii 2, 9 **4974** 2, 4 **4977** 9, 11
δεῖν **4971** 9
δηλοῦν [**4972** 12]
διά **4970** 5 **4971** 2, 17 **4977** 3
διάθεcις **4973** ii 9 **4977** 9
διαλαμβάνειν **4970** 2
διδόναι **4971** 1, 11 [**4975** [1] 16]
δίκαιος **4970** 4
διccός **4972** [35], [39]
δολιχός [**4973** iii 2–3?]
δραχμή **4975** [2] 4, 5 **4976** 1, 1a, 2a, 3, 5, 7 **4977** 1, 4, 5, 6, 15, 16
δύναμις **4971** 18

ἐάν **4971** 11
*ἐγκατατομικός [**4972** 16–17]
ἔγωγε **4970** 2
εἶναι **4970** 2 **4972** 3, 8, 11, 14, 16, 26, 33 **4977** 10
εἰς **4970** 1 **4975** [1] 19
εἰcάγειν **4970** 1
εἶτα [**4971** 1]
Ἑλληνικός **4976** 6–7
ἐμβρυοτομία [**4972** 18]
ἐμετικός [**4978** 6]
ἐμφυcᾶν **4975** [1] 7
ἐν **4970** 3, 6 **4971** 5, 18 **4972** 22 **4975** [1] 15, 16, 18

ἐνικός [**4972** 28]
ἔνιος [**4975** [1] 3]
*ἐντεροκηλίδιον **4975** [1] 8
ἐπαγγελία **4972** [28–9], [35–6?]
ἐπαγγέλλειν **4972** [29], [36]
ἐπαίρειν **4973** ii 6
ἐπεί **4971** 2
ἐπί **4972** 37, 38 **4975** [1] 10
ἐπιβάλλειν **4977** 7
ἐπιδεῖν **4975** [1] 10
ἐπίμεικτος **4972** 25, 33–34, [37–8]
ἐπιπάccειν **4975** [1] 9
ἐπιτήδειος **4972** [4], 8
ἐπιφαίνειν **4973** ii 8
ἐπιφορά **4977** 11
ἐπιχρίειν [**4978** 5]
εὔογκος [**4973** iii 8?]
εὐπρέπεια **4972** [29–30], [41]
ἔχειν **4972** 28, 35, 39 **4973** iii 11 **4975** [1] 19

ζεῖν **4978** 7
ζῆν **4972** 31, 32, 41

ἤ **4971** 13 **4972** 5, 10, 29, 30, [31] **4973** ii 4 **4975** [1] 15 **4977** 12?
ἡλίκος [**4975** [1] 15]
ἡμέρα **4975** [1] 10

θεραπεία **4972** 13
θεώρημα **4970** 2
θηριοῦν **4975** [1] 11

ἰατρεύειν **4970** 6
ἰατρικός **4970** 1
Ἱπποκράτειος **4970** 3
ἴcος **4978** 3
ἱcτάναι **4975** [1] 13
ἱcτᾶν **4977** 10

164   INDEXES

ἰςχυρός **4971** 12

καδμεία **4977** 3–4
καθαρτικός **4978** 8
καθιστάναι **4970** 5
καιρικός **4972** 11
καιρός **4971** 1
κακός **4972** 31
καλός [**4972** 31]
κάμνειν [**4972** 7?]
κάρδαμον **4975** [1] 13 **4976** 4
κατά **4970** 1 **4971** 4 **4972** [12], 14, 21, [24], [25], 37 **4974** [2], 4 **4978** 12
κατακαίειν **4975** [1] 3, 12
καταλύειν **4971** 17
καταπλάςςειν **4975** [1] 2, 6
κατάρροπος [**4972** 6]
κεῖςθαι **4974** 5
κίκινος **4975** [1] 15
κιρνᾶν **4978** 12
κολλύριον **4977** 3
κόμμι **4977** 1, 4–5, 16
κοτύλη **4975** [1] 18, 19
κρᾶςις **4977** 12
κρόκος **4977** 5 **4979** 4
κύαθος **4978** 9, 10, 11, 12
κύαμος [**4975** [1] 15]
κυπάριςςος **4975** [1] 8

λαμβάνειν **4975** [1] 8
λεαίνειν **4975** [1] 9
λέγειν **4972** 5, [9–10], 17
λεῖος **4975** [1] 7
λειοῦν **4975** [1] 6
λευκός **4975** [1] 14
λοβός **4973** ii 13
λόγος **4970** 1
λοξοτομεῖν [**4972** 10–11]
λύειν **4975** [1] 10

μάθηςις **4970** 4
μέγας **4973** ii 13
μεθοδεύειν **4972** 23?
μεθοδικός [**4972** 2]
μέθοδος **4972** 2
μειγνύναι **4978** [4], 11
μελάνθιον **4976** 3
μέλι **4975** [1] 2, 15, 16 **4978** 9
μέν **4972** 24 **4973** ii 5
μέντοι **4971** 7
μέςος **4973** iii 4 **4977** 12

μετά **4972** 12, 14 **4975** [1] 1, 6, 7, 9 **4977** 2, 11 **4978** 4
μέτωπον **4973** ii 15 **4978** 5
μέχρι **4971** 9
μή **4971** 11 **4975** [1] 10
μήκων **4978** 1–2
μόριον [**4975** [1] 1]
μύρον **4978** 4
μῦς **4978** 2–3
μυςταγωγεῖν **4970** 5–6

νάρδος **4975** [1] 7
νέος **4970** 1
νευροχονδρώδης **4974** 1
νήςτης **4978** 13
νίτρον **4976** 6
νόμος **4970** 4

ξηρός **4975** [1] 3

ὀγκώδης **4973** ii 14
ὀδούς **4974** 2
ὀθόνιον **4975** [1] [3], 11
οἶνος **4975** [1] [1], 9, 16
οἱονεί **4973** ii 8–9
ὁμοίως [**4971** 10–11]
ὁμοῦ **4978** 11
ὄνομα **4972** 19
ὄνυξ **4973** iii 3
ὄξος **4978** 10
ὀξύβαφον **4975** [1] 17
ὄπιον **4977** 6
ὀρθόπνοια **4975** [1] 13
ὅρκος **4970** 3
ὄρχις **4975** [1] 5
ὅς **4972** [12], 14
ὅςπερ **4971** 18
ὀςτέον **4974** 5
ὅταν **4972** [5], 9
ὅτι **4973** ii 4
οὖς **4973** ii 13
οὗτος **4970** 5 [**4971** 12–13] **4974** 4

πάθος **4971** 3, 10 **4972** 22
παιδίον **4975** [1] 8
πάλιν [**4972** 30–31]
παράθεςις [**4971** 7–8]
παρακμή [**4971** 10]
παρειά **4973** ii 10
παριέναι **4973** ii 7, 11
παροξύνειν **4971** 3
παροξυςμός **4971** 6–7
παχύς **4973** ii 14 **4977** 12–13

πέπερι **4975** [1] 14 **4977** 15
περί **4971** 12 [**4972** 16]
πίνειν **4978** 13
πήγανον **4975** [1] 5
πιλίον **4979** 2
πλαγιοτομεῖν **4972** 10
πλατύς **4973** ii 12
πλεῖςτος **4971** 4
πληθύνειν **4973** ii 4–5
ποιεῖν **4970** 4 **4975** [1] 9, [2] 2 **4977** 9
ποῖος **4972** 26, 33
πολύς [**4971** 2]
πόνος **4975** [1] 3, 5
πόςος **4972** 21
ποτίζειν **4978** 7
πούς **4973** iii 7
προλέγειν **4972** 15
πρός **4973** ii 15 **4975** [1] 3, 7, 8, 11 **4977** 9
προςάγειν **4972** 40
προςήκειν **4970** 2
προςτιθέναι **4975** [1] 10
πρῶτος **4970** 3
πτερίς **4976** 1

ῥυτιδώδης [**4973** ii 10?]
ῥώθων **4973** ii 14

ςανδαράκη **4979** 5
ςημείωςις [**4972** 15]
ςημειωτικός [**4972** 14]
ςίλφιον **4978** 6
ςπέρμα **4975** [1] 14, [2 6] **4976** 4–5 **4978** 2
ςπόδιον **4975** [1] 7
ςποδός **4975** [1] 4
ςταφίς **4975** [1] 1
ςυμβαίνειν **4971** 19
ςύμφυςις **4974** 3
ςφαῖρα **4975** [1] 10
ςφόδρα **4970** 5
ςχῆμα **4972** 4, 7
ςχηματίζειν **4972** 6
ςχηματικός **4972** 3
ςῶμα **4971** 13 [**4973** iii 10] [**4974** 1]
ςωτηρία [**4972** 39–40]

ταράςςειν **4973** ii 3
τάςςειν **4971** 5
τηρεῖν [**4971** 9]
τις **4971** 16 [**4972** 2]
τμῆμα [**4972** 9]
*τομικός [**4972** 7–8]

I. MEDICAL AND RELATED TEXTS

τρίβειν **4975** ¹ 1, [12], 15 **4977** 8
τρίτος **4971** 2 **4975** ¹ 18
τριώβολον **4976** 2, 2a **4977** 5, 6
τροπή [**4971** 11–12]
τρόπος **4972** 21, 24, 27, 34, 38
τροφή **4971** 4
τρυφερός **4977** 10
τυγχάνειν **4972** 20

ὑγρός **4977** 7
ὕδωρ **4977** 1, 2 **4978** [6–7], 10

ὑοσκύαμος **4975** [¹ 13–14], [² 5–6]
ὑπό [**4971** 16]
ὑποκάμπτειν **4973** ii 7–8
ὑποκάτω **4973** ii 6–7
ὑπόχλωρος [**4973** ii 3–4]
ὕσσωπος **4975** ¹ 17

φλεγμονή **4975** ¹ 5
*φλυκτιδώδης **4973** ii 9?
(-)φύειν **4973** iii 5
φυλάccειν **4971** 8

φύλλον **4975** ¹ 6

χειρουργία **4972** [13], 22, [36–7]
χλωρός **4975** ¹ 9
χρῆcθαι **4975** ¹ 4 **4977** 1

ψιμύθιον **4977** 4

ᾠόν **4977** 3, 6, 11
ὡς **4970** 2 **4971** 2
ὥσπερ **4970** 4 **4972** 4, 9

II. RULERS

Augustus

θεὸς Cεβαcτός **4980** 2–3 [**4981** 5]

Tiberius

[Τιβέριος] Καῖcαρ (. . .) Cεβαcτὸς Αὐτοκράτωρ θεοῦ Cεβαcτοῦ υἱός **4980** 1–3 (oath)
Τιβέριος Καῖcαρ Νέος Cεβαcτὸς Αὐτοκράτωρ θεοῦ Cεβαcτοῦ υἱός **4981** 3–6 (oath)
Τιβέριος Καῖcαρ Cεβαcτός **4980** 15 (year 20) **4981** 16–17 (year 20)

Nero

Νέρων Κλαύδιος Καῖcαρ Cεβαcτὸς Γερμανικὸς Αὐτοκράτωρ **4982** 6–8 (oath), 18–19 (year 8)

Antoninus Pius

Ἀντωνῖνος [**4987** 5] (year 9)

Marcus Aurelius and Verus

οἱ κύριοι Αὐτοκράτορες Ἀντωνῖνος καὶ Οὐῆρος Ἀρμενιακοὶ Μηδικοὶ Παρθικοὶ Μέγιστοι **5000** 12–16 (oath)

Marcus Aurelius

Αὐρήλιος Ἀντωνῖνος Καῖcαρ ὁ κύριος **4989** 7–8 (year 14), 25–7 (oath)
Αὐτοκράτωρ Καῖcαρ Μᾶρκος Αὐρήλιος Ἀντωνῖνος Cεβαcτὸς Ἀρμενιακὸς Μηδικὸς Παρθικὸς Γερμανικὸς Μέγιcτος **4989** 28–31 (year 15)

Commodus

Αὐρήλιος Κόμμοδος Ἀντωνῖνος Καῖcαρ ὁ κύριος **4990** 11–12 (year 28)

Caracalla

Μᾶρκος Αὐρήλιος Cεουῆρος Ἀντωνῖνος Εὐcεβὴς Εὐτυχὴς Cεβαcτός **4991** 12–15 (year 24)

Severus Alexander

Μᾶρκος Αὐρήλιος Cεουῆρος Ἀλέξανδρος Καῖcαρ ὁ κύριος **4992** 11–13 (oath)
Αὐτοκράτωρ Καῖcαρ Μᾶρκος Αὐρήλιος Cεουῆρος Ἀλέξανδρος Εὐcεβὴς Εὐτυχὴς Cεβαcτός **4992** 14–16 (year 3)

Valerian and Gallienus

οἱ κύριοι ἡμῶν Οὐαλεριανὸς καὶ Γαλλιηνὸς Cεβαcτοί **4994** 17–19 (oath) **4997** 14–16 (oath)

INDEXES

Valerian and Gallienus (*cont.*)

Οὐαλεριανὸς καὶ Γαλλιηνὸς Καίcαρες οἱ κύριοι **4996** 17–19 (oath)

Αὐτοκράτορες Καίcαρες Πούπλιος Λικίννιος Οὐαλεριανὸς καὶ Πούπλιος Λικίννιος Οὐαλεριανὸς Γαλλιηνὸς Εὐcεβεῖς Εὐτυχεῖς Cεβαcτοί **4994** 20–25 (year 1) **4995** 16–22 (year 1) **4996** 21–7 (year 2) **4997** 18–24 (year 1) **4998** 22–7 (year 1)

Diocletian and Maximian

Αὐτοκράτωρ Καῖcαρ Γάϊος Αὐρήλιος Οὐαλέριος Διοκλητιανὸς καὶ Αὐτοκράτωρ Καῖcαρ Μᾶρκος Αὐρήλιος Οὐαλέριος Μαξιμιανὸς Γερμανικοὶ Μέγιcτοι Εὐcεβεῖς Εὐτυχεῖς Cεβαcτοί **4999** 17–22 (years 8 and 7 respectively)

III. MONTHS

Φαωφι **5015** 10
Τυβι **4995** 22 **5016** 5
Φαμενωθ (**4980** 16) **4989** 31

Φαρμουθι **5002** 4
Παχων **4981** 17 [**4997** 24]
Παυνι (**4982** 20) **4994** 25 **5014** 10

Μεcορη **4999** 22
Καιcάρειος **5001** 5

IV. DATES

7 March 34 **4980** 15–16
26(?) April 34 **4981** 16–17
28 May 62 **4982** 17–20
145/6 **4987** 5
25 February – 26 March 175 **4989** 28–31

187/8 **4990** 11–12
215/16 **4991** 12–15
223/4 **4992** 14–16
253/4 **4998** 22–7
6 January 254 **4995** 16–22
26 May or 24 June 254 **4994** 20–25

26 May – 24 June 254 **4997** 18–24
254/5 **4996** 21–7
12 August 292 **4999** 17–22

V. PERSONAL NAMES

Ἀδωρᾶ, w. of —ion, m. of —es **4999** 10
Ἀκύλας, s. of Apoleius **5004** 2
Ἀλέξανδρος see Index II s.v. Severus Alexander
Ἄμαεις, s. of Paphib **5010** 3
Ἀμμωνάριον, w. of Diogas, m. of Patermouthis **5003** 3
Ἀμμωνιανός **5009** 5
Ἀμμώνιος **4985** 1; see also Index VI s.v. Ἰβιὼν Ἀμμωνίου
Ἀμοϊτᾶς, Aur., s. of Amoitas and Thaesis, *epitropos* of Vibius Publius **4998** 4, [27]
Ἀμοϊτᾶς, f. of Aur. Amoitas **4998** 4, 28
Ἀμουνι—, f. of Aur. Copreus **5016** 1
Ἀνδρόμαχος, s. of Didyme **4989** 13
Ἀνίκητος, alias N.N., slave of Vibius Publius **4998** 11
Ἀνουβᾶς, shepherd **5012** 2

Ἀντέρως, f. of Aur. Didymus **5015** 2
Ἀντίνοος, Aur., prefect of Egypt **4991** 8–9
Ἀντίοχος, s. of Theon, h. of Hieraciaena, f. of Ploution **4997** 1, 34
Ἀντωνᾶς, h. of Isarion, f. of Aur. Dioscorus **4994** 4–5, 34
Ἀντωνῖνος see Index II s.vv. Antoninus Pius, Marcus Aurelius and Verus, Marcus Aurelius, Commodus, Caracalla
Ἄπεις, f. of Aur. Callinicus **5015** 4
Ἀπίων **4998** 30
Ἀπολήϊος, f. of Aquila **5004** 2
Ἀπολλ— **4981** 2, 18
Ἀπολλωνία, w. of Ptolemaeus, m. of Vibius Publius **4998** 6–7, 9
Ἀπολλώνιος, f. of Tapontos **4982** 4
Ἀπολλώνιος, f. of Sarapion **4983** 8
Ἀριστοῦς, d. of Ariston, w. of Sarapion, m. of Sieapis and Thais **4983** 8
Ἀρίστων, f. of Aristous **4983** 9

Ἀρίστων, s. of Diogenes and Sieapis **4983** 11
Ἁρμίνcις, s. of Didyme **4989** 15
Ἁρμίνcις, s. of Heraclides, h. of Diogenis, f. of Sarapous **4994** 6, 29, 35
Ἀρτεμίδωρος, Aur., s. of Aur. Dioscorus and Sarapous **4994** 14, 33
Ἄρτεμις, w. of Hermogenes, m. of —genes alias Dionysius **4990** 8
Ἀcκλατάριον, w. of Plutarchus, m. of Didyme **4989** 2
Ἀcκληπιάδης, Aur. Theon alias, also called Zoilus **4995** 25
Ἀτρῆς, Aur., s. of Cornelius, president of Thosbis **5015** 1, 17
Αὐρηλία see Ἰcιδώρα
Αὐρήλιος **4993** 12 [**4996** 2]; see also s.vv. Ἀμοϊτᾶς, Ἀντίνοος, Ἀρτεμίδωρος, Ἀτρῆς, Ἀχιλλεύς, Βηcαρίων, Δίδυμος, Διογένης, Διονύcιος, Διόcκορος, Ἡρᾶς, Θέων, Καλλίνικος, Κοπρεύς,

V. PERSONAL NAMES

Κορνηλιανός, Μᾶρκος Αὐρήλιος Ἀχιλλεύς, Οὐηριανός, Πετρῶνις, Πλούταρχος, Πλουτίων, Πολύκαρπος, Σαρᾶς, Τούρβων, Ὡρίων, and Index II s.vv. Marcus Aurelius, Commodus, Caracalla, Severus Alexander, Diocletian and Maximian

Ἀχιλλεύς, Aur., h. of Philous, f. of Aur. Tourbon **4995** 23, [31–2]

Ἀχιλλεύς, vir egregius **5010** 1

Ἀχιλλεύς see *Μᾶρκος Αὐρήλιος Ἀχιλλεύς*

Βησαρίων, Aur. **4994** 30
Βησᾶς, h. of Zoilous, f. of Aur. Saras **4992** 1–2, 17
Βησᾶς, s. of Saras and Sintotoes called Eudaemonis **4992** 4

Γάιος see Index II s.v. Diocletian and Maximian
Γαλλιηνός see Index II s.v. Valerian and Gallienus

Δᾶτος see *Οὐαλέριος Δᾶτος*
Δημέας, s. of Tiberius Claudius Demetrius and Tanechotis **4996** 6
Δημήτριος see *Τινήιος Δημήτριος*
Διδύμη, d. of Plutarchus and Asclatarion, m. of Ploution, Andromachus, and Harmiysis **4989** 1, 12, 17
Δίδυμος, Aur., s. of Anteros, president of Thosbis **5015** 2
Διογᾶς, h. of Ammonarion, f. of Patermouthis **5003** 3
Διογένης, h. of Sieapis, f. of Ariston **4983** 11
Διογένης, adoptive f. of Petear— **4990** 6
Διογένης, Aur., alias Hermias, *laographos* **4999** 2
Διογενίς, w. of Harmiysis, m. of Sarapous **4994** 7–8
Διόδωρος, f. or grf. of Petear— **4990** 5
Διοκλῆς, s. of Ptolemaeus **4985** 3
Διοκλητιανός see Index II s.v. Diocletian and Maximian
Διονύσιος, district-scribe of the Upper toparchy **4983** 3

Διονύσιος, s. of Theon and Ptolema **4984** 3
Διονύσιος, f. of Theon **4984** 4
Διονύσιος, —genes alias, s. of Hermogenes and Artemis **4990** 7
Διονύσιος, Aur. **4997** 28
Διόσκορος, Aur., s. of Antonas and Isarion, h. of Sarapous, f. of Aur. Artemidorus **4994** 4, 11, 26, 33
Διόσκορος, Aur., s. of Heraclas, president of Ibion Ammoniou **5014** 1–2, 6

Ἐπίμαχος, s. of Ploution **4989** 16 n.
Ἐπιτέλης, s. of Epiteles and Thais **4990** 14
Ἐπιτέλης, s. of Epiteles, h. of Thais, f. of Epiteles **4990** 14
Ἐπιτέλης, f. of Epiteles **4990** 14–15
Ἑρμίας, Aur. Diogenes alias, *laographos* [**4999** 3]
Ἑρμογένης, h. of Artemis, f. of —*genes* alias Dionysius **4990** 7
Εὐδαιμονίς, Sintotoes called, w. of Aur. Saras, m. of Besas **4992** 4–5
Εὔφορος **5017** 2
Εὐφράτης, slave of Vibius Publius **4998** 15

Ζωῖλος, f. of Hierax **4982** 13
Ζωῖλος, Aur. Theon alias Asclepiades also called **4995** 26
Ζωῖλος **5001** 4
Ζωιλοῦς, w. of Besas, m. of Aur. Saras **4992** 2
Ζώσιμος, f. of Plutarchus **4989** 2

Ἡρακλᾶς, f. of Aur. Dioscorus **5014** 2
Ἡρακλείδης, f. of Ploution **4982** 15
Ἡρακλείδης **4985** 1; see also *Τιβέριος Κλαύδιος Ἡρακλείδης*
Ἡρακλείδης, f. of Harmiysis **4994** 7, 35
Ἡράμμων, alias Castor, strategus of the Oxyrhynchite nome **4990** 2
Ἡρᾶς, Aur., phylarch of Oxyrhynchus **4994** 2 [**4995** 1] **4998** 2

Θάησις, m. of Aur. Amoitas **4998** 5
Θάησις **5016** 2

Θαΐς, d. of Sarapion and Aristous, sister of Sieapis **4983** 13
Θαΐς, w. of Epiteles, m. of Epiteles **4990** 15
Θεαγένης, comedy actor **5013** 2
Θέων, s. of Dionysius, h. of Ptolema, f. of Dionysius **4984** 3
Θέων, f. of Ptolema **4984** 4
Θέων, Aur., alias Asclepiades, also called Zoilus **4995** 24
Θέων, f. of Antiochus **4997** 1, 34
Θέων, f. of Aur. Horion **4999** 5
Θέων, alias Ptolemaeus **5018** 2
Θιν—, w. of Thot—, m. of Horus **5000** 7–8
*Θινπαύνις(?), w. of Petsemis, m. of Petosiris **5000** 26
Θοτ—, h. of Thin—, f. of Horus **5000** 6
Θρακίδας, f. of Leon **5008** 6
Θῶνις, s. of Paues and Tnepheros **5000** 21

Ἱερακίαινα, w. of Antiochus, m. of Ploution **4997** 2, 35
Ἱέραξ, s. of Zoilus, h. of Tapontos [**4982** 13]
Ἰσάριον, w. of Antonas, m. of Aur. Dioscorus **4994** 5
Ἰσιδώρα, Aurelia **5008** 7
Ἰσίδωρος, Marcus Aurelius Achilleus alias **4991** 5

Καικίλιος Κλήμης **4984** 1
Καῖσαρ see Index II s.vv. Tiberius, Nero, Marcus Aurelius, Commodus, Severus Alexander, Valerian and Gallienus, Diocletian and Maximian
Καλλίνικος, Aur., s. of Apeis, head of troupe of performers **5015** 3–4, 7, 17–18
Καλουίσιος Στατιανός, prefect of Egypt **4989** 5–6
Κάνωπος, citharode **5013** 1
Κάστωρ, Herammon alias, strategus of the Oxyrhynchite nome **4990** 2
Κλαύδιος see *Τιβέριος Κλαύδιος* N.N.; see also Index II s.v. Nero
Κλήμης see *Καικίλιος Κλήμης*
Κολλοῦθος, s. of Tnephersois **5008** 4

Κόμμοδος see Index II s.v. Commodus
Κοπρέας, s. of Ophellius and Tayris, village elder **5003** 4
Κοπρεύς, alias Melas, s. of Ploution and Teclomis **4997** 4, 33
Κοπρεύς, Aur., head of troupe of performers **5014** 4, 7
Κοπρεύς, Aur., s. of Amuni(u)s, president of Sincepha **5016** 1
Κοπρεύς see Τιβέριος Κλαύδιος Κοπρεύς
Κορνηλιανός, Aur., head of troupe of performers **5016** 6 n.
Κορνήλιος, f. of Aur. Hatres **5015** 1–2

Λέων, s. of Thracidas **5008** 6
Λικίννιος see Index II s.v. Valerian and Gallienus

Μαξιμιανός see Index II s.v. Diocletian and Maximian
Μᾶρκος Αὐρήλιος Ἀχιλλεύς, alias Isidorus **4991** 4–5, 22
Μᾶρκος see Μᾶρκος Αὐρήλιος Ἀχιλλεύς; see also Index II s.vv. Marcus Aurelius, Caracalla, Severus Alexander, Diocletian and Maximian
Μέλας, Copreus alias, s. of Ploution and Hierciaena **4997** 5

Νααρωοῦς **5002** 3
Ναύαρχος, f. of Pnepheros **5000** 2
Νεῖλος, s. of Nilus, Alexandrian **5000** 28–9
Νεῖλος, f. of Nilus **5000** 29
Νέρων see Index II s.v. Nero
Νίκανδρος, royal scribe of the Oxyrhynchite nome **4983** 3

Οὐαλεριανός see Index II s.v. Valerian and Gallienus
Οὐαλέριος Δᾶτος, prefect of Egypt **4991** 7
Οὐαλέριος Πρόκλος, prefect of Egypt **4987** 4–5 **4988** 3
Οὐαλέριος see Index II s.v. Diocletian and Maximian
Οὐηριανός, Aur., prefect of Egypt **4990** 10
Οὐίβιος Πούπλιος, s. of Ptolemaeus and Apollonia **4998** 6, [7]–8, 12, 15
Οὐίβιος, f. of Psais **5011** 2
Ὀφέλλιος **4998** 30 n.
Ὀφέλλιος, h. of Tayris, f. of Copreas **5003** 4

*Πάςεμςις **4986** 3?
Πατέρμουθις, s. of Diogas and Ammonarion, village elder **5003** 3
Πανῆς, h. of Tnepheros, f. of Thonis **5000** 21–2
*Παφιβ, s. of Preiteles, f. of Amaeis **5010** 3
Πέςοϊς, f. of Aur. Petronis **5014** 2
Πετεαρ—, surnamed N.N., s. or grs. of Diodorus, adopted s. of Diogenes **4990** 4, 18
Πετέμουνις **5009** 4
Πετόςιρις, s. of Petsemis and Thinpayniis **5000** 23–4
Πετρῶνις, Aur., s. of Pesois, president of Ibion Ammoniou **5014** 2
Πετςειρᾶς/Πεττειρᾶς, f. of Tanechotis **4996** 7–8, 43
Πέτςεμις, s. of Psenesis, h. of Thinpayniis, f. of Petosiris **5000** 24
Πλούταρχος, s. of Zosimus, h. of Asclatarion, f. of Didyme **4989** 1
Πλούταρχος, Aur. **5010** 4
Πλουτίων, s. of Heraclides **4982** 15
Πλουτίων, s. of Didyme, f. of Epimachus **4989** 3, 11, 16
Πλουτίων, s. of Ploution, farmer **5001** 2
Πλουτίων, f. of Ploution **5001** 3
Πλουτίων, Aur., s. of Antiochus and Hieraciaena, h. of Teclomis, f. of Copreus alias Melas **4997** 1 n., 25, 33
Πνεφερῶς, s. of Pnepheros and Tsenth—, *archephodus* of Tychinphagon **5000** 1
Πνεφερῶς, s. of Nauarchus, h. of Tsenth—, f. of Pnepheros **5000** 1–2
Πολύκαρπος, Aur., dependant of Marcus Aurelius Achilleus alias Isidorus **4991** 2–3
Πούπλιος see Οὐίβιος Πούπλιος; see also Index II s.v. Valerian and Gallienus
*Πρειτέλης, f. of Paphib **5010** 3
Πρόκλος see Οὐαλέριος Πρόκλος
Πτολέμα, d. of Theon, w. of Theon, m. of Dionysius **4984** 4
Πτολεμαῖος, f. of Diocles **4985** 3
Πτολεμαῖος, h. of Apollonia, f. of Vibius Publius **4998** 8
Πτολεμαῖος, Theon alias **5018** 3

Ϲαραπάνουβις, royal scribe of the Oxyrhynchite nome [**4990** 2–3]
Ϲαραπίων, village-scribe of Cercemunis **4983** 4
Ϲαραπίων, s. of Apollonius, h. of Aristous, f. of Sieapis and Thais **4983** 7
Ϲαραπίων, f. of —ion **4999** 9
Ϲαραπίων **5009** 4
Ϲαραποῦς, d. of Harmiysis and Diogenis, m. of Aur. Artemidorus **4994** 6, 28, 34
Ϲαρᾶς, Aur., s. of Besas and Zoilous, h. of Sintotoes called Eudaemonis, f. of Besas **4992** 1, 17
Ϲεουῆρος see Index II s.vv. Caracalla, Severus Alexander
*Ϲιέαπις, d. of Sarapion and Aristous, w. of Diogenes, m. of Ariston **4983** 7
Ϲιντοτοῆς, called Eudaemonis, w. of Aur. Saras, m. of Besas **4992** 4
Ϲοντωους, h. of Thaesis, f. of N.N. **5016** 2
Ϲτατιανός see Καλουίϲιος Ϲτατιανός

Τανέχωτις, d. of Petteiras, w. of Ti. Claudius Demetrius, m. of Demeas **4996** 7, 42–3
Ταποντῶς, d. of Apollonius, w. of Hierax **4982** 3
Τάϋρις, w. of Ophellius, m. of Copreas **5003** 4
Τέκλωμις, w. of Ploution, m. of Copreus alias Melas **4997** 6
Τιβέριος Κλαύδιος Δημήτριος, s. of Ti. Claudius Copreus, h. of Tanechotis, f. of Demeas **4996** 3–4, 40–41

V. PERSONAL NAMES

Τιβέριος Κλαύδιος Ἡρακλείδης, strategus of the Oxyrhynchite nome **4983** 2

Τιβέριος Κλαύδιος Κοπρεύς, f. of Ti. Claudius Demetrius **4996** 4–5, 41–2

Τιβέριος see Index II s.v. Tiberius

Τινήϊος Δημήτριος, prefect of Egypt [**4990** 9]

Τνεφέρςοϊς, m. of Colluthus **5008** 5

Τνεφερῶς, w. of Paues, m. of Thonis **5000** 22–3

Τούρβων, Aur., s. of Aur. Achilles and Philous **4995** 10, 30

Τςενθ—, w. of Pnepheros, m. of Pnepheros **5000** 3

Χενάνουπις **4987** 2

Φιλοῦς, w. of Aur. Achilles, m. of Aur. Tourbon **4995** 11, [31–2]

Ψάϊς, s. of Vibius, priest of Athena **5011** 2

Ψένςις, f. of Petsemis **5000** 25

Ὠρίων, Aur., s. of Theon **4999** 5

Ὧρος, s. of Thot– and Thin–, *eirenophylax* **5000** 6

—*ατίων* **5009** 6

—*γένης*, alias Dionysius, s. of Hermogenes and Artemis **4990** 7

—*ης*, s. of —ion and Adora **4999** 10

—*ίων*, s. of Sarapion, h. of Adora, f. of —es **4999** 9

—*ίων*, mime actor(?) **5013** 3

—*τᾶς* **5009** 4

—*ωρίων*, *bouleutes* (or son of a *bouleutes*)

VI. GEOGRAPHICAL

Ἀλεξανδρεύς **4980** 10 (**4981** 11) **5000** 29–30

Ἀντινόου (*πόλις*) **4986** 2

Ἀράβων (*κώμη*) **5011** 4

Ἀρμενιακός see Index II s.vv. Marcus Aurelius and Verus, Marcus Aurelius

Βερκυ (*κώμη*) **5010** 6

Γερμανικός see Index II s.vv. Nero, Marcus Aurelius, Diocletian and Maximian

Δρόμου Θοήριδος (*ἄμφοδον*) **4990** 13–14

Ἑρμαίου (*ἄμφοδον*) **4989** 10

Θοήριδος see *Δρόμου Θοήριδος*
Θῶςβις (*κώμη*) **5015** 3

Ἰβιῶν Ἀμμωνίου (*κώμη*) **5014** 3, 28

Ἱππέων Παρεμβολῆς (*ἄμφοδον*) **4997** 32

Ἱπποδρόμου (*ἄμφοδον*) **4997** 8–9, 31

Κερκέμουνις (*κώμη*) **4983** 5, 6
Κρητικοῦ (*ἄμφοδον*) **4995** 29

Μενδ( ) (*κώμη*) **4987** 2
Μερμέρθων (*κώμη*) **4999** 26
Μηδικός see Index II s.vv. Marcus Aurelius and Verus, Marcus Aurelius
Μητρώου (*ἄμφοδον*) **4991** 1, 22
Μικρὸν Ταρουθίνου (*ἐποίκιον*?) **5010** 4

Ναουέως (*κώμη*) **5002** 2
Νέμερα (*κώμη*) **5001** 1
Νεμεςίου (*ἄμφοδον*) **4998** 17

Ὀξυρυγχίτου (*νομός*) **5014** 19, 26 [**5015** 21]
Ὀξυρυγχιτῶν (*πόλις*) **4994** 2–3 [**4998** 2] **4999** 3–4, 6–7 (**5016** 7)
Ὀξυρύγχων (*πόλις*) **4983** 9 **4989** 4 [**4990** 8] (**4992** 2) **4994** 8 **4996** 8 **4997** 3 **4998** 5 **5015** 4

Πακερκη (*κώμη*) **5003** 1 **5008** 3 (*ἀπηλιώτου*)

Παμμένους Παραδείςου (*ἄμφοδον*) **4998** 14 **4999** 11 n., 23 n.
Παραδείςου see *Παμμένους Παραδείςου*
Παρεμβολῆς see *Ἱππέων Παρεμβολῆς*
Παρθικός see Index II s.vv. Marcus Aurelius and Verus, Marcus Aurelius
Πάωμις (*κώμη*) **5007** 2–3
Πλατείας (*ἄμφοδον*) **4994** 12, 32 **4996** 11

Ῥωμαῖος [**4980** 9] **4981** 10 [**4998** 21] **4999** 16

Ϲιγκεφα (*κώμη*) **5016** 3
Ϲύρων (*κώμη*) **5006** 3

Τ— (*κώμη*) **5005** 5
Τακονα **5004** 1
Ταρουθίνου see *Μικρὸν Ταρουθίνου*
τοπαρχία (**4982** 5) (Eastern) **4983** 4 (Upper)
Τυχινφαγων (*κώμη*) **5000** 4, 9

Φοβωου (*κώμη*) **4982** 5

VII. RELIGION

Ἀθήνη **5011** 2

Ζεύς **5017** 1 **5018** 1

Ἥλιος **5017** 1 **5018** 1

θεός [**4980** 2] [**4981** 3] **5015** 21 **5017** 2 **5018** 2

Θόηρις see Index VI s.v. Δρόμου Θοήριδος

ἰβιών see Index VI s.v. Ἰβιὼν Ἀμμωνίου

ἱερεύς **5011** 2

Μητρῷον see Index VI s.v. Μητρῴου

Σάραπις **5017** 1 **5018** 1

VIII. OFFICIAL AND MILITARY TERMS AND TITLES

ἀγορανόμος **4984** 2 **4985** 2

ἀπὸ γυμνασίου [**4993** 14] **4994** 14–15, (36) **4996** 9–10 **4999** 13 n.

ἀρχέφοδος **5000** 4–5 **5002** 1 **5003** 1 **5004** 1

βασιλικὸς γραμματεύς (**4983** 3) [**4990** 3]

βενεφικιάριος (**5011** 1)

βουλευτής **5012** 3

γυμνασιαρχ— (**4986** 2)

δεκαδάρχης (**5005** 1) (**5006** 1) (**5007** 1) (**5008** 1) (**5009** 1)

δημόσιοι **5005** 4 **5006** 2 **5007** 2 **5010** 6

δωδεκάδραχμος (**4994** 14, 36) (**4995** 12) (**4996** 9, 39) **4999** 13 n.

εἰρηνοφύλαξ **5000** 9–10

ἐξηγητεύειν **5009** 6

ἐπιστάτης εἰρήνης **5008** 2–3 **5009** 2 **5011** 4

ἡγεμονεύειν [**4990** 10]

ἡγεμονία (**4991** 11)

ἡγεμών **4987** 4 **4988** 3 **4989** 6 (**4990** 10) (**4991** 8)

κράτιστος **4987** 4 **4988** 3 (**4991** 10) **5010** 1

κωμάρχης **5006** 2 **5007** 1 **5008** 2 **5009** 2 **5010** 6 **5011** 4

κωμογραμματεύς (**4983** 5)

λαμπρότατος **4989** 6 [**4990** 9] (**4991** 8)

λαογράφος (**4983** 6) (**4991** 1) **4999** 1

νομοφύλαξ **5002** 1 **5007** 7

οὐετρανός **5012** 2

πρεσβύτερος (**5003** 2)

προστάτης (κώμης) **5014** 3 **5015** 3 **5016** 4

στρατηγός (**4983** 3) [**4990** 2] **5002** 1

στρατιώτης **5005** 3 **5006** 5 **5010** 2

συστάτης **4999** 27 n.

τοπογραμματεύς (**4983** 4)

φύλαξ **5005** 4

φυλάρχης **4994** 2 **4998** 2

IX. PROFESSIONS AND OCCUPATIONS

αὐλητής **5014** 5 **5015** 5

γεωργός **5001** 3

ἐπίτροπος **4998** 5–6

ἴδιος **4991** 3

κιθαρῳδός **5013** 1

κροταλίστρια **5015** 5–6

κωμῳδός **5013** 2, 5

μῖμος **5013** 3 n.

μουσικός **5014** 5

ὀρχηστής **5013** 4

ποιμήν **5012** 2

πραγματευτής **5016** 6 n.

προεστώς **5014** 4 **5015** 4–5

πρωταύλης **5014** 4

X. MEASURES

(a) Weights and Measures

κεράμιον **5014** 14, 15 **5015** 15

κοτύλη **5014** 13 **5015** 13–15 n.

(b) Money

δραχμή **5014** 11, 17 **5015** 12, 18–19

XI. GENERAL INDEX OF WORDS

ἀγοράζειν **5019** 1
ἀγορανόμος see Index VIII
ἀδελφή **4983** 13 (**4989** 18)
ἀδελφός **4981** 9, (13) (**4989** 13) **5012** 1 n.
ἀδιαίρετος **4985** 7
αἰτιᾶσθαι **5012** 2
ἀκολούθως **4990** 16
ἀλήθεια [**4980** 4] [**4981** 6–7] (**4982** 9)
ἀλλήλων **4994** 13 **5014** 1 **5015** 1
ἄλλος [**4980** 11] **4981** 12
ἅμα **5005** 2 **5006** 4 **5007** 6 **5015** 19
ἄμφοδον **4989** 9–10 **4990** 13 **4994** 11 **4996** 10–11 **4997** 8 **4998** [10], 14, [16] [**4999** 10–11]
ἀμφότερος **4989** 4, 23 (**4990** 8) **5014** 3 **5015** 2
ἀναγράφειν **4984** 2 (**4992** 8) **4994** 9–10 **4996** 10, 14–15 **4997** 7, (11) (**4998** 10, [13], 16, 19)
ἀναζητεῖν **5000** 19–20
ἀνακτᾶσθαι **5017** 3
ἀναπέμπειν **5003** 1 **5004** 1 **5010** 2
ἀνεπηρέαστος **5014** 22
ἀνέρχεσθαι **5004** 3 **5006** 3–4
ἀνήρ **4981** 8
ἀντί **4998** 11
ἄνω **4983** 4
ἀξιοῦν **4992** 8 [**4999** 14] **5017** 2 **5018** 2
ἀπελεύθερος **4980** 9 **4981** 11
ἀπηλιώτης **5008** 3
ἀπό **4983** 9 **4987** 2 **4989** 4 **4990** [8], 15 **4992** 2 **4994** 8 **4996** 8 **4997** 3 **4998** 5 [**4999** 6] **5000** 4, 8, 18, 27 **5014** 8, 10, 19 **5015** 4, 9, 10, 21 **5016** 3, [6]; see also Index VIII s.v. ἀπὸ γυμνασίου
ἀπογράφεσθαι **4983** 12, 16 **4987** 3 **4988** 2 (**4989** 7, 11) **4990** (11), [17] (**4991** 11) **4999** 7–8
ἀπογραφή (**4989** 9) [**4990** 12] [**4991** 16]
ἀποκαθιστάναι **5014** 20, 25
ἀποστέλλειν **5010** 2 **5011** 2
ἀρραβών **5014** 17 [**5015** 18]
ἄρτος **5014** 13 **5015** 12
ἀρχέφοδος see Index VIII

ἄσημος (**4989** 12, 14, 15)
ἀσφαλής **5014** 21
ἄτεχνος (**4989** 12, 14, 15) **4997** 6–7 **4998** 10, 13, 16
αὐλή **4985** 5
αὐλητής see Index IX
αὐτόθι **5014** 16 **5015** 16
Αὐτοκράτωρ see Index II s.vv. Tiberius, Nero, Marcus Aurelius and Verus, Marcus Aurelius, Severus Alexander, Valerian and Gallienus, Diocletian and Maximian
αὐτός **4982** (5), 16 **4983** (6), 15 **4989** 4, (13, 15) **4990** (15), 18 **4992** (7), 9 **4994** 30 **4995** 27 **4996** 15 **4997** 11, 29 [**4998** 19] **4999** [2], 14 **5000** 5, 8, 10, 27–8 **5004** 3 (bis) **5014** 7, 21, 24, 26 **5015** 7–8, [10], 11 [**5016** 4]

βασιλικός see Index VIII s.v. βασιλικὸς γραμματεύς
βενεφικιάριος see Index VIII
βία **5015** 21
βούλεσθαι **4994** 9 [**4999** 7]
βουλευτής see Index VIII

γεωργός see Index IX
γίγνεσθαι **4994** 12
γράμμα **4982** 17 **4994** 31 **4995** 28 **4997** 30 **5007** 4
γραμματεύς see Index VIII s.v. βασιλικὸς γραμματεύς
γράφειν **4982** 16 **4994** 30 **4995** 26–7 **4997** 29
γραφή **4980** 5 n. [**4981** 7] **4982** 10
γυμνασιαρχ— see Index VIII
γυμνάσιον see Index VIII s.v. ἀπὸ γυμνασίου
γυνή **4980** 6 [**4981** 8] **4982** 3 **4994** 5–6 **5008** 5

δάνειον (**4984** 2)
δέ **4980** 14 **4981** 15 **4982** 2, [12] [**5000** 34] **5014** 16 **5015** 16
δεκαδάρχης see Index VIII
δημόσιος see Index VIII s.v. δημόσιοι

διά **4998** 30 **4999** 1 **5010** 2 **5015** 21
διαδέχεσθαι **4991** 10
διαθήκη (**4990** 16)
διαλύειν **5018** 4
διαπέμπειν **5009** 3
διατιθέναι **4985** 4
διαψεύδεσθαι **4981** 14
διδόναι **5017** 3 **5018** 5 **5019** 3
διέρχεσθαι (**4989** 7) (**4990** 11) (**4991** 12)
δίκαιον **4990** 16
διό **4992** 7 **4995** 14 **4996** 13 **4997** 10 **4998** 18 **4999** 13
δοῦλος **4998** 12, 15
δραχμή see Index X(b)
δύο **5000** 27
δωδεκάδραχμος see Index VIII

ἐάν **5014** 26
ἑαυτός **4985** 7–8 [**5000** 34]
ἐγγυητής **5004** 2
ἐγκαλεῖσθαι **5002** 3 n.
ἐγώ **4980** 6, 13 (bis) **4981** [8], 13, 15 **4982** 3, 11 **4983** 13 **4989** 9 **4990** 18 **4992** 3 **4996** 6 **4997** 4 **4999** 8 **5005** 3 **5007** 5 **5017** 3 **5018** 3, 5 **5019** 3
ἔθιμος [**4998** 21] [**4999** 16]
εἰ **5017** 3 **5019** 1
εἰδέναι **4982** 17 **4994** 31 **4995** 27–8 **4997** 30 **5019** 1
εἴκοσι **5014** 12 **5015** 12, 19
εἶναι **4980** 13 **4981** 15 **4982** 11 **4994** 15 **4999** 11 [**5000** 32–3] **5004** 3 **5014** 10, 15 **5015** 16 **5018** 3
εἰρήνη see Index VIII s.v. ἐπιστάτης εἰρήνης
εἰρηνοφύλαξ see Index VIII
εἰς **4985** 5 **4987** 5 **4988** 4 **4989** 10 **4992** 5 **4999** 14 **5014** 16, 25
εἷς [**4999** 2] **5014** 14, 15 **5015** 15 (bis)
εἴσοδος **4985** 6
ἐκ [**4980** 3] [**4981** 6] **4982** 8 **4989** 4 **4990** 13 **4994** 13 **4996** 6, 44 **4997** 36 **4999** 10
ἕκαστος **4980** 7–8 **5014** 11 **5015** 11

ἑκατόν **5014** 11 **5015** 12
ἐκεῖ **5014** 20
ἐκπέμπειν **5002** 2
ἔκτακτον **5014** 24
ἔλαιον **5014** 12 **5015** 13
ἐν **4982** 2, [5] **4983** 15 (bis) **4992** 9 **4996** 15 **4997** 12 [**4998** 19] **5010** 3
ἐναντίος **4980** 14 **4981** 16 **4982** 12
ἐνιαύϲιοϲ **4981** 1?
ἐνιϲτάναι **4988** 4 (**4992** 6) **4994** 3, 15–16 **4995** 13 **4996** [2], 12 **4997** 9 **4998** 3 **4999** 4, 11 **5000** 18–19 **5016** 5
ἔνοχοϲ **5000** 32
ἐντάϲϲειν (**4990** 1)
ἐντόϲ **5000** 17
ἐντυγχάνειν **5001** 4 **5008** 6 [**5009** 4–5]
ἐξαυτῆϲ **5004** 1 **5005** 2 **5006** 3 **5007** 3 **5008** 4 **5009** 3 **5010** 2
ἐξηγητεύειν see Index VIII
ἑξήκοντα **5000** 17–18
ἔξοδοϲ **4985** 6
ἑορτή **5015** 9, [14–15]
ἐπί **4980** 4 [**4981** 6] **4982** 9 **4990** 13, 17 **4994** 11 **4996** 10 **4997** 8 **4998** 10, 14, 16 **4999** 10 **5014** 9 **5015** 9 **5016** 11
ἐπιβάλλειν **4985** 4
ἐπιδιδόναι [**4980** 4] **4981** 7 **4982** 9, 13 **4992** 7, 18 **4994** 26–7 **4995** 14, 23–4 **4996** 13 **4997** 10, 25–6 **4998** 18, [28] **4999** 13
ἐπικαλεῖϲθαι **4990** 6 (**4992** 4) **4995** 25–6
ἐπίκριϲιϲ **5018** 4
ἐπίξενοϲ **4980** 10–11
ἐπιορκεῖν **4980** 14 **4981** 15 **4982** 11
ἐπιϲτάτηϲ see Index VIII s.v. ἐπιϲτάτηϲ εἰρήνηϲ
ἐπίτροποϲ see Index IX
ἑπτά **5014** 9, 23
ἐργαϲτήριον **5015** 5
ἕτεροϲ **4980** 8 **4981** 10 (**4989** 15)
ἔτοϲ (**4980** 15) (**4981** 16) (**4982** 17) **4987** 5 (**4988** 4) (**4989** 7, 12, 14, [15], 18, 24, 28) (**4990** 11) [**4991** 12] (**4992** 6, 7, 14) (**4994** 2, 16 [bis], 20, 36) (**4995** 13, 16) **4996** [2], 12, (21) **4997** 9, (18) (**4998**

3, [9, 12, 15, 22]) (**4999** 4 [bis], 12, [27], 24)
εὖ **4980** 13 **4981** 15 **4982** 11
εὐορκεῖν **4980** 13 **4981** 14–15 **4982** 10
εὐϲεβήϲ see Index II s.vv. Caracalla, Severus Alexander, Valerian and Gallienus, Diocletian and Maximian
εὐτυχήϲ see Index II s.vv. Caracalla, Severus Alexander, Valerian and Gallienus, Diocletian and Maximian
ἔχειν **5014** 16
ἕωϲ **5015** 10 **5016** 5

ζεῦγοϲ **5014** 12 **5015** 13

ἤ **5000** 32 **5004** 2, 3 **5011** 3
ᾖ [**4980** 3] **4981** 6 **5018** 3
ἡγεμονεύειν see Index VIII
ἡγεμονία see Index VIII
ἡγεμών see Index VIII
ἥκειν **5005** 2 **5011** 3
ἡμεῖϲ **4990** 13 **4994** 12–13, 18 **4997** 15
ἡμέρα **5000** 17, 19 **5014** 9, 11, 14, 23 **5015** 9, 11–12, 13–15 n.

θεόϲ see Index VII
θέϲιϲ **4990** 6
θηϲαυρόϲ **4983** 14

ἴδιοϲ see Index IX
ἱερεύϲ see Index VII
ἴϲοϲ **4990** 13

καθαρόϲ **5014** 16 **5015** 16
καθήκειν **4992** 10 **4994** 16 **4995** 15 **4996** 16 **4997** 13 [**4998** 20] **4999** 15
καθόλου **4980** 11–12
κατά **4987** 3 **4988** 2 **4989** 5, 9 **4990** [8], 12 **4991** 6, [15]
καταγίνεϲθαι **4982** 2 **4983** 17]
καταγράφειν **4985** 2
καταμένειν **5010** 3
κελεύειν **4987** 3 (**4988** 2) (**4989** 5) **4990** 9 (**4991** 6)
κεράμιον see Index X(a)
κιθαρῳδόϲ see Index IX
κληρονομικόϲ **4990** 15–16
κοινόν (noun) [**4999** 1]

κοινόϲ (adjective) **4985** 7
κόλλημα **4994** 37
κοτύλη see Index X(a)
κράτιϲτοϲ see Index VIII
κροταλίζειν **5016** 10
κροταλίϲτρια see Index IX
κύριοϲ **4983** 10 (**4989** 3); see also Index II s.vv. Marcus Aurelius and Verus, Marcus Aurelius, Commodus, Severus Alexander, Valerian and Gallienus
κωμάρχηϲ see Index VIII
κώμη **4982** 5 **4983** 15 **4987** 2 **5000** 5–6, 11, 28 **5002** 2 **5006** 2–3 **5007** 2 **5014** 8 **5015** 3, 9 **5016** 3, [4]
κωμογραμματεύϲ see Index VIII
κωμῳδόϲ see Index IX

λαμβάνειν **5007** 3
λαμπρόϲ **4999** 3 (bis), 6 (bis) **5016** 6, 7; see also Index VIII s.v. λαμπρότατοϲ
λαογράφοϲ see Index VIII
λέγειν **4983** 14
λειτουργεῖν **5014** 8 **5015** 8
λόγοϲ **5014** 16
λύειν **4990** 16–17

μᾶλλον **5019** 1
μέγαϲ **4999** 25 **5017** 1 **5018** 1; see also Index II s.vv. Marcus Aurelius and Verus, Marcus Aurelius, Diocletian and Maximian
μείϲ **5001** 5 **5014** 10 **5015** 11 (**5016** 5)
μέν **4980** 13 **4981** 15 **4982** 11 **5014** 6 **5015** 6
μέροϲ **4985** 5 **4989** 10 **4990** 17
μετά **4983** 10 (**4989** 3) **5014** 22 **5016** 8
μεταβάλλειν **5015** 17
μεταλλάϲϲειν **4999** 8–9
μέχρι **5007** 5
μή **4982** 16 **4989** 27 **4992** 18 **4994** 19, 31 **4995** 27 **4996** 20 **4997** 17, 29 **4998** 22 [**4999** 17] **5014** 26
μηδέ **4980** 9, 10 (bis), 11 **4981** 11 (bis), 12
μηδείϲ **4980** 8, 11 **4981** 10, 12, 14
μήν [**4980** 3] [**4981** 6]
μήτε **4980** 9 **4981** 10

XI. GENERAL INDEX OF WORDS

μήτηρ **4983** 8 **4984** 4 [**4986** 3-4] (**4987** 2) (**4989** 2, 12, 13, 15, 17 [*bis*]) **4990** 5, [7], (15) (**4992** 2, 4) **4994** (5), 7, (34) **4995** 11, [31] **4996** 6-7, 42 **4997** 2, 5, (35) **4998** [4], 7, 9 (**4999** 5, 10) **5000** 3, 7, 22, 25-6 (**5003** 3, 4) (**5016** 2)
μικρός see Index VI s.v. Μικρὸν Ταρουθίνου
μῖμος see Index IX
μιcθός **5014** 10, 24 **5015** 11
μουcικός see Index IX

νέος see Index II s.v. Tiberius
νομοφύλαξ see Index VIII

ξενία **5014** 21

οἰκεῖν **4980** 7, 12-13 **4981** [9], 13
οἰκία **4982** 4 **4983** 14 **4985** 5 (**4989** 9, 10) [**4990** 12] [**4991** 15] **4994** 12
οἰκίδιον **4990** 17
οἶνος **5014** 14 **5015** 15
ὀκτώ **5015** 13-15 n.
ὅλος **5014** 13 **5015** 13-15 n. **5016** 12
ὁμήλικος [**4999** 14-15]
ὀμνύειν [**4981** 3] **4982** 6, 13 **4983** 17 [**4989** 24] **4992** 10, 18 **4994** 17, 27, 29 **4996** 17 **4997** 13-14, 26 **4998** 21, [28] [**4999** 16] **5000** 11
ὅμοιος **4996** 15-16 **4997** 12 [**4998** 20]
ὄνος **5015** 22 n.
ὄξος **5014** 15 **5015** 15
ὅρκος **4982** 15 **4992** 19 **4994** 28, [30] **4997** 27 **4998** 22, 29 **4999** 16 **5000** 33
ὀρχηcτής see Index IX
ὅς **4980** 7 **4983** 15 **4989** 10 **4990** 16, 17 [**4998** 11]
ὅτι **5019** 1
οὐ **5019** 2
οὐδέ **4983** 16
οὐδείς **4983** 15-16
οὐετρανός see Index VIII
οὗτος **4985** 5 **4994** 5 **5014** 18 **5015** 19 **5017** 3 **5018** 5 **5019** 3
οὕτως **5019** 2

παιδίcκη **5019** 2
—παίζειν **5016** 9-10
πανηγυρίζειν **5014** 9
παρά **4980** 6, 13 **4981** [8], 13 **4983** 7 **4989** 1 **4990** 4 **4991** 2 **4992** 1 **4994** 4 **4996** 3 **4998** 4 (**4999** 5, 8] (**5005** 1) (**5006** 1) **5007** 1 (**5008** 1) (**5009** 1) (**5010** 1) (**5011** 1)
παραδιδόναι **5008** 4 **5009** 3 **5011** 2
παρακεῖcθαι **4980** 7
παραλαμβάνειν **5014** 6, 19 **5015** 6-7, 20 [**5016** 7-8]
παρέξ **4980** 12 **4981** 12
παρέχειν [**5000** 33-4] **5014** 20-21
παριcτάναι **5000** 20-21
πᾶc **5014** 15 **5015** 16
πατήρ (**4989** 18) **4996** 44 [**4997** 36] **5004** 2
πέμπειν **5001** 2 **5005** 2-3 **5006** 4 **5007** 7
πέντε **5015** 9-10
περί **5014** 6 **5015** 6, 17
πληροῦν **5014** 23 **5016** 11
ποιμήν see Index IX
πόλις **4983** 10 **4986** 2 **4989** 4 **4990** [8], 15 **4992** 3 [**4993** 1] **4994** 3, 8 **4996** 9 **4997** 3 [**4998** 2, 5] [**4999** 4, 7] **5015** 4 **5016** 7
πραγματευτής see Index IX
πρεcβύτερος see Index VIII
προγράφειν **4980** 12 **4981** 3, 13 **4982** 14
προεcτώς see Index IX
προκεῖcθαι [**4980** 4] **4997** 27-8 [**4998** 29]
πρός **4985** 7 **4988** 4 **4989** 7 **4990** 11 **4991** 11 **4993** 13 **4994** 15 **4995** 13 **4996** 14 **4997** 11 **4998** 19 **4999** 11
προcβαίνειν **4992** 5
προcγίγνεcθαι (**4989** 16)
προcέρχεcθαι **5010** 4
προcτάτης see Index VIII
πρότερος (**4990** 14)
πρωταύλης see Index IX
πρώτως **4994** 9 **4999** 7

ῥαφάνινος **5014** 13 **5015** 13-14

Cεβαcτός see Index II s.vv. Augustus, Tiberius, Nero, Marcus Aurelius, Caracalla, Severus Alexander, Valerian and Gallienus, Diocletian and Maximian
cημαίνειν (**5010** 5) (**5012** 3)
signare **5007** 8
cτρατηγός see Index VIII
cτρατιώτης see Index VIII
cύ [**4999** 8] **5004** 3 **5016** 8
cυγγραφή **4984** 3
cυγκυρεῖν **4985** 6
cυμπανηγυρίζειν **5016** 9 n.
cυμφέρειν **5019** 1, 2
cύμφορος **5018** 3
cυμφωνία **5014** 5, 7, 18 **5015** 8, 19-20 **5016** 8, 12
cύν **5010** 3 **5014** 7, 18 [**5015** 7]
cυναντᾶν **5007** 5
cυνεπιδιδόναι **4994** 29
cύνναος **5017** 2 **5018** 2
cυνορία **5007** 6
cυcτάτης see Index VIII

τάξις [**4992** 10] **4996** 16 **4997** 12 [**4998** 20] [**4999** 15]
τάccειν [**4999** 14]
τε **5014** 5 **5015** 5
τέλειος **4997** 6, 31 (**4998** 13)
τελευτᾶν **4992** 6, (9) **4996** 11-12 (**4997** 9) (**4998** 17)
τεccαράκοντα **5014** 17-18 **5015** 13
τεccαρεcκαιδεκαετής (**4992** 5)
τιθέναι **4990** 16
τοπαρχία see Index VI
τοπογραμματεύς see Index VIII
τρεῖς **5000** 30 **5016** 3
τύχη **4989** 27 **4992** 13 **4994** 19 **4996** 19 **4997** 17 **5000** 16

ὑγιής [**4980** 3] [**4981** 6] **4982** 8
υἱός [**4980** 3] **4981** 6 **4983** 11 **4989** 3 **4992** 3 **4994** 13 **4996** 6, 41 **4997** 4 **4999** 9, 25 **5008** 4-5 **5010** 3
ὑμεῖς **5007** 6 **5011** 3
ὑπάρχειν **4983** 12 (**4989** 9) **4990** 13 [**4991** 16-17]
ὑπέρ **4982** 16 **4994** 30 **4995** 27 **4997** 29 **5015** 18
ὑπό **4987** 3 **4988** 2 **4989** 5 **4990** 9 **4991** 7 **5002** 3 n. **5005** 3 [**5012** 3]

ὑπόμνημα **4992** 8 **4995** 15 **4996** 13–14, (44) **4997** 10–11, (36) [**4998** 18] **4999** 13–14

φάναι [**4994** 30]
φίλος **4999** 8
φροντίζειν **5007** 4
φύλαξ see Index VIII
φυλάρχης see Index VIII

χαίρειν (**4984** 2) (**4985** 2) [**5016** 7]
χρᾶςθαι **5019** 3
χρηματίζειν (**4989** 4, 11, [17]) (**4991** 6) [**4998** 7]
χωρίς **5015** 20

ψεύδεςθαι **4989** 27 **4992** 18 **4994** 19–20 **4996** 20 **4997** 17 **4998** 22 [**4999** 17]

ὠνή **4985** 3
ὡς **4989** 24 **4991** 6 **4992** 10 **4994** 16 **4995** 15 **4996** 16 **4997** 13, 27 **4998** 7, [20], 29 **4999** 15

XII. CORRECTIONS TO PUBLISHED TEXTS

II **255** = W. *Chr.* 201.17–18	**4980** 5–8 n.
P. Col. VIII 222.2	**4994** 8 n.
P. Fouad 52.2	**4994** 8 n.
P. Palau Rib. 10	**4983** 16–17 n.
P. Wisc. I 16	**4982** 13–15 n.
P. Wisc. I 18.8	**4983** 16–17 n.

4970

```
των ινεων τοι̣     ]ν αλλο το μη εστιν ιατρικη[      ]ο̣  ]μεν
θεωρημα τα σ[    ]ηκον εστιν ως επω̣ς δι αλλα βαν
εν πρωτοις αν[    ]τ̣ο ιπποκρατιος ορκου την αρχην τη̣
μαθησεως πολ̣[   ]εν ως τ ε νομολογικα ιο τα του κα
σφοδρα βιωφελ̣[  ]κ̣ αθεσ τ.ντος τοις εμ υρ[  ]  του τον
  τ̣α τω μη θεισαν[    ]ν̣ισ τον αλλα το μεν τω ιατρευει
```

4971

```
          τοις κ.ροις ιδοντας ε[
          επει δ ιατρ   ως τη π[
          προτ  μ ε τ    αι αθητ[
          τροφην και τοπ .εισ[
          εν τη αργυ[    ]  ας τε ου[
          ποσε    αι ε    οντα[
              αλο   τινα στοι[
           ειν περ υλα μεν ιπ[
           εισθαι δε ισ ε ιπτιο̣[
           κ   ης των ιπλ θων  [
           ιδοντας ο  ωνη τ[
             ταν .χρα σ ε πι τ[
                ωντ  ην απος[
             του αλ    σ εν εα[
               γεν η    κεισε[
                ηνο        σ ης
                 ην τω  δια[
                 υριοι   μερεν
                  β       νει το[
                  ν      οσα σ .[
                   κ      ο ν[
```

PLATE II

4968 (reduced)
fols. 1b, 8a

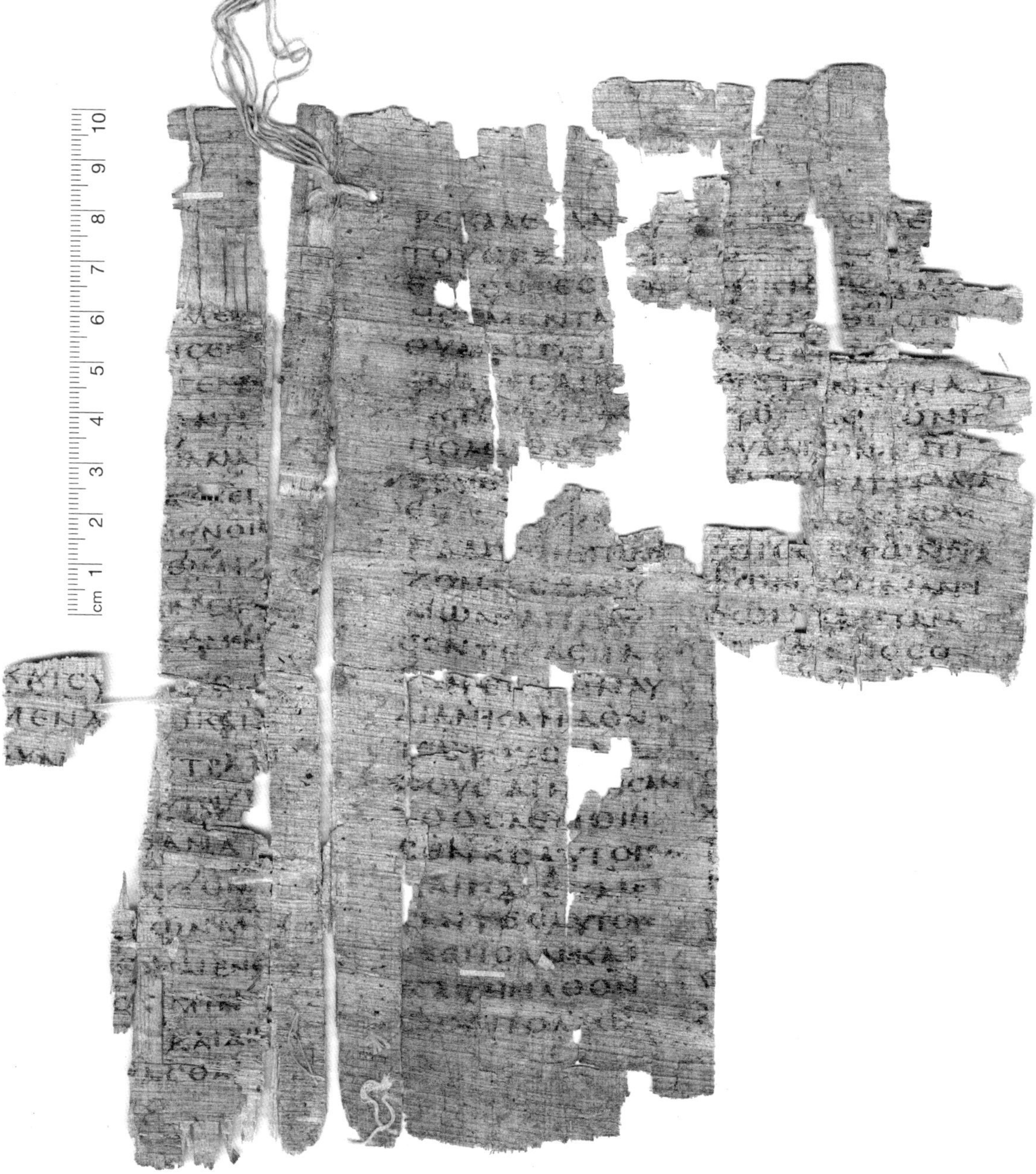

PLATE III

4968 (reduced)
fols. 8b, 1a

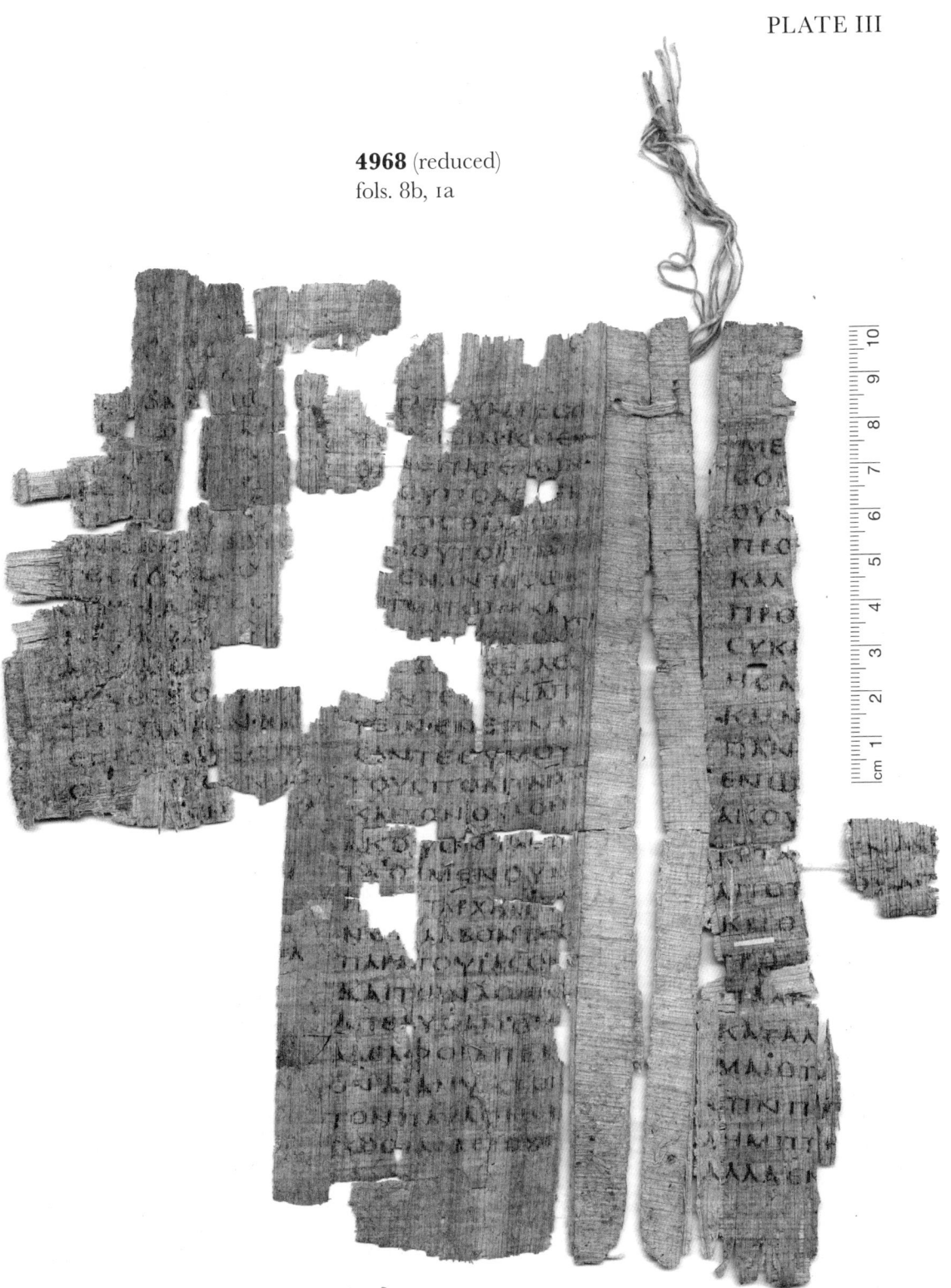

4968 (reduced) fols. 6b, 7a

PLATE VI

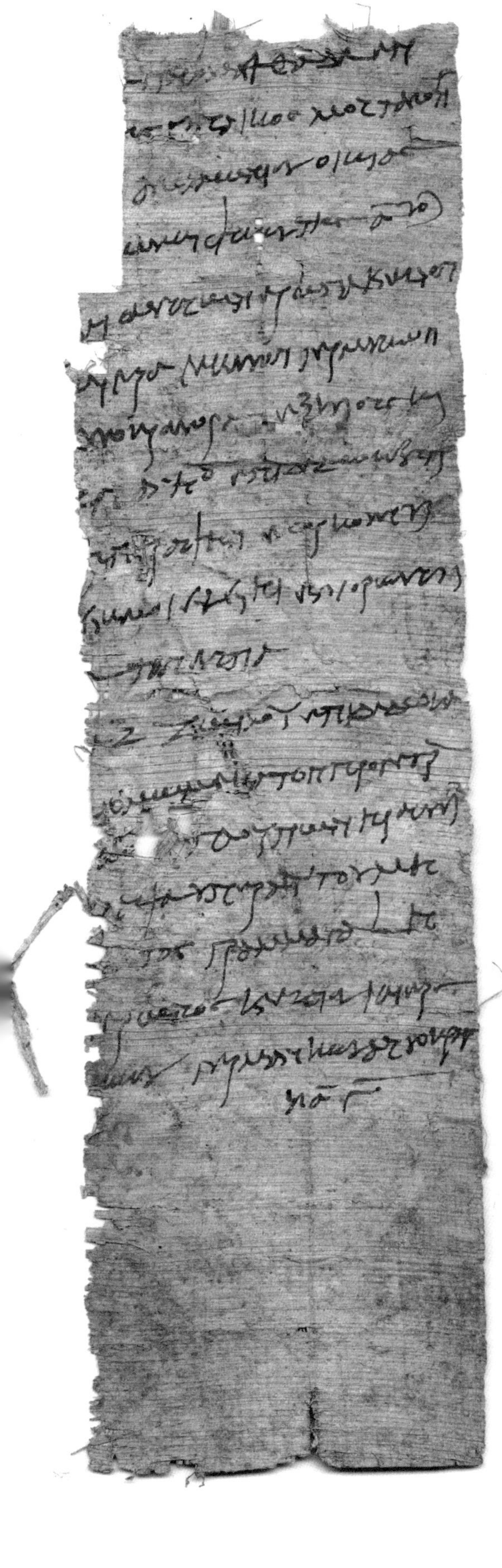

PLATE VII

4982

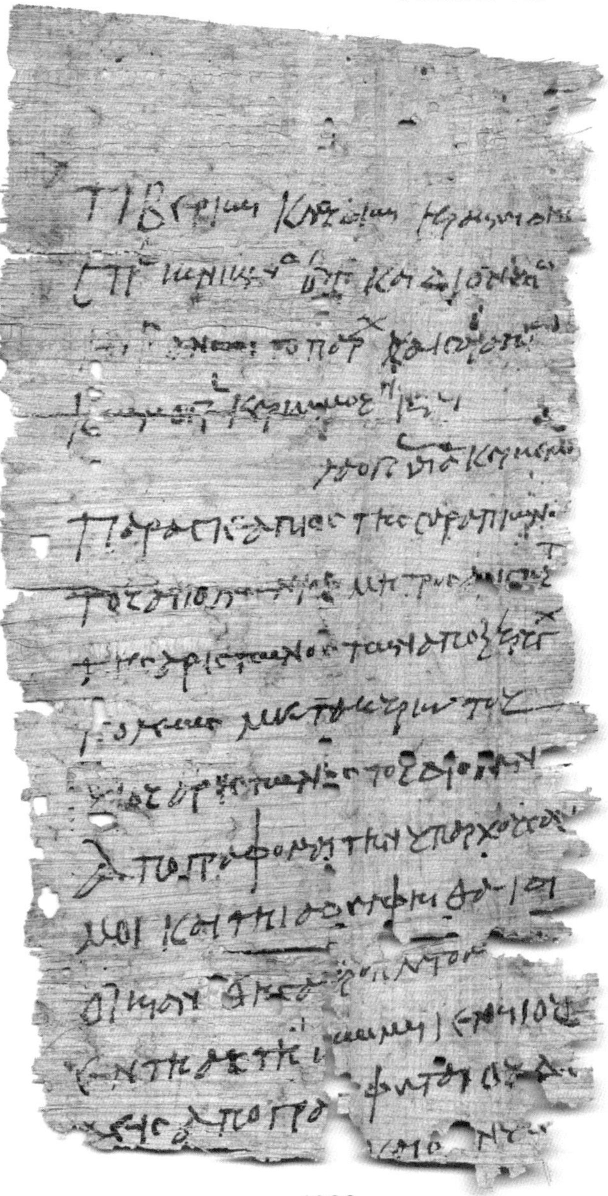

4983

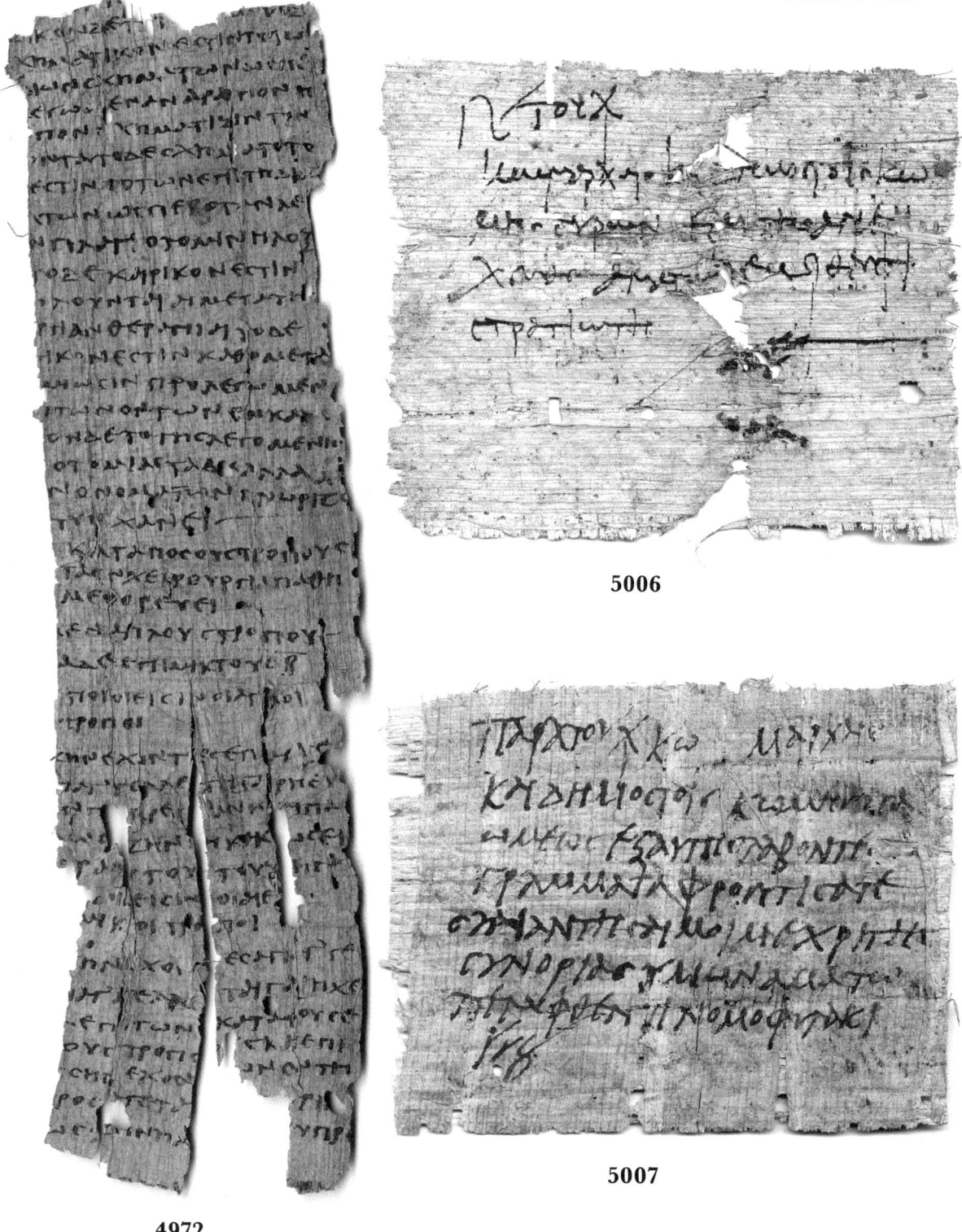